Force & lucidity

As it were,
but no desire, ✓

What would J. P. Sartre
call Maze?

Apply his anti-relational arguments
contra intention to cognitive
states?

Direct realist re perception (Gibson)

Perception & belief?
What is a cognition?

Is his objection to desire that it is
relational, or the direction of the relation

Inverted spectrum   Pg 103
   No sympathy
No attempt to explain away
   subjectivity of experience
Comes alive in hachet jobs

determinism, physicalism,
   empiricism

The meaning of behaviour

J. R. Maze

Senior Lecturer in Psychology
University of Sydney

London
GEORGE ALLEN & UNWIN
Boston   Sydney

George Allen & Unwin (Publishers) Ltd,
40 Museum Street, London WC1A 1LU, UK

George Allen & Unwin (Publishers) Ltd,
Park Lane, Hemel Hempstead, Herts HP2 4TE, UK

Allen & Unwin Inc.,
9 Winchester Terrace, Winchester, Mass 01890, USA

George Allen & Unwin Australia Pty Ltd,
8 Napier Street, North Sydney, NSW 2060, Australia

First published in 1983

British Library Cataloguing in Publication Data

Maze, J. R.
  The meaning of behaviour.
1. Human behaviour
I. Title
150'.1   BF121
ISBN 0-04-150081-4

Library of Congress Cataloging in Publication Data

Maze, J. R.
  The meaning of behaviour.
Bibliography: p.
Includes indexes.
1. Personality. 2. Psychology–Philosophy. I. Title.
BF698.M345 1983   155.2   82-20670
ISBN 0-04-150081-4

Set in 10 on 12 point Times by Fotographics (Bedford) Ltd
and printed in Great Britain
by Biddles Ltd, Guildford, Surrey

Preface

This book had its beginnings in a proposal by W. M. O'Neil, at that time editor of a projected series of short volumes on the history of modern psychology, that I should write a critical history of dynamic depth psychologies. But as the work progressed, it developed beyond historiography into a radical rethinking of the most fundamental concepts not only of personality theory but of the whole theory of the origins of action. I had always been inclined in favour of dynamic depth theories, by which I mean those that seek the origins of all behaviour in genetically determined primary drives, rather than in rationality, or in 'conditioning', but I was forced to believe that their explanatory bases were unstable, because almost without exception their motivational concepts actually consisted of *strivings towards goals*, rather than of drives. Such concepts may have persuasive descriptive force, but the notions that people can adopt or abandon goals, choose what path they will take towards them, and direct their own behaviour towards those ends, carry so much open or concealed voluntarism that they are of no use for scientific explanation. The answer to the basic psychological question 'Why did this person do that?' seemed for these theories to be, in the long run, just 'Because he or she wanted to', which is too easy altogether.

   The outstanding counter-example to that kind of voluntarism was in Sigmund Freud's conception of instinctual drives. His methodological principle that these must be identified by their physiological source, rather than by their aim or object, still offers great promise for a deterministic theory of motivation, provided that his hydraulic model can be modified to fit in with modern neuroscience, and the effort to show that that can be done became one of my major concerns.

   Apart from that, the only currently available deterministic alternative to dynamic depth theories, that is, conditioning theory, has no adequate account of human nature to offer, because it retreats from the issue altogether. Organisms in that view are characterised only by teachability; there is no attempt at a general account of what reinforces behaviour, or of what kinds of things organisms do by nature. They are just neutral material malleable by reinforcement contingencies – an assumption the falsity of which is now becoming plain. Further, the denial by such theories of any efficacy to mental processes is not essential to determinism; if thinking is one of the natural processes occurring in organisms, then an account of its causes, and its effects in behaviour, can in principle be given.

   In this book I argue that determinism is essential for psychology, as it is for every field of empirical enquiry, and that an understanding of the role of cognitive processes is an essential aspect of a general deterministic psychology. The widespread conviction that cognition is inseparable from purposefulness is criticised in detail, but the currently fashionable computer-simulation approach to cognition, deterministic though it may be, is rejected as simply a branch of technology having no bearing on epistemology. In particular, its claim to establish that human cognition proceeds by the use of internal representations is argued to be untenable. Computational devices may work by having representational entities provided by their creators; persons are not so equipped. Computer designers and programmers implicitly exempt themselves from their own theories. They know not only the internal representations but the external objects to which they refer; the computational device does not, and indeed knows nothing at all.

Phenomenology and existentialism are here argued to make an unjustifiable leap from self-knowledge to self-creation, as a result of their subjectivism and their needless conflation of cognition with purposefulness. Examination reveals the essential vacuity, as an account of the springs of behaviour and the constitution of the self, of the existentialist doctrine that we 'choose our being' at every – or any – moment. On the other hand, the 'intention plus belief' type of action theory proposed by mental philosophers as a causal account of apparently voluntary behaviour is also found to be deficient, in that 'intention' conceived as a mental state cannot be a legitimate causal variable. The revised version of Freud's theory of instinctual drives with their consummatory behaviours fills this gap in action theory.

The book is addressed to philosophers of the mind as well as to psychologists, and to anyone who is seriously concerned with the origins and meaning of behaviour. Its conceptual arguments are developed by examining current psychological theories of motivation and cognitive processes. Psychology has suffered too long from its self-created insulation against philosophical criticism. Whether it likes it or not, psychology is inescapably concerned with epistemology and action-theory, and the attempt to restrict its scope to supposedly atheoretical fact-gathering does not preserve psychologists from falling into perennial fallacies. Because of these, a great proportion of psychological research has been misdirected, to pseudoproblems on which no conceivable data could throw any light. Perhaps this book will help clear away some of the unnecessary hindrances to the progress of the science.

I am grateful to all those who have offered constructive or destructive comments on parts of the book, and especially to R. M. Henry, T. McMullen, J. A. Meacham, J. Michell, W. M. O'Neil, W. W. Rozeboom, E. R. Valentine, N. E. Wetherick, and R. Wollheim. Richard Wollheim also gave me the hospitality of the Department of Philosophy, University College London, for the study leave during which I completed the final version, and I am very grateful to him.

J. R. M.
Sydney 1982

Contents

Acknowledgements

The author wishes to thank the following publishers for permission to quote excerpts from the works mentioned, the full citations for which are to be found in the bibliography.

Academic Press, Inc. for J. M. Davidson, 'Hormones and reproductive behavior' in S. Levine (ed.) *Hormones and behavior*; George Allen and Unwin for E. Husserl, *Ideas*; Basic Books for selections by L. Binswanger in R. May *et al.* (eds) *Existence*, and S. Freud, 'Instincts and their vicissitudes', *Three essays on the theory of sexuality* and 'Project for a scientific psychology'; Basil Blackwell for G. E. M. Anscombe, *Intention*, M. Heidegger, *Being and time*, R. Harré and P. Secord, *The explanation of social behaviour*, J. Shotter, *Journal for the Theory of Social Behaviour*, 1973, and J. Searle, *Mind*, 1979; Brooks/Cole for selection by A. H. Maslow in E. A. Southwell and M. Merbaum (eds) *Personality: readings in theory and research*; Cambridge University Press for A. Woodfield, *Teleology*, D. M. Armstrong, *Belief, truth and knowledge*, selection by C. Taylor in R. Borger and F. Cioffi (eds) *Explanation in the behavioural sciences*, S. Ullman, *The Behavioral and Brain Sciences*, 1980, and R. Puccetti and R. W. Dykes, *The Behavioral and Brain Sciences*, 1978; Elsevier Biomedical Press for M. J. Morgan, *Trends in Neurosciences*, 1979; W. H. Freeman for U. Neisser, *Cognition and reality*; Lawrence Erlbaum Associates for selection by R. M. Shiffrin in W. K. Estes, *Handbook of learning and cognitive processes*; The Harvester Press for M. Boden, *Artificial intelligence and natural man*; The Hogarth Press for S. Freud, *The standard edition of the complete psychological works of Sigmund Freud*; Houghton Mifflin for J. J. Gibson, *The ecological approach to visual perception*; Hutchinson for K. H. Pribram and M. Gill, *Freud's 'Project' reassessed*; Methuen for selections by M. Boden, N. Bolton, and P. Pettit in N. Bolton (ed.) *Philosophical problems in psychology*; W. W. Norton for S. Freud, *New introductory lectures on psychoanalysis*; Philosophical Library and Methuen for J.-P. Sartre, *Being and nothingness*; Martinus Nijhoff for E. Husserl, *The idea of phenomenology*; Penguin Books for K. H. Pribram, 'The foundation of psychoanalytic theory: Freud's neuropsychological model', in *Brain and behaviour 4: Adaptation: selected readings*, K. H. Pribram (ed.), copyright K. H. Pribram, 1969; Experimental Psychology Society for A. Dickinson, *Quarterly Journal of Experimental Psychology*, 1979; Routledge and Kegan Paul and Humanities Press for D. M. Armstrong, *A materialist theory of the mind*, C. Taylor, *The explanation of behaviour*, and F. Brentano, *Psychology from an empirical standpoint*; Routledge and Kegan Paul for A. Gauld and J. Shotter, *Human action and its psychological investigation*, J. Hornsby, *Actions*, and E. Wilson, *The mental as physical*; Tavistock Publications for R. D. Laing, *The divided self*; and Universitetsforlaget for J. Searle, *Inquiry*, 1979.

1
Introduction

During the latter part of the 1970s academic psychology underwent a rather ragged paradigm shift. It is clear enough what the shift was away from; it was away from behaviourism. It was away from stimulus–response (S–R) psychology, away from S–R learning theory, away from 'conditioning', away from every stance, whether it called itself 'merely methodological' or outrightly 'metaphysical' behaviourism, that tacitly or overtly treated mental processes as non-existent by assuming that they play no part in the determination of behaviour. It can be called a paradigm shift because non-cognitive behaviourism had not been nor could have been *proven* wrong; it protected itself in the classical manner of Kuhnian paradigms by declaring that any data that conflicted with its presuppositions were illegitimate or imaginary. Mental processes were unobservable, thus not data; introspective reports were just vocal-motor habits; no evidential connections could be posited between observable movements and unobservable mental processes, and so no disconfirming evidence could be brought against behaviourism's founding premise (repeatedly repudiated yet always there, since it was the only thing that gave behaviourism any pretence to substance as a theory) that *there are no mental processes*. Admittedly, during the 1970s many clever experiments were developed in the operant learning tradition (e.g. Hearst & Peterson 1973) that made S–R explanations look strained, and the observation of reliable unreinforced changes in behaviour ('autoshaping', 'sign-tracking', etc.) in modern Pavlovian conditioning (cf. Morgan 1979a) seemed also to fit more kindly into some sort of cognitive learning view, but there has probably been nothing that an inventive S–R theorist of the old school, a Clark Hull, could not have accommodated within his non-cognitive principles, conjuring with constructs such as 'pure stimulus act', 'stimulus-generalisation', 'response-generalisation', and so on. These manoeuvres could continue to be used successfully while the principle that cognitive processes could not be the object of empirical observation was accepted, and indeed to a large extent it still is widely accepted. Instead of that principle being subjected to critical scrutiny, attempts have been made to find indirect ways around it, by treating cognitive processes as theoretical constructs, perhaps, or by trying to dispute the whole concept of objective empirical science. Thus, the paradigm shift was the consequence of some obscure change in sympathies, rather than of formal disconfirmation of S–R psychology.

But the paradigm that is to replace behaviourism is as yet not at all clearly formulated. There is wide agreement that it is to deal with cognitive functioning and the intentionality of behaviour, but the basic conceptual parameters of these content areas still call for clarification, and pose many problems of a logical, not merely empirical nature. Unfortunately, professional psychologists, because of the strongly praxis-oriented nature of the discipline, are in large measure uninformed and amateurish in their approach to these matters, and bravely hurl themselves into venerable philosophic blunders, believing that their new doctrines are the logical opposite of the principles of behaviourism and so are rendered victorious by its collapse. Thus, in the revulsion against behaviourism's 'objectivism' we find in the study of cognitive processes the postulation of every variety of subjectivist epistemology, with givens ranging from the sensa of information-processing theory to the visual images and propositional tokens of information-retrieval models and the total world-designs of phenomenology; all this without the smallest recognition of the intractable problems that have been pointed out in representationism and correspondence truth theories throughout the entire history of philosophy.

The other half of the problem, intentionality or goal-directedness, is virtually an unopened book for psychology; non-behaviourists have never recognised it as the problem it is at all. Psychological behaviourism, with the sole exception of E. C. Tolman's (1932) 'purposive behaviourism', has been steadfastly opposed to purposivism, interpreting the goal-directedness of behaviour as the causal consequence of past contingencies of reinforcement rather than the anticipation of future consummations, because it saw that psychology must be deterministic, and held (rightly as I shall argue) that purposivism was incompatible with determinism. But outside behaviourism goal-directedness has hardly ever been identified as a problem for science. In abnormal psychology, for example, although there have been some more or less explicit attempts to trace the multiplicity of behaviour back to a small number of basic drives, nevertheless the ability of the person to direct his or her own behaviour towards the gratification of those drives, by whatever well or ill judged means, is accepted without demur, indeed without reflection. Similarly, most social psychology is permeated with some variant of utilitarianism, assuming that its actors cast up the costs and benefits of the various options available to them and *elect* the course that maximises satisfaction. Yet, as I shall try to show, entities that can direct themselves towards a certain outcome, entities that generate their own behaviour *for a purpose*, simply cannot be dealt with in the categories of the natural sciences.

Well, then, it may be asked, is that not so much the worse for the natural science approach? Why should psychology be confined within that arbitrary strait-jacket? There is no lack of psychologists who call for some more liberal mode of apprehension, especially from within the movements of both humanism and existentialism. Both schools reject as unnecessary and indeed unfulfillable for psychology the requirement that the scientific explanation of an event depends on the discovery of its cause; if scientific explanation is of that kind, then it is inappropriate for psychological events since they have no cause, it is said. Again, the authority of Thomas Kuhn is invoked, with a freehand interpretation of his concepts, to support the contention that determinism may be a suitable 'paradigm' for some disciplines and not for others, or that determinism in general is only a subjective world-view which is already under stress from accumulating anomalies (here an invocation of quantum mechanics) and is about to be replaced by a more accommodating paradigm. An examination of the great range of arguments that have been brought forward under the heading of determinism versus indeterminism is too large a project for this book; what I shall do, however, is to examine in detail some proposed alternatives to psychological determinism to see whether they can even in principle enlarge our understanding of organismic behaviour. Though they may reject the label 'science' for psychology, and though they may reject explanation in favour of *understanding* through empathy or openness-to-experience – i.e. in favour of *intuiting* what it is that a person is trying to get at – nevertheless, existentialists and humanists plainly feel that they have a great deal of useful information to impart about the vicissitudes of human life, information that can be generalised and applied to the care of families, friends, or patients. The question will be to discover the conditions of that usefulness, and to examine whether, in so far as their psychological assertions are useful and informative, they do not contravene the authors' distinctive commitment to the concept of individual spontaneity, or of 'choosing one's being'.

In philosophy proper also, amongst philosophers of mind, a movement has developed of dissent from the philosophical–behaviourist way of dealing with mental events; that is, from the line of thought most commonly associated with the names of Ryle and Wittgenstein, which seeks to treat the names of mental events as referring only to dispositions towards certain kinds of behaviour. In particular, the behaviourist analysis of teleological processes, of those sequences of behaviour which at first glance we unreflectingly interpret as occurring in order to bring about predictable outcomes – an analysis that for decades has been pretty well established orthodoxy for the biological sciences (Russell, Braithwaite, and latterly Charles Taylor being the leading proponents) – has been subjected to detailed and forceful criticism in recent years, most notably in Woodfield's *Teleology* (1976). In my next chapter I shall be commenting in some detail on that book and on some later contributions to the same stream of thought. Woodfield contends that any list of externally observable features of behaviour – lists whose contents have become fairly familiar by now, harking back to McDougall's 'marks of behaviour' (1936), typically including persistence with variation, or plasticity of means in arriving at an allegedly identifiable terminus – cannot give an adequate account of what is ordinarily meant by 'purposive behaviour', perhaps because it will turn out to be applicable also to the behaviour of certain inanimate systems that we would not ordinarily accept as having purposes, and again because we will believe some behaviour to be purposeful that does not come up to those criteria – that does not ever arrive at its apparent 'goal', for example. Woodfield believes that in order to capture the meaning of 'purposive' and cognate terms we must recognise the determining role of processes internal to the organism – specifically, its *desire* for a certain condition and its *beliefs* about how to arrive at it. Woodfield himself disclaims any originality in the content of this conclusion, claiming that virtue only for his method of analysis, as revealing what is essentially involved in the concept of teleology and what is inevitably lacking in any 'externalist' account. Indeed, a number of other philosophers and philosophical psychologists on both sides of the Atlantic have advanced roughly similar 'internalist' (belief plus desire) accounts, with varying accents, in recent years: for example, Davidson (1963, 1973), Audi (1979), and Dennett (1979) in the United States, and in Britain, Gauld and Shotter (1977), Pettit (1978, 1979), McGinn (1979), and Wilson (1979).

But, in my opinion, none of these thinkers has committed himself sufficiently firmly (if at all) to a programme of psychological determinism, to be able to see just what large questions are raised and what great lacunae are left by these contributions. They really constitute nothing but a clearing of the ground before a start is made, the merest prolegomena. If one is to make good the rescue of 'belief', 'desire', and 'intention' from the merely dispositional status to which they had been consigned by philosophical behaviourism, then one must give some indication, in however general or schematic terms, of what kind of thing the substantive basis of the behavioural dispositions might be – that is, what kind of intrinsic property, process, or state these internal entities 'belief', 'intention', and 'desire' might turn out to be. It is no use, it seems to me, just to declare oneself to have a 'realist' conception of dispositions, because that leaves open the move – which has been actively advocated by Armstrong (1973), for example – of saying that the disposition itself is the 'real' term, the causal property, which (in the requisite external conditions) produces the behaviour. This, I shall argue, is merely tautological, and it seems to me an odd direction for Armstrong to take, in view of the immense contribution that he has made to the systematisation and clarification of central state materialism (Armstrong 1968). Central state materialism, or the mind–brain identity thesis, which has been given a rather more technical treatment by Wilson (1979), seems to me the only scientifically viable view now possible of the ontological status of 'mental entities', yet it is remarkable how many philosophers who nominally embrace the identity thesis still allow themselves to use such terms as 'mind', 'thought', 'wish', 'sensation', 'intention', and so on, as nouns, as if they were the names of mental rather than physiological entities mediating the various mental functions. It is a quite inadequate shift to say that they are using those terms only until the brain states to which they really refer have been identified – the details of these being safely left to the physiologist – because what is distinctive of these mentalistic concepts and quite alien to brain states is their *intentionality*, i.e. their supposed intrinsic relatedness to intended objects. The concept of intentionality enables the 'provisional' identity theorist to slide away from thorny problems concerning the causes of behaviour, problems that present themselves in the most immediate way when we take seriously the proposal that it is non-intentional *brain* processes which are at work. I shall try to show that intentionality as currently conceived (cf. Searle 1979b, for example) is not a coherently formulated notion, and must be radically revised.

Not only can there be no mental entities with relations intrinsic to them, but the arguments supporting the mind–brain identity thesis, properly understood, entail that there cannot be any intrinsic, non-relational mental properties *whatever*, and it is a salutary exercise to try to discuss mental processes without using any of those traditional mind-type nouns. One is compelled to realise what a profound reorganisation of psychological theory is required before one can tentatively identify, or even imagine, the kinds of brain structure that might subserve and *integrate* the related functions of knowing the environment, carrying out various programs of action on the known objects, and modifying those programs in the light of past experience so as to be more effective, all in such a way as to give a believable, deterministic account of a partly rational, partly irrational, conflict-prone yet remarkably adaptive human being.

Intimately wrapped up with this failure to sketch in a conceivable physiological realisation of 'intention' in particular is an hiatus in the causal sequence from material antecedents, external and internal, to behaviour. Even those thinkers who, like Davidson, insist that reasons can be causes, that is, that these internal psychological processes play a part in the efficient causation of behaviour, have been reluctant firmly to grasp the implications of saying that those internal events are themselves caused. If there is an unbroken causal sequence, if we are *thrown into* these internal states, motivational and informational, and, being in them, have our behaviour *produced* in us by external stimulation, then that must cause a radical reappraisal of what can be meant, if anything, by 'acting intentionally'. Almost without exception these authors avoid the crunch of this hard confrontation by retaining, as if nothing can or need be done about it, the concept of agency. Typically, lip-service is paid to the causal principle by agreeing that I can be caused *to act*, but never that my action (i.e. my behaviour) is caused. I call that lip-service because what is retained inviolate, preserved from criticism, is precisely the concept that whatever brought it about, *I act*, that is, I generate my behaviour in pursuit of my goals (and the origin of those goals remains shrouded in mystery, the mystery of 'human nature'). But this is to undercut what is absolutely the most central concern of psychology, the answer to the question 'Why did he do that?' In the natural sciences such questions – 'Why did this litmus turn red?' 'Why does this flower close its petals in the evening?' – are answered by finding the internal structures and the external cause, but if we accept that human beings simply are able to direct their own behaviour towards whatever goals they choose, then the answer to the 'Why?' question will invariably be, after perhaps a number of clauses specifying interim goals, beliefs about ways and means, and so on, simply 'Because he chose', and that will be that. Such an answer is final, unchallengeable, and totally inscrutable. If there were such a realm of events, there could not be a science of it.

Complacency about the problems of determinism in psychology is made easier by the unchallenged currency of the term 'behaviour'. The 'behavioural scientist' of today is one who is aggressively confident of the observability of his subject-matter – none of those fairy-tales about 'the science of mental life' for him – and the plain matter-of-factness and unproblematic status of behaviour as data is widely accepted. Yet the question of what we can see a person doing raises the most awkward epistemological and ontological issues. To say that we can see a person crossing the street or waiting for a bus or signing a contract or indeed *doing* anything whatever is a quite different kind of claim from saying that we can see a metal ball rolling down an inclined plane. All that we can actually *see* in the literal-minded sense of the behavioural scientist is the person's movements. We may see, for example, that a woman's hand is holding a pen which is being driven across the bottom of a printed sheet of paper, leaving a pattern of marks that other observations may persuade us is characteristic of her in similar situations. But, of course, to say that she is signing a contract entails a great deal more than that. It entails that she is moving the pen in that way in order to produce a recognisable signature which she agrees will constitute prima-facie evidence that she has willingly made herself legally obliged to carry out the commitments specified in the print above, which we assume she has read and understood, and so on – things that certainly cannot be 'seen' in the positivist, behaviourist sense, yet we claim, to others or to ourselves, to be able to make such observations scores of times every day, and could not begin to function socially if we did not believe we could make them. Every name of a behavioural act one can think of, however simple, can be interpreted in this way, that the person is making certain movements because he or she *believes* they will bring about a certain result ('hewing wood', 'drawing water', 'answering the telephone'); thus, the behavioural scientist, along with the rest of us, since he cannot avoid using such terms if he is to say what someone is doing, commits himself at every moment to the premise that he can see what that person *thinks* he or she is doing. This poses a staggering problem for any psychologist, even one who recognises a determining role for cognitive processes, in trying to give (as I claim must be done in the name of explanation) a deterministic account of behaviour. Not only do these behaviour-names implicitly attribute thought-processes to persons, but they seem also to assume that those persons can direct their own movements towards the result in question. The problem is to explain deterministically not only how a particular action comes about but why on successive performances it is likely to be done more and more effectively. One necessary preliminary to opening up such problems will be to disentangle the various confusions and illegitimate conflations concealed in the everyday and the professional usage of the term 'behaviour' itself.

But to convince the reader of the necessity of this task requires in the first place to show what is essentially involved in all 'teleological explanations' and why a science even of human behaviour cannot accept them as valid, nor, by the same token, accept 'purposive' or 'goal-seeking' as scientifically meaningful terms. As I suggested above, even the analysis of teleological explanations into the actor's desire for something and belief in how to get it does not go far enough towards an acceptable causal theory, because for that the concept of desire must be turned round from 'striving towards' something to 'being driven by' something else, and the nature and number of these driving engines be discovered, if we are to avoid that instantly available and completely trivial form of pseudo-explanation, 'Because he wanted to'.

Behaviourism, for quite ill founded reasons, has taken it that any theory of primary drives is just the invention of imaginary forces, comparable to the demons with which primitive man explained the workings of nature (Morgan 1979b). Along with every other postulated internal state of the organism, drives were to be emptied of all content other than the contingency of behavioural changes on manipulations of the environment – on deprivation of food, for example, and its availability on the performance of certain behaviours. But as we shall see in more detail later, behaviourists' practice contradicts their theory; they have always operated as if they had an implicit understanding of at least some primary drives, of what activated the drives and what sorts of behaviour they might be expected to give rise to, if only in that they deprive animals of food or water, for example, and then expect that eating or drinking will function as a reinforcer. Their reluctance to acknowledge the reality of these internal driving processes arose from their conviction that the notion of them was inescapably teleological, that they were forces directed towards a certain goal, seeking it out. But although the history of motivation theories and instinct psychologies is indeed littered with useless concepts of that kind – 'the acquisitive instinct', 'will to power', 'need for achievement', 'need for self-actualisation', and an endless list of others – nevertheless, it need not always be so. The concept of a set of 'biological engines' that drive the behaviour of a human being is no more metaphysically suspect (though it is a great deal more complicated) than that of the motors that drive the mechanical monsters in Disneyland. What makes human beings and many other species of organism different from mechanical monsters is that the operation of their motors is modified by that special form of feedback known as cognition, by which I simply mean their recognition of relevant facts, but, despite the explicit arguments of such authors as Gauld and Shotter (1977) and the unexamined presupposition of others (Rychlak 1975), to say that organismic behaviour is guided by cognition does *not* entail that it is not caused in every detail, nor that it exhibits some privileged kind of self-generated 'causality' not enjoyed by the ordinary objects of nature.

In the history of psychology the one grand systematic attempt at a deterministic theory of human motivation that would embrace all its variety and turbulence has been <u>Freud</u>'s unfinished metapsychology. When I say that a theory is deterministic that does *not* mean that the theory claims to be able to determine, i.e. to predict, everything that a person will ever do; nor does it entail some sort of fatalism, as if to say that it is no use people's contemplating the outcomes of various courses of action that seem open to them because what they are going to do has already been determined in advance by everything that has happened in the universe up to date. For one thing, the phrase 'everything that has happened in the universe' has no determinate referent, since 'the universe' is infinitely extended in space and time, and full of an infinite complexity of things, so that no complete list of everything that is going on could conceivably be drawn up. 'Everything' is open-ended in every dimension. Further, if I do contemplate the outcomes of my courses of action, then that contemplation is itself one of the things going on in the universe, and not only must it have a cause but it must also have effects, since nothing happens in a vacuum, even though those effects may not always be what I expect. <u>'Determinism', in the usage I am adopting, just means that every event has a cause, and is a cause of further events.</u> (The meaning of 'cause' will be elaborated in the following chapter.) So, then, Freud's metapsychology, I am claiming, was based on the premise that all human behaviour, bodily and mental, thoughts, wishes and actions, is caused, and it attempted to rough in the schematic outlines and name the identity of the main internal mechanisms, what I am calling 'biological engines', which in interaction with the pressures of the environment, give rise to all our behaviour. It must be stressed that Freud's concept of instinctual drive was not (leaving in abeyance for the moment his final version of Eros and Thanatos) in any sense that of a disembodied force sweeping us towards some fore-ordained consummation regardless of the conditions of existence; on the contrary, <u>his drives</u> (he always insisted on their plurality) <u>were thought of as physiological mechanisms with in-built, though modifiable, ways of working</u>. A certain confluence of internal and external conditions was required to make them start working and another to make them stop. His attempt (begun in the posthumously published 'Project for a scientific psychology', 1895) at providing a model of such physiological structures had to be

Bad argument

suspended because the contemporary understanding of neurological functioning was too limited to make such a model possible, but it certainly was not an inherently unachievable project. In the following chapters I shall be trying to show how, in broad outline, Freud's concept can be recast to make it compatible with the principles of present-day neurology (though that will be only to claim that some such mechanisms are possible, or scientifically conceivable). My turning to Freud does not in this connection entail a commitment to the details of his theories of mental structure or of the major complexes, nor does it repudiate them; his importance here lies in his fundamentally sound understanding of the methodological requirements for a scientifically viable theory of primary or instinctual drives, and in his daring to flesh out that abstract schema with psychological content of potentially the profoundest significance. That wealth of observation and insight should not be passed over, simply because in his time he had to try to relate it to a conceptually limited neurology.

A theory of primary or instinctual drives is required to fill that gap in philosophical action theory which is barely papered over by the use of the term 'desire'. It is needed to finish off the interminable chain of 'wanting A because it leads to B', and 'wanting B because it leads to C'; it is the only way, as we shall see, of giving empirical content to the notion of the inherently desirable. It will help bridge the gap between thinking of something to do and *doing* it. It will get rid of the implicit appeal to 'the will'. And it will get rid of the mere anti-theoretical particularism left behind by the behaviourist retreat from motivation theory. The recognition of the unifying and fundamentally explanatory function of such a theory of drives is the positive contribution to psychological theory offered by this book.

2
Teleological and causal explanations

The descriptive properties of animate behaviour

The notion that behaviour needs to be explained by reference to its purpose is, of course, age-old and did not arise wantonly. The behaviour of organisms does exhibit features that distinguish it from that of all inanimate objects except perhaps those governed by negative feedback. It shows a special sort of unity in diversity, or convergence mediated by variability. A hungry organism (from any of a great range of species) can be set down at a wide diversity of starting points and in each case will show behaviour that in a physical–geographical sense is different from that which occurred in the others, but, if the physical conditions make it possible, each of these trains of behaviour is likely to arrive at a common phase, that is, getting and eating food as soon as possible under the circumstances. If the starting point was originally unfamiliar, and the organism is allowed several trials from the same start, then again its behaviour can be expected to vary from one occasion to the next, and by and large it will change in such a way as to arrive at the food more quickly and economically. If the animal is heading towards a dish of food in view and someone moves the dish, the animal will change course to follow the food. All this is so familiar that if we come upon an organism whose behaviour is highly stereotyped, not modifiable by changes in the conditions and in consequence 'ineffective' or 'maladapted', then we think there is something wrong with it. It is this convergence on a common outcome, an outcome that is usually defined more or less explicitly as the reversal of some common (and stressful) starting condition, as hunger is reversed by eating, which is held to distinguish animate from inanimate behaviour.

But these differences between animate and inanimate behaviour are actually more difficult to specify than it seems at first glance, if we try to restrict ourselves to a positivistic conception of what is externally observable. Thus (as is regularly pointed out), even the weariest river winds somewhere safe to the sea, finds it way around obstacles, and reverses its starting condition of being higher to that of being lower. We seem as much, or as little, entitled to say that height is 'stressful' to water as that food deprivation is to animals, and that the stream takes the path it does in order to get lower. However, it is only in a metaphorical sense that water 'finds its way' around obstacles. We know that it is physically pushed this way and that by the interaction of the contour of the land and the gravitational effect of the Earth. The behaviour of organisms *appears* to be, to a degree, independent of direct physical pushing and pulling, and if we did not mean that organisms literally, not metaphorically, *find* their way around obstacles then there could not be such a metaphor. Finally, it is the improvement relative to reversing the starting condition – improvement of a different order from that of the river in sweeping aside obstacles and settling into a smooth course – which provides the most persuasive support for the proposition that animate *behaviour* is different from inanimate *happenings*.

The question is, in what terms can one give an intelligible account of how the apparent goal-directedness of behaviour comes about? By 'intelligible' I mean, of course, something more than that the sentences in which it is couched be linguistically understandable. I mean that the manner of working of these entities be of a kind that we can understand; of which we can feel, yes, I see *how that works*; and not of a kind that we must accept simply as a mystery, not graspable, not explicable in any workaday sense of those terms. To draw such a distinction presupposes a theory of viable explanation, which in this case is essentially a theory of causality, but it would be counter-productive to presume to begin by laying down an apodeictic theory of causality, a standard to which any candidate for explanatory legitimacy must conform. There has been too much argument about the nature of causality, too many accusations of *a priorism*, for any such account to be accepted as analytically necessary, or an iron law of nature. What I shall rather do is to try to unfold the main kinds of thinking about goal-directed behaviour, to show how they envisage the coming to be of these behavioural events. Of course, what I shall really be asking is whether they allow for the identification of a believable sort of efficient cause for the events, but if they do not, one will not be entitled to say, therefore they are *mistaken*, but can only try to persuade the reader that they present a kind of happening that cannot be understood.

The kinds of theory to be examined offer themselves as programmes for an empirical science of goal-directed behaviour, since for psychology a mere mystical celebration of the wisdom and harmony of nature does not promise any enlightenment. Consequently, they claim in their various ways that the concept of goal-direction is compatible with determinism. Some accept teleological causation as a special variety of causality, open to study (Charles Taylor's view, for example); others, rejecting that conception, offer an explanation, supposedly one of efficient cause, of goal-directedness as the outcome of a pair of states internal to the organism and determining its reaction to its environment – i.e. a desire or intention to bring something about, plus a belief about how to do it. Both, I shall contend, fail because at bottom they assume the concept of agency, and that is a concept that is simply unintelligible, one that cannot offer any useful information.

I begin by directing my attention to Woodfield's (1976) discussion of these types of theory, largely because it seems to me that he offers easily the most detailed working out of the desire plus belief model – to such an extent, indeed, that its deficiencies begin to be revealed, though that is not his intention.

Teleological explanations – externalism

Woodfield (1976) divides teleological theories into 'externalist' and 'internalist' types, i.e. into those which hold that goal-directed behaviour can be identified and explained by reference only to its external form, and those which hold that reference to processes internal to the behaving entity is necessary. Although, as usual with such divisions, the components of each package of ideas are not all logically inseparable from one another, and some migrate across the boundary, nevertheless it is a useful partitioning of the issues.

The major works cited by Woodfield as putting the externalist or behaviourist view of goal-direction are those of Russell (1945), Sommerhoff (1950, 1974), Braithwaite (1953), Nagel (1961), C. Taylor (1964), and Wright (1972). He holds, with reason, that this trend of thinking was historically linked with the emergence of behaviourist psychology and organismic biology, and its distinctive notion was 'that the hall-mark of a goal-directed process is the constancy of the final state in the face of variations in the initial conditions and starting-points' (Woodfield 1976, p. 39). Its authors wanted to supply objective, non-mentalistic criteria of purposive action, holding that such behaviour was discriminably different from the mechanical–causal behaviour of ordinary inanimate systems, as I was saying at the beginning of this chapter. There are differences of detail in their lists of criteria, but the central conception is that of the plasticity of behaviour with reference to a goal. As Russell says, 'The same goal may be reached in different ways, and from different beginnings' (Russell 1945, p. 110), and on any particular occasion, if one method or path is closed off, another may be employed. Woodfield characterises these as the 'lens' pattern, in which a variety of paths may be taken from one starting point to the goal point, and the 'fan' pattern, in which the object may start from a variety of different points, yet on each occasion arrives at the same goal.

As Woodfield points out, these criteria do not adequately distinguish purposive from non-purposive behaviour. If we start a boulder rolling down into a valley from the same point several times, it is quite unlikely to take just the same path on each occasion; if we close off its original path by putting a large rock there, then when it 'finds' that way closed it is quite likely to 'try' another route and get to the bottom all the same. If it is started from different points on the valley's rim, then, if the terrain is favourable, it will still get to the same terminus, at the bottom. (Even the most 'purposive' entity will not be able to get to its goal under just any circumstances.)

But, as I suggested in the case of the river, the reason why we are ordinarily not deceived into thinking that a boulder's rolling downhill is goal-directed behaviour is that we believe we can *see* that it only began rolling because it was pushed, that it rolls until something stops it, and that its variations of direction are caused by its being physically deflected by objects. McDougall's earlier list of 'marks of behaviour' (1936), though in the long run unavailing, was more sophisticated than those of these authors, if only because it began by saying that the behaviour of organisms exhibits 'a certain spontaneity of movement' as distinct from being simply pushed or pulled, and each of his succeeding marks can be read as just a more specific elaboration of that first one; thus, the animal is assumed to persist *of its own accord* until it gets to the goal and stop of its own accord when it does so; it varies its own direction to get around obstacles and prepares itself in advance for what is to come; and finally, actively adopts more effective means for getting there (instead of being mechanically pushed along the path of least resistance).

Such self-activation and self-direction would certainly distinguish purposive behaviour from mechanical–causal events, but to list them as *evidence* for purposiveness is a *petitio principii*; they are not evidence for it but the whole substance of it, as I shall try to show in more detail later. Certainly, self-activation in the full sense of an event that has no external cause but is 'self-generated' cannot be listed as an objectively observable aspect of behaviour. We can see, say, a sprinter leap from the starting-blocks without being pushed or pulled by anything else, and we can see a rocket hurl itself from its launching pad also without being externally pushed or pulled, but we cannot claim to *observe* that the former event was uncaused any more than we can claim it about the latter. The causal processes may well be concealed.

Yet, if McDougall had allowed that he was talking only about appearances, in terms of 'as if', then it is just that descriptive feature, the *appearance* of spontaneity, the appearance of self-direction, that marks off animate from inanimate action. To approach the matter in another way, if we *should* want to say that the presence of an object in its path *caused* the animal's detour around it (as against saying that the animal changed its own path), then that would look like a case of action at a distance, since the animal does not have to run into and bounce off the obstacle but turns aside before it reaches it, and causal action at a distance is an uncomfortable concept. Furthermore (depending, of course, on the species of organism), we can directly see that it is the movements of its own limbs or fins or wings, thrusting against the ground or water or air, which bring about the change in direction, so that at that first descriptive, holistic level, the organism does 'turn itself' away from the obstacle. The attribution of self-direction, of the absence of external causality, is reinforced by our native reluctance to believe literally in action *at a distance* – it sounds almost a contradiction in terms. Everyone's primitive image of causality seems to derive from the experience of physical pushing, or seeing things actually bang each other about in predictable directions the way billiard balls do; causal effects, according to this image, are produced only by physical contact, and perhaps that notion is not to be despised. Even physical scientists, dealing with apparent cases of action at a distance – electromagnetism, for example, or gravitational attraction – are regularly impelled to conjure up notions of some sort of physical medium, 'fields' of one sort or another, which, though they may be invisible and intangible to our senses, nevertheless spread through space, embrace objects and push them together or apart, changing action at a distance into physical contact, though of a strange kind. The scientist, presumably, fears that without some such medium to provide for causal explanation of physical events he may be forced back into a teleological, Aristotelian physics, in which bodies move because they have a natural tendency to move (of themselves) in their own characteristic way, and stop when they get to their natural resting places.

But the scientifically untrained person, and perhaps the scientist when he is relaxing, lets his thoughts run in the opposite direction when he sees a happening that, if it had been caused, must have been caused by action 'at a distance', so hard to comprehend; he slips into the magical mode of thinking, and sees it as having *no* external cause, but as a case of spontaneous activity, self-generated. It is reported that the great American comedian, W. C. Fields, used to go on tour in vaudeville with an act that included demonstrations of skill on a pool table. At the climax of the act, after a good deal of patter and a few suspended preparations for making a shot, he would set the balls racing about the table at the same time, helter-skelter, but all finally scuttling into the pockets 'like rabbits', miraculously, leaving the audience convulsed with incredulous laughter. They could see it but they could not believe it. Now, of course, if the billiard balls had actually been rabbits, then it would not have been incredible, nor even very funny, but just a good piece of animal training. The point is that a billiard ball is not the *kind of thing* that finds its way into the pocket, whereas rabbits are. If, by the same token, the audience had been able to see the network of fine wires on the pool table, by which the effect was achieved, then again the mystery and the delight would have disappeared along with the suggestion of self-direction. The action would no longer have seemed magical, but just the immediate physical effect of the wires guiding the balls to the pockets.

What has emerged from these various examples and counter-examples is that we are naturally inclined to attribute goal-directedness only to certain kinds of object, living organisms being the paradigm case, and the first distinguishing characteristic to emerge so far is that their parts are articulated in such a way as to enable them to push themselves around in their environment. Not to make a mystery of the matter, a second necessary characteristic which will shortly appear (and this will not complete the list) is that these goal-directed entities must have sense organs that will fill the gaps in the most obvious cases of action 'at a distance' by enabling the organisms to react to distant objects without being physically pushed by them, though, of course, some physical stimulus must leave the distant object and reach the organism's sense receptors.

If that is the case, then the externalist or behaviourist approach to the identification of goal-directedness just in terms of observable patterns of movement, and without its being necessary to consider the intrinsic properties of the behaving object at all, cannot be successful. Further, as we shall see from a number of examples, to ignore the intrinsic nature and ways of working of the behaving object is, whether wittingly or not, to commit oneself to some theory of the origin of the behaviour that is opposed to that of efficient causality.

Most of Woodfield's criticisms of the behaviourist theories proceed in much the same way as those above, i.e. by finding counter-examples in patterns of behaviour that would fall within the descriptive formula and yet would not be accepted as teleological, or others that would be excluded by the formula but do seem to be examples of goal-directedness. In the course of this discussion he moves from the description of goal-directed behaviour to the question of what it is for something to be a goal, and indeed the one concept is meaningless without the other. To call the convergent patterns of behaviour 'teleological' is precisely to say that they take the forms they do *in order* to arrive at the terminus, which is what distinguishes goals from *de facto* terminations. It is simply disingenuous for anyone to claim that he is using teleological concepts merely in a 'descriptive' rather than an explanatory way, because to describe a behaviour sequence as teleological is to claim that its occurrence is *explained* by the fact that it was likely to bring about, or was required to bring about, a certain outcome. Accordingly, before going on to discuss Woodfield's own proposals about what 'being a goal' means, I shall turn briefly to Charles Taylor's contribution to the behaviourist approach and to Woodfield's criticisms of it, because out of certain ambiguities in Taylor's views it begins to become plain that teleological explanations are directly incompatible with causal ones – an indispensable point in my argument.

In calling Taylor's conceptions 'behaviourist', one must hasten to add that he is directly and explicitly hostile to psychological behaviourism of the mechanistic S–R type. He insists that goal-directedness is a real force in certain classes of natural event, notably of course the behaviour of organisms, and that it is not to be reduced to concatenations of deterministic movements.

In Taylor's *The explanation of behaviour* (1964) his basic principle of teleological explanation is given thus:

The condition of an event *B* occurring is, then, not a certain state of *P* [a disembodied Purpose], but that the state of the system *S* and the environment *E* be such that *B* is required for the end *G*, by which the system's purpose is defined (Taylor 1964, pp. 9–10).

The import of that last phrase, that *G* is that 'by which the system's purpose is defined', is obscure, as Woodfield also notes, but on reflection it seems to me just a part of Taylor's denying that there is any large extrinsic Purpose that governs the development of the universe. Only some systems can be said to be purposive or goal-directed and for each one its goal-directedness is intrinsic to itself, arising as its natural way of working where that way of working is best described as working *towards* a particular nameable kind of goal state.

The passage quoted shows that Taylor is attributing a special kind of causality (as distinct from a special kind of cause) to teleological processes: 'The condition of an event *B* occurring is . . . that *B* is required for the end *G*'. This is, naturally, later qualified by saying that *B* must be physically possible for this *S* in this *E* at this time. Let us call this special causality T-causality. Its nature is obscure. Taylor does not commit himself to the incoherent conception of backward causation, as if some still non-existent event, one still in the womb of time, could cause something to happen now. Yet he continually uses phrases such as 'an event's occurring is held to be *dependent* on that event's being required for some end' (Taylor 1964, p. 9, my italics). It is as if 'requirement' were an active force in the current situation.

Taylor holds that the condition of being required for *G* is observable *ex ante*, without waiting to see what *S* does. He says:

. . . the fact that the state of a system is such as to require a given event if a certain result is to accrue can be perfectly observable, and the fact that this antecedent condition holds can be established independently of the evidence provided by the occurrence of the event itself (Taylor 1964, p. 10).

Now, that assertion seems to me to be perfectly unexceptionable, but its import for teleological theory has been vastly overrated both by Taylor and his critics; this observability *ex ante* of the necessity of a certain kind of *B* if *G* is to come about has no implications whatever as to whether *B* will *occur*. To take one of the literally endless possibilities, a car engine from which the rotor of the distributor has been removed cannot be started because the electrical impulses are not being delivered to the spark plugs. The replacement of the rotor is necessary if the engine is to be started, but that does not imply that it *will* be replaced; nobody may ever be concerned to start this engine again.

But Taylor wanted to draw some important distinction between 'intrinsic' descriptions ('the rotor is missing') and his 'requiring B for G' descriptions ('the rotor must be replaced if the engine is to be started') because he wanted to be able to claim that teleological explanations could account for behaviour when simple causal explanations could not. He says that:

> ... any given antecedent condition of B which fulfilled the conditions for the description 'requiring B for G' (let us call this T) would also fulfil some other 'intrinsic' description, E. But this is not to say that B's occurring is a function of E's occurring, i.e. that B depends on E (Taylor 1964, p. 13).

Plainly, what Taylor wants to say is that B cannot be accounted for by *any* set of intrinsic antecedent conditions, but so far he has not adequately stated the causal theorist's case; no determinist would claim that the absence of the rotor was sufficient to cause its replacement. Taylor goes on:

> For it may be that in other circumstances a situation which fulfils the description E is not followed by B, the circumstances being precisely those in which the situation does not also fulfil the conditions for the description T; whereas all cases of T may be followed by B (Taylor 1964, p. 13).

But it is quite mysterious how a situation describable by E ('rotor is missing') could sometimes also be describable by T ('rotor must be replaced if engine is to start') and sometimes not. Conceivably, someone might provide an ingenious mechanism that would bypass the rotor and still deliver the spark to the cylinders, but surely the availability of such a mechanism would have to be included in E, i.e. in the relevant antecedent causal conditions. That sort of difference was not what Taylor had in mind, I think; in the background is the notion that on the one occasion the organism chooses to pursue G and on the other not. In reply to Noble (1967), Taylor agreed that the intrinsic description of the antecedents should include the state of the behaving entity or system S, so that 'E' in the passage above should read 'SE'. Woodfield's comment on this revision sums up the position justly:

> Now the passage seems to assert that it is possible that two cases may obtain, in which the system and the environment are in precisely the same state, intrinsically characterised, but in one the teleological description T holds, in the other it does not. In one, SE is followed by B, in the other not ... But surely it is obvious that in a pair of cases with identical antecedent conditions, if a response of type B is required for G in one, it must equally be required for G in the other ... It may, indeed, be conceivable that only in one of the two cases does an instance of B

actually *occur*. But the reason why *B* occurred in that case could not be simply that the antecedent situation required *B* for *G*. That would have been a sufficient reason for *B* to have occurred in the other case too (Woodfield 1976, p. 76, notation adjusted to conform to Taylor's).

But, in fact, for the determinist it is *not* conceivable that *B* could occur in the one case and not in the other if the system and the environment were in exactly the same state in all the relevant causal conditions. Because of this, Noble went on to argue that 'whenever a teleological explanation of the kind described by Taylor can be given, it is necessarily the case that a non-teleological (*SE–B*) account can also be given' (Noble 1967, p. 103).

Now, presumably by 'non-teleological (*SE–B*) account' Noble means an ordinary efficient-causation account, which would be a way of arguing that Taylor had shown his own teleological account to be unnecessary and, indeed, empty in contending that the sufficient conditions for the occurrence of the behaviour were observable *ex ante*. If Noble did not mean that, then there would have been no good reason for Taylor to find anything in this criticism that called for a reply, because it would be quite unnecessary for him to claim that there could be situations describable as 'requiring *B* for *G*' for which he could not also give an intrinsic description. Indeed, that would be quite inconceivable; one could not possibly say 'This situation requires *B* for *G*' without being able to see *what kind of situation it was*, and how it related to the causal conditions of *G*. That he did feel called on to find some answer may have been due to his reluctance to declare that goal-directed behaviour *is not caused*; i.e. that teleological explanation is incompatible with causal explanation of the same events. For if Noble had claimed that the regularity of the *SE–B* relationship (conceded by Taylor) showed that it was a causal, not a teleological one, it was open to Taylor simply to declare that such a conclusion was unjustified, and that the relationship, however regular, was not an example of efficient causality but of *occasionalism*; that is, that finding itself in a situation *E* in which *B* was required for *G* would be an occasion for *S* spontaneously to emit *B*, directing its own movements towards *G*. In no instance would it be the case that for such an *S*, *E caused B*; rather, *S* is conceived of by Taylor as generating in itself the movements necessary to bring about *G* in *E*. This difference between efficient causality and occasionalism (or what I previously called T-causality) would need to be directly observable for Taylor's purposes, otherwise the difference between the two positions would become simply a verbal one. If *S* always does *B* in *E*, what does it matter whether we call *E* the cause or the occasion?

The notion that we can just observe the difference between efficient causality and T-causality, however regular the relationship between *SE* and *B*, is implicit in Taylor's (1967) reply to Noble. He claims that when we have identified a *T–B* relationship, that relationship allows us to formulate a general law predicting that in some as yet unobserved situation

E_{n+1}, a known S will produce a novel set of movements adequate to bring about G, whereas, he says, the mere SE–B connections cannot be generalised beyond observed particulars. I cannot see that the latter is the case. It is just as open to the determinist to predict on the basis of past observations that some novel G-producing event will occur, but he will regard that as just the beginning of his enquiry, as a fascinating fact of nature crying out for explanation, whereas the teleologist takes it as primitive, not further to be explained. T-causality is *sui generis*. Event B is supposed to be generated by the fact that it is required for G, and that is the end of the matter. Woodfield says that in Taylor's theory 'the T-law is a kind of causal generalisation, and teleological explanation as Taylor defines it turns out to be a kind of causal explanation' (Woodfield 1976, p. 81). In addition, Wright, who sympathises with Taylor's approach and offers a modified version of it, calls teleological explanations 'etiological' (Wright 1976). But it is a quite different kind of 'causality' from efficient causality.

Taylor proposes that an event could be explained at one level by efficient-causal laws and at another by teleological laws, the latter being more basic. But, in fact, one cannot consistently say of the one event both that it was caused and that it occurred in order to bring about its consequences; that would inflict an unacceptable level of violence on the meaning of either 'cause' or 'in order to'. To take an example from the popularised kind of physiological writing, it might be said in describing the 'emergency pattern' of physiological discharges that the adrenal glands secrete adrenaline in order to procure the release of red blood cells from the spleen, and that the spleen releases these red blood cells in order to provide for the more rapid distribution of oxygen (in case this should be required for the energetic use of the muscles in fighting or fleeing). Now, if we consider these two statements about the spleen, we can see that one of them must be given up. If the adrenaline *causes* the release of the red blood cells, then on any particular occasion (leaving aside the matter of the survival value of such a mechanism making it genetically more common over many generations) the consequences of the spleen's behaviour would be perfectly irrelevant to its occurrence. The attribution of goal-directedness to the spleen's behaviour entails that it is in some sense free to release or not release the red blood cells – that they were not simply jolted out of it, as it were, by the adrenaline.

One can imagine the determined compatibilist asking, but *why* does the arrival of the adrenaline cause the red blood cells to be released? Why in general does event-type A cause event-type B? Perhaps a superior agency has dictated this causal connection precisely in order that some overall scheme will be realised, thus making causality compatible with, indeed an integral part of, teleology. But for the determinist, that would be just a play-acting kind of causality. He does not regard the question 'Why does A cause B?' as legitimate; causal connections, once we have discovered what fills in any spatial or temporal gaps, are the brutest of brute facts. The interacting entities cause effects in each other because of their own intrinsic properties, not because of some external licensing agency. That would make nonsense of the whole idea of causality.

Taylor got into this problem about the apparent coextension of causal and teleological explanations because of his desire to show that teleological behaviour was predictable and its conditions observable *ex ante*, thus disposing of the two most frequent objections, that it is unpredictable and only capable of pseudo-explanation *a posteriori*. The reason why his attempt failed, as Woodfield has helped to make clear, is that giving an externalist account of the objective characteristics of goal-directed behaviour necessitates giving an externalist account of what it is for something *to be a goal*, and it seems impossible to encompass everything that is ordinarily meant by 'having a goal' in the externalist way. Taylor is not explicit about the concept of goal, but the general externalist tendency, as Woodfield points out, is to take a goal as being a kind of activity common to a species, one that has obvious biological utility, and one that appears to be the focus of convergent behaviour. Woodfield's general criticism of this definition is that if S's having a goal G at a particular time is supposed to explain why S behaves 'appropriately' at that time, then his having the goal cannot *consist in* that appropriate or convergent behaviour, because the *explanans* must be distinct from the *explanandum* (Woodfield 1976, p. 157). The externalist also faces the problem of saying why a particular sequence should be regarded as *terminated*, since every action will be followed by some further one, and perhaps it was that later one which was the actual focus of the convergence. Behaviourally, it would be impossible to tell. Woodfield advances a number of other considerations, especially those of goal-failure and the changing of goals in midstream, to which I shall return shortly, which he believes prompt an 'internalist' conception of having a goal, i.e. the notion that the goal actually engaged must be somehow represented in S's internal state; but in much of this he was anticipated briefly, yet forcefully, by Borger, commenting on a paper of Taylor's in 1970.

In his 1970 paper Taylor took a significant step away from the externalist approach by introducing the condition that 'in applying teleological explanation to animate beings . . . we have to take account of the way that the agent sees the situation' (Taylor 1970, p. 59). He goes on:

Plainly, explanations of human behaviour, for instance, can only be teleological if we interpret 'requiring B for G' as 'requiring B for G in the view of the agent'. That an action is required in fact for a given goal will not bring it about unless it is seen to be such; and many actions can be accounted for in terms of the goals of the agents concerned which in no wise really serve those goals (Taylor 1970, p. 59).

Taylor seems not to have seen how large an admission this is. It actually means that *B* is not *at all* brought about by its being required, but only by the antecedent belief in the agent's mind that it is required. The teleological aspect of the explanation resides in the fact that the agent, believing *B* to be necessary for *G*, *chooses* to do *B*, or does *B* by an exercise of agency (a conception to which I shall return later).

This recognition of the instrumental role of state variables which are ordinarily taken to be internal to the organism, its beliefs, which may be true or false, about what needs to be done for *G*, obviously introduces a large constraint on the observability *ex ante* of the requiredness of *B*. There are great practical difficulties in finding out in advance (unless we rely on asking), without waiting to see what behaviour actually occurs, whether the agent has a certain conception (especially if it is a mistaken one) of how to go about things. Further, if the agent's conception is mistaken, then the behaviour is unlikely to arrive at or even converge on the goal; yet, as Taylor said above, such misguided actions 'can be accounted for in terms of the goals of the agents concerned', which requires that not only the mistaken beliefs but the goals as well be identifiable independently of the behaviour. In this paper Taylor had nothing to say about what turned a certain possible outcome into a *goal*; that concept was still unexamined. The question is begged when he says that the situation must be seen as requiring behaviour *B* for goal *G* 'in the view of the agent', for the expression 'goal *G*' simply assumes without explanation that the agent already sees this outcome as his goal. Taylor sometimes uses expressions such as 'the goals of the agent', but his preferred formula, and the one that suits his theory best, is to say that the *situation* requires *B* for *G*. In ordinary discourse 'the demands of the situation' is usually a rationalising cliché disclaiming self-interest; situations do not literally demand or require anything, it is only organisms which can properly be said to do that. The point is that from any situation at all quite a large (perhaps endless) variety of outcomes could be produced by different behaviours; what determines which one will be produced?

This question was raised by Borger (1970), and though he did not labour the point it seems to me to reveal at one stroke how inadequate and peripheral in its explanatory role is Taylor's formula for the explanation of goal-directed behaviour, that it occurred 'because it was required for *G*'. Borger's paper gives the instance that he had just made a cup of coffee, and points out that 'the situation was also such that it "required" a quite different series of events to produce a cup of tea, or a ham sandwich – yet somehow only the coffee producing events occurred' (Borger 1970, p. 83). That is, let us imagine Borger standing in his kitchen, where all the materials and equipment for producing a cup of coffee, or a cup of tea, or a ham sandwich, or a three-course meal, or a batch of coloured stuff for finger-painting, and so on, are available, and Borger knows all this and has a fair idea of how to do any of those things, yet contents himself with making a cup of coffee. How is that selectivity to be understood? The natural answer is that it was something in the agent, not in the external situation; that at that moment he wanted coffee, not the other things, or had some other good reason for making coffee; and this leads us back to the 'internalist' account of goal-directed behaviour advanced by Woodfield. The general point is that the abstract causal fact that one event (B) leads to another (G) is not in any material sense a condition of B's occurring; it has, in fact, absolutely *nothing* to do with B's occurring; the only way it can, if at all, be mentioned among the causes of B is in the event that the agent concerned believes 'B promotes G'; it is the belief, not the fact believed, that figures among the causal conditions, and not the belief alone but also a motivational state to which the event-type 'G' is relevant.

Teleological explanations – internalism

Woodfield argues towards the position that internal states of belief and intention are required for goal-direction by analysing the *meaning* of 'S did B in order to do (or bring about) G'. Included in that meaning, he insists, is the possibility of goal-failure; that is, it could be true that S did B in order to do G even though S did not ever succeed in doing G. Also, it could be true that in the course of doing B, S changed his mind about doing G, thus never did do it, yet at the time he undertook B he undertook it in order to do G. These two possibilities are among the chief ones that the externalist approach cannot handle, since it defines goal-directedness in terms of the plasticity of behaviour in *arriving at* the goal. It seems plain that if an organism can still have a goal even though it does not arrive at it, then we must regard the having of the goal as some kind of internal state that the organism has antedating or at least contemporaneous with its undertaking B, and Woodfield's fully spelled out paraphrase (with regard to systems capable of goal-directed behaviour) of the meaning of 'S did B in order to do G' is:

> S did B because S wanted to do G and believed that B [promoted] G, and this desire–belief pair initiated and sustained a desire to do B, which, after joining forces with a belief that the time was ripe, gave rise to an internal state that controlled the performance of B (Woodfield 1976, p. 182).

Although all the clauses of this are relevant to his discussion, he says that for convenience it can be shortened to:

> S did B because S wanted to do G and believed that B [promoted] G (Woodfield 1976, p. 182).

Woodfield also offers paraphrases of natural function statements ('The heart beats in order to circulate blood') and artefact function statements ('The knife is sharp in order to cut'), but I shall not be directly concerned with these. His account of natural functions is in terms of an efficient-causality conception (though quirkily and idiosyncratically formulated) of their survival value, and that of artefact functions is very much a subspecies of his view of goal-directed behaviour, with the artefact serving as an instrument for goal achievement, in the view of the agent.

In general, then, Woodfield aims to give a causal account of how goal-directed behaviour comes about, or at least to show programmatically how such an account could be given. The final-causality role of events to come, implicit in Taylor's approach, has supposedly been transposed into the efficient causality of current states of the organism. But, unfortunately, that laudable program is hindered by Woodfield's restricting himself to his professional analytic philosopher's role of unfolding what '*S* does *B* in order to do *G*' means, because, as I have argued above, what it *means* is something incompatible with an efficient-causality explanation of the events to which it is applied; one cannot say of the one event both that it was caused and that it occurred in order to bring something about. Woodfield (as with almost everyone who takes this line) manages to conceal this incompatibility from himself by accepting the concept of 'intention' (or 'desire' or 'purpose' or 'goal' – he takes all these to be more or less cognate terms) as the kind of intrinsic internal state that can function as one of the causal conditions of the organism's behaviour. Intentions, along with beliefs, are accepted as 'intentional states' of the person, i.e. as states that essentially contain within themselves a reference to or representation of some possible type of situation or event external to themselves. This conception of intentionality is accepted quite complacently, without any exception that I can find, by philosophers currently writing about these matters, but what I want to argue is that it is a fundamentally incoherent ~point~ conception, one that cannot be genuinely understood, and that some radically revised account of the facts to which the concept of intentionality has been applied must be given. The supposed intentionality of intentions and that of beliefs raise rather different, though interconnected, problems, and I shall deal with them separately as far as possible, taking intentions first and leaving a fuller discussion of beliefs until later in this work. This will clear the ground for me to show schematically what form the description of the relevant internal causal states must take.

The intentionality of intentions and their supposed role as causes

The standard objection to treating intentions as efficient causes of behaviour has been that efficient causes and their effects must be logically independent of each other – 'distinct existences' as Hume says – and, so the argument runs, an intention is not logically independent of the intended action resulting from it; consequently, it cannot be an efficient cause of it. But, due in large measure to Davidson's analysis (1963), this argument is now widely seen to be ineffective. As Mackie puts it, it is little more than a bad pun on the phrases 'logically distinct' and 'logically connected' (Mackie 1974, p. 287). The intention would need to be 'logically connected' with its intended effect only in that it contained a representation of that event-type in it, and that certainly would not make it logically impossible that one could occur without the other. Or as Pettit argues:

> It may be that my intending to do X and my doing it, described as such, are logically connected but they are not so connected when the first event in the pair is redescribed as 'the intending which I went through at time t' or 'the intending that was uncharacteristic of me' (Pettit 1979, p. 8).

However, it is a little too easy, having rejected the 'logical connection' argument, to go on, as Pettit does (following Davidson), to say that:

> The question of status then appears to be settled. The explanation of actions by reference to states of belief and concern [i.e. intention or desire] represents those actions as the determined causal issue of the mental states (Pettit 1979, p. 8).

The disability of the concept of intention (and of intentionality in general) is that it essentially involves the incoherent notion of intrinsic relatedness, i.e. the notion that the relation to its object is built into the mental 'entity', intention, itself. Anything that can stand in a causal relation, or in any relation at all, must have at least some intrinsic properties. If that were not the case, if the supposed entity consisted solely of relatedness to something else, as the 'self' is held so to consist in existentialist psychology, then we could not understand what it was that was said to have these relationships. A relation can hold only between two or more terms, and a part of what is involved in seeing those terms as related is being able to see them as distinct, that is, as each having its own intrinsic properties, so that we can say what the terms *are* that are related. That means that each term of the relation must be able in principle to be described without the need to include any reference to its relation to the other. Further, a thing's relations are not to be found *in it*; they cannot be found just by examining its own nature. Nothing can have its relations intrinsic or internal to itself. (Of course, the relations between a thing's parts may be said to be internal to it, but they are not *its* relations; they are the relations of the parts and they are external to those parts.) So, then, if 'intention to do B' is to be able to stand in a causal relation to B-type behaviour (or in any relation to anything), then it must be of such a nature that it conceivably could be described just by reference to its intrinsic properties, without referring to its relation to anything outside itself, which of course means *without referring to its relation to B-type acts.* But, surely, that is impossible from the nature *Pictures* of the concept. One cannot subtract all reference to *B* (or to possible *B*-type *Rep in φ* acts) from 'intention to do *B*'. And if that internalised relationship is *of Art* incorporated in the concept, then it is an incoherent concept.

Searle came close to recognising this difficulty in a recent article (1979a), only to sheer away from it again. He begins by drawing a parallel between intentional states and speech acts, in that the distinctive feature of each is representation. Declarative speech acts represent a certain state of affairs as being the case, and intentions to act represent a certain state of affairs as possible and desirable. In the one case the condition of satisfaction is that the content of the speech act should fit the world, and in the other that the world should come to fit the state represented in the intention (though as we shall see later the *manner* in which that satisfying state comes about is most important, and difficult to define, if we are to say that it was achieved intentionally). But Searle declares that the question of what is an intentional state, is not an ontological one, because only its 'logical properties' are important. It is simply not relevant to ask how such states are realised. 'Are they neural configurations in the brain, modifications of a Cartesian ego, Humean ideas and images floating around in the mind, words occurring to us in thought, or causal dispositions to behave?' (Searle 1979a, p. 81). It simply does not matter, he says, just as it does not matter whether a speech act is realised in speaking or in writing, in French or in German. 'We should, with justification, regard someone who was obsessed by the question whether speech acts were identical with physical phenomena such as sound waves as having missed the point' (Searle 1979a, p. 81).

But that is too easy. Of course a speech act is not identical with the physical events used on any particular occasion to convey it, but *some* such physical phenomena must be employed, and whatever they are, they must be able to be described in terms that make no reference at all to their function of representation. That *is* an ontological matter, since it deals with the categorial properties of things that we can conceive of as physically existing, whereas the question of which physical medium a given speech act employs is merely a technical one. Later in the paper Searle does recognise that the representational function is not intrinsic to the physical medium in which the speech act is realised, but he does not see that this is a perfectly general categorial necessity which applies to 'intentional mental states' as well. He says:

> ... speech acts have a physical level of realization, *qua* speech acts, that is not intrinsically Intentional. There is nothing intrinsically Intentional about the utterance act, that is, the noises that come out of my mouth or the marks that I make on paper ... How does the mind impose intentionality on entities that are not intrinsically intentional, on entities such as sounds and marks that are, construed in one way, just physical phenomena in the world like any other? (Searle 1979a, p. 89).

Now, there is nothing mysterious about how that happens; putting it briefly, intentionality is imposed by the language community's coming to agree that a given physical entity (sound, mark, etc.) shall be conventionally used to stand for another bit of the physical world. But such agreed-upon relations cannot confer intentionality upon *mental* entities (if such there be) since they are not public property. Searle says that:

> Beliefs, fears, hopes and desires on the other hand are intrinsically Intentional. To characterize them as beliefs, fears, hopes and desires is already to ascribe intentionality to them (Searle 1979a, pp. 88–9).

With this I have already agreed, but Searle does not see that it is a logical defect in those concepts. In the long run he has nothing to tell us about the nature of an 'intentional state', and could not very well do so:

> If the characterization of Intentionality in terms of representation were intended to be an analysis . . . then it would be hopelessly circular . . . I do not believe it is possible to give an analysis of Intentionality. Any attempt to characterize Intentionality must inevitably use Intentional notions (Searle 1979a, p. 90).

But the reason for that circularity is that 'intentional states' as conceived have not, and could not have, any intrinsic properties to which one could point without having to make reference to direction-towards-an-object. If one asks, what is the nature of the mental state that intends this intentional object, the only possible answer, in the present way of thinking, is, the *intending* of it – the 'intention' to do it, if it is an object of pursuit, or the 'representation' of it, if it is an object of belief. No other nature is attributed to these intentional states, apart from their serving these functions – they are 'that which' does the job. The reasons why no intrinsic nature *can* plausibly be attributed to them are rather different in the two cases, intentions and representations. For representations, the status of substantive entities (or 'mental states' – this being only a verbal shift) cannot be granted to the various forms of mental image that have been proposed because then they could not do their job of explaining how we manage to know the world; the problems of knowing these substantive entities and their relations would be just the same as those of knowing external substantive entities. (This cursory comment will be elaborated later on.) In the case of intentions, if they were substantive entities, intrinsically describable internal states, then they could not do the job that even people like Woodfield still (inexplicitly, perhaps) want them to do, namely, explaining how we *actively direct ourselves* towards goals, because once they are given substance, once they are given intrinsic properties, then causality lays its hold upon them and self-direction ('intentional action') is pushed out. This does not mean that those 'intentional states' must therefore be retained with all their faults; what I am going on to argue is that the problems to

[margin notes, left side, handwritten:]
All prop atts? All intensional states? An eliminative materialist? (No, just appetitive, motivational states) PD 66

which they are addressed – how we break out of subjectivity; how we direct our actions – are unnecessary inventions, based on false premises.

To put it bluntly, what I am contending in the case of the origins of behaviour, is that if no intrinsic properties can be found for 'intention', if we must regard it as a concept defined essentially by intrinsic or constitutive relations, then it is an improperly formulated, incoherent concept. Not only can it find no place in a deterministic psychology, but it is a concept which is not really intelligible, for exactly the same reasons that the 'will' that we are constantly enjoined to exercise is not an intelligible concept, however much it is bandied about, and so it should be discarded. (I cannot exercise my 'will' in the sense in which I may exercise my muscles or my lungs because it is not an organ having any substance. Its whole nature is to be 'that which produces my actions'.) Now, I have admitted from the beginning that the behaviour of organisms has distinctive characteristics, those which are (however misleadingly) referred to as 'being goal-directed', and my own goal is not to explain them out of existence but to give an empirically understandable account of how they come about. The first step is to get rid of 'intentions'.

Further, I am grouping the concept of 'desire' as a causal condition of behaviour along with 'intention' as calling for critical scrutiny. 'Desire' and 'intention' are separable concepts because one can be said to have a desire to do something yet have no intention to do it, in fact, positively intend not to do it if one has competing motives. But 'desire' along with 'intention' suffers the disability that it is supposed to be an internal state that is nevertheless essentially characterised by its relation to a projected event or event-type; it is always a desire *for* something, this relation being intrinsic to it as conceived. Like 'intention to act', 'desire to act' also has the notion of self-generated movement towards its intentional object built into it, even though it may await the forming of an intention (in the theory I am criticising) before it becomes translated into action. In the case of 'desire' one can manage much more readily than in the case of 'intention' to form a conception of what actual processes are going on that would do the job for which the concept of 'desire' is called into play. But what causes me to feel some reserve about the supposedly causal explanation of action which proceeds by postulating a desire to do G and a belief that B will promote G, and asserts that the concurrence of these and various contextual factors *causes* the action, is my suspicion that hidden in the background is the notion that when those antecedents occur, then the agent *decides to act*, and if not that, then at least *directs his own movements* in such a way as to perform B. That is not a causal explanation of behaviour, and it is the lack of any suggestion, however schematic, of what desires consist of, where they come from, and how their existence produces the movements they are said to cause, which turn the 'desire or intention plus belief' model embraced by Woodfield and several others into something that is not much more than a distant and polite nod towards a causal theory.

Woodfield himself is not insensible of the possibility of such a criticism. He says:

Having G as a goal amounts to having G as the intentional object or content of desire, and type-identifying an internal state as 'a desire to do G' involves, [some philosophers] would say, classifying it on the basis of a teleological taxonomic principle. Instead of explaining observable behaviour straightforwardly by reference to a future goal, I am (they would say) explaining it by invoking an internal state which has a reference to the future goal built into it. The problematic forward orientation is still there (Woodfield 1976, pp. 204–5).

But his defence against this anticipated criticism misses the main point, since it refers only to the intentionality of cognitive representation of the goal, and not to the equivocal causal status of 'desire to do G'. He says:

This line of criticism rests on a serious misapprehension. Desires are not type-identified retrospectively, according to their outcomes . . .
   It is terribly tempting to think of a goal as a concrete future event, and to think of the present desire as involving a conception of that future event, with the conception of the goal being in some sense logically or ontologically derivative from the goal itself. But this is the wrong way round. A goal just *is* the intentional object of the relevant kind of conception. Admittedly, in a loose sense of 'refer', a man's desire to do G tomorrow does refer to a future time, and to an act-type G. The man may envisage a possible future doing of G. But the description of the desire does not make a reference to a particular action in the actual future (Woodfield 1976, p. 205).

Wright takes Woodfield to task for this defence, pointing out what a tangle he gets himself into by saying, as he does later on in elaborating his argument, that goals 'are mental entities, living permanently inside intentional brackets' (Woodfield 1976, p. 212), and that 'intentional objects . . . can never become real objects'. If that were the case, then, as Wright points out, once we had formulated the image of the goal then we would *have* 'the goal', and nothing would be left to be done. '. . . if G is a mental entity which antedates B, then there is nothing left for B to bring about' (Wright 1978, p. 228). Wright points out that in the great majority of cases (the minority including only things like trying to achieve a state of 'inner peace', for example) our goals are types of physical event and achieving them means bringing about an actual instance of the type.
   But Wright's motivation is different from mine. He wants to argue that '*B* occurs because it is appropriate for *G*', G being a certain type of physical event, is a self-sufficient form of 'etiological' explanation, and I am contending that it is a type of explanation which presents us with a mystery,

and that it is a strange form of 'etiology' which is incompatible with efficient causation. My criticism of Woodfield is that what is 'problematic' in the 'forward orientation' of his explanatory use of goal as internal state is not that it presupposes that the agent can think about the future, which is not a problem at all, but that he can impel himself *towards* the future.

Since experience has informed me that the proposition '*there are no intentions*' cannot be expected to win instant assent, I am going on to elaborate what I have been saying about the unimaginability of finding intrinsic properties of intentions. That immediately raises the question, why one should bother to do so, why should that be a requirement for the explanation of behaviour? This will call for an explication of what is involved in giving a causal explanation of an event, and an attempt to point out what a painful void is left if one contends that such an explanation is impossible. What will emerge from unfolding the nature of causal explanation is the revelation of how extraordinarily difficult the development of a thoroughly deterministic psychology is once we are jolted out of the complacency of thinking we can use intentions as causes. The conventional employment of the concept of 'behaviour' itself plays a large role in concealing the extent of this difficulty, because that conventional usage glosses over the question of how the *movements* are put together that bring about the *achievement* for which any piece of behaviour is named. Accordingly, the title of this book will have to be, in part, justified by dissecting that concept itself.

The non-existence of intentions

In forming hypotheses about the nature of some causal factor that has not yet actually been observed, one requirement for a useful hypothesis is to sketch in the notion of a kind of thing or property that we can imagine *finding*, and in fact the notion of a kind of thing that someone could have stumbled on without having the least idea what effects it might have, just as a chemist might have identified a certain kind of molecule in opium without knowing that molecules of that kind would put people to sleep if swallowed in sufficient quantities. That is, we should be able to offer a description of the causal property that does not refer to its causal role.

Armstrong, in *A materialist theory of the mind*, disputed the force of that requirement with regard to our thinking about intentions as mental causes. He says that: 'my direct awareness of this mental cause is simply an awareness of the sort of effect it is apt for bringing about' (Armstrong 1968, pp. 134–5). The strangeness of saying that our awareness of a cause *is* our awareness of its effects is obscured by his saying 'the sort of effect it is apt for bringing about', but the use of 'apt' is unjustified here. We could only informatively say that something was apt for a certain function if we could directly see the sort of thing it *was* – it is like saying 'That's well designed', or, for example, 'That's just the shape of chisel I want for this bit of carving'. But in Armstrong's sentence 'the sort of effect it is apt for bringing about' could be changed to 'the sort of effect it *does* bring about', which in turn could be boiled down to 'its effects', and, to repeat, being aware of certain effects is not being aware of their cause. But Armstrong's view of intentions is encapsulated within a wider theory of dispositions as causes which is not peculiar to him, and since that theory is directly relevant to my theme it is worthwhile looking at it in a little more detail.

Armstrong draws an analogy with the brittleness of glass, saying that brittleness is

> . . . an actual state of the glass, and so a causal factor in its subsequent breaking. Although speaking of brittleness involves a reference to possible breaking, the state has an intrinsic nature of its own (which we may or may not know), and this intrinsic nature can be characterized independently of its effect. And it is a mere contingent fact that, in suitable circumstances, things with this nature break. Now may not the relation of the intention to the occurrence of the thing intended stand in much the same relation as brittleness stands to the actual subsequent breaking? And if so, intentions may still be causes of the occurrence of the thing intended (Armstrong 1968, p. 134).

But there is an obvious tension between saying that *brittleness* is an actual state of the glass, which I take to mean an intrinsic state, and saying that we may not know the intrinsic nature of that state, that is, that we may have to discover it *after* we know that the glass is brittle. And if he does mean that the intrinsic state *is* brittleness, then it is certainly not 'a mere contingent fact that, in suitable circumstances, things with this nature break'; it is analytically true (cf. Tuomela 1977). That this is not simply a verbal infelicity on Armstrong's part is shown by his explicitly arguing in a later work that a disposition can be regarded as an intrinsic state (Armstrong 1973). Beginning with the proposal that it seems hard to believe that a thing's dispositions could change without some change in the thing (with which I readily concur), he develops an argument the actual import of which, in my opinion, is that if an object has a disposition, then that disposition must be based in some non-relational property, or intrinsic state, of the object. But he goes on to contend that one can

> . . . *identify* the disposition with this state of the disposed object. It is linguistically proper, for instance, to say that brittleness *is* a certain sort of bonding of the molecules of the brittle object (Armstrong 1973, p. 15).

Armstrong's authority for saying that this is linguistically proper is that physical scientists speak that way, but if they do, it is simply a conceptually loose way of speaking, not licensed by their professional success in identifying the physical properties that determine brittleness. However much we know or do not know about its physical base, to say that an object is brittle means *only* that if it is struck sufficiently hard in suitable circumstances it will break. If we believe that the object must possess some specific physical state causally related to this, that is because we are thinking as determinists, and do not like disembodied powers or potentialities; and because we believe that the object possesses this state even when it has not been struck we say that it *is* brittle; but the potentiality for the outcome is conceptually distinct from the intrinsic state. 'Brittleness' is just a promissory note for a causal law which will only be made good when we *discover* the relevant intrinsic state. Armstrong recognises that if we did seek to fill out the law in that way, then we should 'expose ourselves to Molière's ridicule', but he might also see that if in the meantime we allow ourselves the expedient of saying that the disposition is its own base, then that is an active discouragement from the scientific endeavour to find out what the base really is. Smith brings another argument against Armstrong's position, contending that a disposition like brittleness might come and go depending on environmental changes rather than internal ones, and claiming that because of this 'it is out of the question to *identify* a disposition with the physical structure of an object, as Armstrong suggests that we should' (Smith 1977, p. 445). But then, it would also be out of the question to identify it with environmental conditions, however relevant. A dispositional statement in itself means nothing more than the 'if . . . then . . .' contingency. Anything else that seems to be entailed is simply added on because of a certain understanding of what is required for a fully fleshed-out causal law.

Thus, this is not simply a linguistic quibble but a principle of scientific method, the importance of which becomes especially acute when dealing with mental or psychological dispositions, precisely because it is so difficult to think of intrinsic properties of the *mental* kind that might turn out (contingently) to be the substantive base of the behavioural disposition (the problem that Searle encountered, as we saw above), and in their absence, and in the absence of any adequate knowledge of their *neurological* basis, the temptation to regard the intention or desire to do *B* as the causally explanatory basis of the behavioural disposition to do *B* is virtually irresistible. But although 'intention' and 'desire' may seem not *mere* dispositions of the kind of 'brittleness' since they have the special feature of including a cognitive representation of the state of affairs to be brought about, nevertheless that cognitive representation does not itself explain the translation of thought into action, since we may cognitively represent to ourselves things that we find attractive, repellent, or perfectly indifferent. The missing component, whatever it is that determines the direction, if any, of behaviour, cannot be called 'the intention to do that behaviour' without indeed being 'exposed to Molière's ridicule', i.e. without being guilty of reification, and without slipping away from an adequate notion of causal explanation.

It may reinforce the foregoing point to compare 'intention' with kinds of organismic state variable that would generally be accepted as legitimate causal factors in behaviour. Biochemical processes provide the most clear-cut examples. For example, if a person has been given an adequate dose of chlorpromazine, it will have an inhibitory effect on the central adrenergic synapses, producing an alteration in the person's responsiveness which is called 'being tranquillised'. Plainly, it would be possible in principle, if unlikely in practice, to identify the presence of chlorpromazine without knowing about its effects on the synapses, and without knowing what its effects on the person's behaviour might be. No reference to them is necessary in specifying the state variable.

Turning to the psychological order of variables as distinct from the biochemical order, and waiving for the moment the implication as I see it of a thorough-going central state materialism that there are *no* intrinsic mental properties (no mind-stuff), let us provisionally accept the proposal of some authors in the history of psychology (notably Freud and McDougall) that emotions are qualitative states of mind. That is to say, a person's mind may be suffused with anger, for instance, as his brain may be suffused with chlorpromazine; thus, states of emotion could be conceived of as intermittent state variables affecting the way a person perceives and reacts to his environment, yet, conceivably, capable of an intrinsic description (to the extent to which colours, for example, are capable of it) that does not need to make reference to their effects.

Turning now to the view that intentions could be state variables, let us suppose that we have identified an intrinsic property which we name IP_B, analogous to chlorpromazine or state of anger, which is the intrinsic property constituting the supposed causal state 'intention to do B'. It may be either a particular neurological state or process, or some supposed mental state, but whichever it is it should in principle be describable without any reference to its tending to do B. (We have already seen how awkward that is; however, let us suspend that objection for a moment and imagine such an IP_B has been found.)

Pursuing the formal analogy of IP_B with chlorpromazine, we accept that once chlorpromazine reaches a person's brain in sufficient concentration then it automatically alters the functioning of the adrenergic synapses and this determines that certain stimuli will not be able to produce the effects in his or her behaviour that they otherwise would have produced. There is no problem in thinking of that as a causal sequence.

With a little more difficulty we can conceive (if we really accept determinism and also believe that there are emotions) that a person can be caused to suffer a state of anger, be 'thrown into a rage', and being in that condition cannot help responding as he or she does to the surroundings.

But if we extend this line of thought to IP_B, saying that someone was *caused* to suffer the state IP_B, and being in that state *could not help* behaving precisely as he or she did (that is, being in state IP_B and having whatever other properties are necessary for B, then the person was *caused* by environmental stimuli to manifest B), then that does seem to leave out an essential feature of what we ordinarily mean by saying that someone did B for a purpose, or on purpose, or intentionally. Surely a part of that meaning is that one chose to do B when other alternatives were available. But does not the notion of being *caused* to 'choose' the alternative that one took make the notion of choice vacuous, and mean that there were no actual alternatives? It is true that there are machines, agreed to be deterministic, that are programmed, through the incorporation of some randomising device, to 'choose' a chess move out of the range of legally possible and undiscriminably attractive moves available at a given time, but of course such outcomes are as determined, though unpredictable in practice, as the outcome of the toss of a coin (which does not 'choose' how to land).

Woodfield also asserts that it is impossible to analyse statements about the role of intentions into statements about the causal role of intrinsic properties of the organism without losing the core meaning of 'acting intentionally'. His view of the import of this, however, is quite different from mine. He says that:

> All internalists agree that a TD [teleological description] is an empirical explanatory hypothesis which asserts that S did B because S was in a certain state. Any analysans of a TD must itself be a sentence used to assert a hypothesis, therefore. But in order to be an analysans, it must be a paraphrase that captures the meaning of the original. This means that it must not speculate about the nature of the internal state any more or any less or on any other level than the TD itself does. In particular, it must not be a sentence used to propose a theory about the brain mechanisms responsible for producing that behaviour. If every statement of the form 'S has goal G' were matched to a statement of the form 'S has property P' [my IP_B], which had the same truth-conditions, where the expansion of 'property P' involves making references to parts of S's brain standing in certain relations, then for each statement of the form 'S did B *because* S had goal G' there would be a matching statement of the form 'S did B *because* S had property P'. But the physiological explanatory statement is no more an analysis of the meaning of teleological explanatory statement than the simple statement about S's brain state is an analysis of the simple statement about S's having a goal. Each asserts that S is in an internal state, but whereas the former describes the state as a state of some of S's internal parts, the latter describes the state holistically, without referring to parts (Woodfield 1976, pp. 161–2).

This passage shows the virtues and the severe limitations of the merely linguistic approach to substantive philosophical issues. In Woodfield's conception of method it is not possible to analyse the concept of 'having a goal' as an internal state in any way that would show that the concept of *intentional* internal state which ordinary usage treats it as being is the notion of something that *cannot be*. The analysans, he says, must not speculate about the nature of the internal state 'any more or any less or on any other level than the TD itself', because then it would mean something different. But it is quite possible for an expression to mean something that could not actually exist; that it can have meaning but no referent; that in a loose sense of 'understand' we understand what the expression means, yet that it means something that is internally inconsistent, self-contradictory, incoherent in some way. If we feel that because a certain concept has wide currency and a received meaning, then its content must be true, must correctly represent some part of the world's furniture, then we should have to feel that there had never been any wrong-headed, conceptually con-fused, yet respectably institutionalised beliefs in the history of society.

What goes unstated in the passage above is Woodfield's acceptance of the concept of an intrinsically intentional state as a viable one, and as the correct one in this case. This is evaded, for the time being, by the imprecise term 'holistically' in the last sentence – i.e. the physiological statement 'describes the state as a state of some of *S*'s internal parts, the latter [teleological statement] describes the state holistically, without referring to parts'. There is a peculiar aura of sanctity attaching to the word 'holistic', especially when talking about organisms, which discourages people from asking unsympathetically what, if anything, it means. What could it mean in Woodfield's sentence, where the holistic states are said to be internal but are distinguished from states of parts? The 'internal' (as distinct from relational) properties a person might have as a whole include, for example, being of a certain mass, or being Jane Smith, or being green all over if a Martian, but that is hardly the kind of thing Woodfield has in mind, since what he is looking for is something internally or intrinsically *relational*. What 'holistic' typically does, and what I think it is surreptitiously doing here, is to exempt the process in question from the claims of efficient causality. Whatever the behaviour is ('goal-seeking' behaviour in this case), it is supposed to be something that the organism as a whole can just *do*, it is one of *its* powers, not to be reduced to the interactions of its parts. The interaction of parts is the way we explain the behaviour of machines – this part pushes that, and that part the next, and so on – and machines are very suspect as goal-seekers.

In offering my own analysis of the meaning of 'intention', I said that it is the notion of some thing or state that has its relations internal to it, being type-identified by, and only by, its intentional object, so that 'to do *B*' cannot be separated off from 'intention to do *B*'. But I also argued that there are no internal relations and therefore *no such states*; that it is not really understandable to say that a thing's relations are internal to it when it can only be related to things other than itself. One symptom of this lack of intelligibility is that when people do try to describe the nature of such a state they can find nothing to say about it except 'its' relatedness – but what 'it' is remains perfectly obscure. All that can be produced is some kind of disguised tautology. Searle confessed, as we have seen, that 'Any attempt to characterize Intentionality must inevitably use Intentional notions.' Woodfield, earlier in his book, had said:

> Might it not be possible to paraphrase statements of intention in turn by stating *their* truth-conditions? Now an analysis of this kind cannot continue beyond statements of intention unless there is some method, available to any competent maker of such statements, of identifying and describing the state of affairs that constitutes a person P's intending to do A, independently of the identification and description of it as 'P's intending to do A'. But the concept of intending may be primitive (Woodfield 1976, p. 35).

And, in fact, all he can find to say in his later discussion is that:

> The most obvious kind of mental state with which to identify the state of having a goal is the state of wanting or desiring. . . . The core-concept of a goal is the concept of an intentional object of desire (Woodfield 1976, p. 166).

Now, in saying this, Woodfield has at least transported the notion of having a goal away from the externalist definition of it as the final outcome on which performances converge, to the having of an internal or intrinsic state. But if we relate the quotation just above to the long paragraph quoted earlier from pp. 161–2 of his book, we see that what he has to tell us about the nature of the internal state is a form of tautology. We find that the 'holistic' description he referred to before of the internal state of having a goal is the state of wanting or desiring. It is having an intentional object of desire. But Woodfield says several times (e.g. p. 202) that he treats the terms 'want', 'desire', and 'intention' as meaning very much the same thing. 'Wanting G', 'intending G', and 'having G as a goal' (last quote, from p. 166) are synonymous, and their only content is that S is in an allegedly internal state describable, let us say, as 'striving towards G' and not describable in any other way. So the explanatory teleological statement comes down to saying that S's behavioural striving towards G ('does B in order to do G') is caused by S's having an internal store of strivingness-towards-G. The only bit of Woodfield's concept that is additional to this reification is that there must also be an internal representation of G, but that does not provide an explanatory basis for the striving, simply because one can picture to oneself any number of situations towards which one would never dream of striving. It has only an instrumental role auxiliary to the motivation, which is what is at issue here.

I argued above, in comparing 'having an intention' as a supposed internal state with 'being suffused with chlorpromazine' as an internal state, that no genuine internal state account of the origins of behaviour will allow one to retain the characteristic meaning of 'acting intentionally' because it will make possible an efficient-causality account of behaviour, and the essential meaning of 'acting intentionally' is that such action *is not caused*. And that I think is also the basis of the incompatibility of meaning Woodfield finds between the physiological and the teleological analyses, though he is reluctant to say so, because he professes to be giving an internalist causal account of teleological behaviour. Even if he should claim to be distinguishing only between *physiological* intrinsic states and *mental* intrinsic states, then, even supposing that he could conjure up an example of the latter, as I tried to do just for argument's sake by giving a certain version of 'state of anger', then that too would not match the meaning of 'intention', because (a) it would still allow an efficient-causality account of the resultant behaviour, and (b) 'intention' is conceived as intrinsically relational, as having the striving-towards relation to its object built into its nature, and not as a plain intrinsic (or qualitative) state. That is the kind of constitutive-relations concept which I have claimed to be incoherent and not genuinely intelligible, however common its usage may be, and Woodfield's inability to give any but a tautological description of this 'internal state' is a neat confirmation in practice of the unintelligibility of that 'meaning'.

Accordingly, although Woodfield and I are agreed on the incompatibility of meaning as between physiological and mental, our conclusions as to what should follow from it are quite different. He thinks that 'intention to do *B*' must be retained as a viable explanatory concept and that no physiologically based account of the causes of goal-directed behaviour can be substituted for it; I think that it is a pre-scientific, pseudo-explanatory, inescapably obscurantist concept which must be discarded if we are to have a scientific psychology, and that only an adequate model of the physiological bases of behaviour will enable us to understand those distinctive features of animate behaviour which lead people to call it goal-directed. This is not a physiological reductionism; as we shall see, it provides a framework for *a deterministic psychology of mental life*.

Why does Woodfield, and why do countless thousands of like-minded if less articulate and thoughtful persons, refuse even to contemplate the abandoning of 'intention' as a real possibility? The linguistic philosopher's, and, allowing for differences of literary style, even the typical layperson's, reaction to such a proposal is given expression by Charles Taylor. He finds it 'preposterous' to suggest that purposive explanation is mistaken and useless and should be discarded, because it would mean that 'the very language we use for action and feeling ... is systematically inappropriate and misleading. And this is just too much to swallow' (Taylor 1970, p. 91).

It is hardly necessary to point out that this is not a philosophic argument at all, merely an emotive one. Hard though it may be to swallow, it is a fact that a very great part of the language we use for action and feeling *is* systematically misleading. Yet the consequences of accepting explanation by purpose, or by intention to act, or by agent-causality, are even more unpalatable to an empirical cast of mind, as I hope will become progressively more clear, since it leaves the origins of behaviour an impenetrable mystery – inexplicable and unpredictable.

The argument of this chapter has been that the teleological explanation of behaviour is directly incompatible with efficient-causal explanation, and therefore deprives us of the only enlightening way of saying just how a behavioural event comes about. However, the alternative model that is currently proposed, which purports to explain goal-directed behaviour as being efficiently caused, and lists as internal causal factors the organism's intentions and beliefs, was rejected because the concept of intention is that of something that possesses internal or intrinsic relatedness (to its object) and therefore is logically incoherent. The relevant internal states that help to determine behaviour remain to be specified.

The range of concepts that can find no place in a deterministic psychology without the most radical reinterpretation – choice, decision, free action, altruism, selfishness, in fact every motive defined by its aim – is wide indeed, and the prospect of persuading people that those notions cannot have the content they seem to have is daunting. Of course, in my own personal life I am as familiar as anyone with the *feeling* that I do often enough deliberate and choose, decide, try, brace myself against faint-heartedness as best I can, yet the analysis of what is required for an efficient-causality explanation of behaviour persuades me that all such feelings must be illusions – illusions whose psychodynamic basis one may not always have enough insight to explain, but illusions nevertheless. In the following chapter I proceed with this enterprise of reinterpretation, and attempt to disarm some objections, by examining first the concept of free action, then that of behaviour itself. There are constant ingenious attempts to reformulate 'freedom of action' to make it compatible with determinism, but ingenuity cannot evade the question of whether every event is caused, unless it is by the mere verbal expedient of postulating a class of . . . happenings? . . . which are not events.

3
Analysis of 'Agency'

The incompatibility of freedom of action with determinism

There seems to be a plain, recognisable difference between actions (behaviours, rather) that one performs under duress, under coercion or compelling threat, and those which one does without such external compulsion – which one seems to do by choice. But, to state baldly my contention in this chapter, it is that if there is a class of behaviours that are not the effect of an external cause, then they consist of, or are the consequences of, the *self-changing* of the actor. That is, they begin with, or are, changes in the actor that are not caused by anything but himself or herself. There may be such changes, but if there are, they are totally unpredictable, and what is much worse, inexplicable.

Notions such as freedom of action, exercise of will, agency, and so on have been closely bound up with ethical traditions, because ethical traditions consider moral responsibility to be their stock in trade, and it is usually a cardinal principle that persons can be held morally responsible only for actions that they chose to do when they might have chosen otherwise. Thus they specifically exempt from praise or blame such behaviour as a person could not avoid; that is, which she or he was caused to do, or, simply, which was caused to occur in her or him. I take those last two clauses to mean just the same thing, though some authors, e.g. Davidson, think there is an important distinction to be drawn. According to Davidson,

> . . . there can be a great difference between 'The heat caused Samantha to return to Patna' and 'The heat caused Samantha's return to Patna.' The former implies, or strongly suggests, a limitation on Samantha's freedom of action; the latter does not (Davidson 1973, p. 141).

With the best will in the world I cannot see that one of those assertions is more unpleasantly deterministic than the other. If the second (or should it be the first?) is supposed to mean that she was caused *to choose* to return, then that does not suggest to me either a greater or lesser limitation on freedom of action; it simply makes nonsense of the notion of choosing.

Moral judgements apply only to agents, to creatures who are believed to be in a fundamental sense the authors of their acts. I mention this to illustrate that in ordinary language the concept of intentional action essentially includes the notion of spontaneity, of self-direction, of being able to originate one's own behaviour, something that, I argued, would be explicitly ruled out by any serious attempt to give an account of 'intentions' as *causes* of behaviour.

Yet there is a persistent philosophical tradition that freedom of action is compatible with determinism, with a causal account of behaviour. One well known if idiosyncratic version of compatibilism was given by MacKay (e.g. 1960, 1967). He takes determinism to entail that it is possible to make scientific predictions, derived from law-like statements, of what a particular individual will do at a given time. That, of course, is a counsel of perfection, demanding an impossibly detailed knowledge of the initial conditions for the particular case, as has, for example, been recently pointed out by Wilkes (1981). MacKay, however, although not recognising its perfectly acceptable impossibility in practice, finds such predictability to be impossible in principle for the behaviour of agents. For example, he says: '*There would not exist* (even unknown to anyone) a determinate *complete* specification of the future of a cognitive agent which had a well-founded unconditional claim to the assent of anyone and everyone if only they knew it' (MacKay 1973, p. 405). The special case is that the agent as such could not justifiably assent to such a specification of his or her future. This is not merely the familiar point that if the agent were informed of the prediction, and were of a contra-suggestible nature, or a dedicated proselytiser for the free-will doctrine, then the prediction would be self-disconfirming, because he or she would act in such a way as to disconfirm it. For the determinist, such a falsification of a specific prediction would not disconfirm determinism; one can simply say that the knowledge of the prediction entered as a new causal variable (subsequent to the making of the prediction) bringing about the disconfirming behaviour. But MacKay's view is that 'our choice is logically indeterminate, until we make it. For us, choosing is not something to be observed or predicted, but to be done' (MacKay 1960, p. 37). He elaborates this (MacKay 1971) by saying that, even though independent, ideally informed observers may be able correctly to predict an agent's choices so that determinism is true for them, it can never be true for the agent, if only because there are relevant states of his cognitive system that are systematically unknowable by him, namely, those states which 'would be *necessarily disturbed* by the changes necessarily concomitant with *believing the specification* of them' (MacKay 1971, p. 275).

Now, it is not clear to me that a cognitive state of mine is *necessarily* disturbed by my believing a specification of it, because that believing would be a *separate* cognitive state, and there is no reason to believe that it would have to displace or disrupt the other. Not being a Turing machine, I can think of more than one thing at a time, and one of my cognitive states can pay attention to another. But even allowing MacKay's point, it says only that the limitation of prediction is due simply to unavoidable ignorance, which has no bearing on the determinist premise that all events are caused, though we may not always know what the causes are. A behaviour-event cannot be caused from one point of view and uncaused from another, and MacKay's argument for the compatibility of the two views is unsuccessful. In the long run he simply assumes that human behaviour is not caused, in that he continually refers to the agent's 'choosing', or 'making up his mind'. If our behaviour in taking one course rather than another is caused, it is pointless to say that we choose.

Another failure to grasp the ramifications of determinism is to be found in the work of Davidson, who holds that 'free actions are caused by states and episodes like desires, beliefs, rememberings and the promptings of passion' (Davidson 1973, p. 139). The immediate puzzle is to understand what the word 'free' can mean in that sentence, since to give it what seems its most obvious meaning, 'uncaused', would be to suspend the Law of Contradiction. Morriston points out that for the traditional compatibilist, 'Internal causation by psychological factors is distinguished from external causation or compulsion, and only the latter is held to be incompatible with freedom and responsibility' (Morriston 1979, p. 266). This at least is more understandable than saying that an action can be both caused and uncaused. It is true that the law will not regard me as being bound by a contract that I signed under duress, one that I 'could not refuse' because a gun was being held at my head and my brains would have been blown out. The presence or absence of the gun is a readily discriminable, objective factor which does not raise any metaphysical puzzles. In this sense, to say that an act is 'free' just means that it occurs free *from* certain specifiable kinds of causal factor, notably, external duress. If duress is present, I am held *not responsible*. But if duress is absent, that does not mean that my action was *not caused*.

Although the distinction between gun present and gun absent is easy enough to make, that between acts for which I am 'responsible' and those for which I am not is actually not so easy to draw; it does not follow automatically, except by legal stipulation. Even with the gun at my head it was not physically impossible for me to refuse to sign the contract; I could have refused and accepted the consequence of being shot dead. The point is that the fear of death recruits very powerful motives in me which are so deep and strong that they are likely to prove supervalent over whatever interests are elicited by the costs (financial loss, it may be) of signing; consequently, I sign. If we accept the concept of 'intentional act', then this is just as intentional as signing without duress; it is simply that the motivation has been altered. On the other hand, in the event that I sign without duress, the determinist will argue that I have been thrown into a certain motivational state by an externally presented opportunity for financial gain, and my signing is caused by the perception of the favourable implications of the contract. Thus there seems no ground for distinguishing between the two actions just in terms of their causal status; depending on the position one was advancing, both could be seen as 'free' or both as caused.

In the traditional compatibilist view the ground of the distinction between free and coerced actions is sometimes put as a *preponderance* of causal factors as between those internal to the agent and those external to him; if they are preponderantly internal the action is said to be free, if external then caused. But that notion of preponderance shows a misunderstanding of the causal relation, like that underlying the now outmoded terms 'agent' and 'patient'. If X impinges on Y and causes a change in it, then X used to be called the agent and Y the patient. That line of thinking encourages one to say that if a gun is thrust at my head and causes me to sign the contract then I am a patient, not an agent. However, it is a distinction that cannot really be sustained. In any causal interaction the properties of the 'patient' are just as necessary for the production of the effect as those of the 'agent'. Thus, acid may turn blue litmus red, but it cannot turn just anything red, only things with the causally relevant properties possessed by the litmus. There are no degrees of necessity or activity; the properties of the litmus are just as necessary and just as active in producing the red-turning as are those of the acid; and when I sign the contract under duress, my motivational state plays just as large a role as the presence of the gun.

Thus, in terms of their status *as caused*, there is no ground for distinguishing between 'free' and 'coerced' actions. For the determinist the expression 'freedom of action' is simply misleading. It may be held to point to a difference in *kinds* of causal condition, but to call behaviour that is *caused by* one kind of condition 'free' is a misuse of language, and the question of whether 'freedom of action' is compatible with determinism is not a properly formulated one. All kinds of behaviour are caused, for the determinist, and all are caused by a confluence of external and internal factors; for him the 'free' (or self-generated) kind of behaviour does not exist. On the other hand, a defender of self-determination could claim that my arguments have only shown that all actions, even 'coerced' ones, are motivated and thus 'free' in his sense of being self-generated. In the immediately following section I am going on to argue that the notion of self-determined behaviour, which seems to him so perspicuous, is in fact totally obscure. What is required of me eventually is to give an account of motives as intrinsically characterised states of the organism (which I have argued is not possible for 'intentions' and 'desires'), in such a way as to make it intelligible that those states can be *caused* to occur, and that being in them the organism has its behaviour *caused in it* by its perception of its immediate surroundings, which is to say that it is in no sense generated by the organism. My dispute with those who want to employ 'intentions' as explanatory causal states rests not only on the fact that 'intentions' cannot be conceived of as intrinsic psychological states but also on my contention that 'intentional behaviour' cannot be regarded as caused at all, because it is inseparable from that concept that the behaviour occurs in order to bring about the intended goal, i.e. that it is generated and directed by the agent.

Some philosophers, for example Chisholm (1976) and R. Taylor (1966), taking it as self-evident that some human actions are 'free', yet wanting also to say that they are caused, since if my actions were not caused (i.e. were random or chaotic), they could not usefully be said to be *mine*, something that I positively did, have drawn a distinction between the 'event-causality' of the ordinary physical world and the 'agent-causality' of human action. The former relates antecedent to consequent events, but the latter relates *persons* to events. I cause my behaviour. That causing is supposed not to be an *event* in me, because then one might ask how that event was caused, and so on; rather, the correct way of expressing the matter, as Richard Taylor has it, is just to say that the cause of my action is *I*. But, as I am about to argue, an action must in part at least consist of changes in me, i.e. of my bodily movements (cf. Hornsby 1980), if it is to eventuate in any changes in the world; thus, to say that I cause my behaviour is to say that I change myself, am a self-changing entity. The notion of self-change is the core-concept of every version of goal-seeking, and the ways of working of such a self-changing entity would be perfectly mysterious; it is a notion that is quite incompatible with any useful concept of causality. To bring this out I shall proceed to unfold the hidden complexities in the everyday notion of doing something, and in the behavioural scientist's notion of response.

The meaning of behaviour

Even the most deterministic of psychologists must expose himself to a charge of covertly falling back into teleological thinking in the very terms that he uses in naming responses. Almost always (the exceptions being very few in number and atypical – such things as emotional reactions and smooth muscle contractions), responses are named, not by listing bodily movements, but by saying, in effect, 'producing a specific outcome by whatever movements are suitable'. The kind of event that is ordinarily called an action or response or bit of behaviour is a complex of (a) changes in the organism and (b) changes in the environment. For example, the bodily behaviour involved in signing one's name consists mainly of an observable set of movements of the arm and hand holding the pen, and other postural adjustments. But 'signing one's name' also includes the fact that these movements result in a recognisable pattern of ink marks on the paper. There are two series of events here, then, one in the organism (the movements of its parts) and one in the environment (the appearing of the marks on the paper). The relation between them is a complex causal one. The movements produce the marks and the perception of the marks made so far affects the further course of the movements. The two sequences may be in almost constant interaction with each other at each moment as they run their course, through a feedback loop of this kind; however, that is not to say that there is some special *kind* of causality involved – a notion that is sometimes concealed in certain uses of the term 'circular causality', as we shall see. It is not as if the two series of events dissolve into one another and form just one self-constituting process. To say that the next segment of the motor activity is partly dependent on the perception of the effects of the previous one (when that is the case) is to specify a causal interaction between distinct happenings. Yet these two distinct sequences (changes in the organism and their effects on the environment) are very frequently run together in the naming of kinds of behaviour: signing one's name, answering the telephone, turning to the left, even such things as eating and swimming, which, when we distinguish them from just making eating or swimming movements, are kinds of achievement. When the movements and their effects are run together and treated as one happening, as something the organism can do, the way is open for thinking that the movements occur the way they do in order to produce their effects.

In a much-quoted paper by Rosenblueth *et al.* (1943) there is a notable case of this compounding of cause and effect, notable because it occurred not in the ordinary way of talking about items of behaviour but in trying to say what the term 'behaviour' itself means. The authors regarded their paper as a schematic programme for a new science, cybernetics. One of their professed aims was to stress the importance of the concept of purpose in the classification of behaviour, and a related one was to define and advocate 'the behavioristic approach to the study of natural events'. This 'consists in the examination of the output of the object and of the relations of this output to the input' (Rosenblueth *et al.* 1943, p. 18). That can be done, they assert, without needing to concern oneself with 'the specific structure and the intrinsic organization of the object' (Rosenblueth *et al.*1943, p. 18). The specific structure is the concern of what they call the 'functional' method of study (an idiosyncratic usage, since 'functionalism' is ordinarily understood to mean precisely the 'behavioristic' method which they oppose to it). Of course, the study of structure is legitimate, they agree, it is just not necessary to behaviouristics – a view that is also embraced by most psychological behaviourists.

In trying to say what behaviour or 'output' is, their belief in the value of a teleological conception is protected by their uncritical fuzziness about what we might call the *locus* of a thing's behaviour. There are three possible positions to take about this, and we find each of them clearly expressed in the paper by Rosenblueth *et al.* without the smallest recognition that they are incompatible, or even that they are different. Within the space of three paragraphs they say, first:

The behavioristic approach consists in the examination of the output of the object and of the relations of this output to the input. By output is meant any change produced in the surroundings by the object (Rosenblueth *et al.* 1943, p. 18).

That is to say:

(a)   The locus of behaviour is in the environment. It is those changes produced *in the environment* by the object. This seems to me a position no one could seriously maintain. If a person is sharpening a pencil, then the fact that the pencil becomes sharp is not in itself the person's behaviour, it is the effect of it.

Later they say:

By behaviour is meant any change of an entity with respect to its surroundings (Rosenblueth *et al.* 1943, p. 18).

I take that to mean:

(b)   The locus of behaviour is in the organism's relations with its environment. It is the compound of changes in the organism and the consequent changes in its environmental relationships. This variant of the 'compounding' conception will be further discussed below.

Finally:

. . . any modification of an object, detectable externally, may be denoted as behavior (Rosenblueth *et al.* 1943, p. 18).

That is:

(c)   The locus of behaviour is in the organism. It consists of changes in the organism's intrinsic properties. That is the usage of 'behaviour' which I am adopting.

Ignoring (a) as not worth serious attention, I shall focus critical attention on (b), preparing the ground for the advocacy of (c), which will further illuminate the issue of whether there is any sense in which purposive behaviour can be said to be caused (if one accepted that there was any such thing).

Behaviour is 'any change of an entity with respect to its surroundings'. What can that mean, to change 'with respect to' the surroundings? One could conceivably say that John grew taller with respect to his surroundings, but that would not add anything to saying that he grew taller. In any case, growing taller is not the sort of change that one would call behaviour. If we introduce a behavioural event in place of growing taller, then the purposiveness implicit in this definition begins to emerge. Suppose the change in the object is that its right hand begins to move back and forth. 'John's right hand moved back and forth with respect to his surroundings.' Probably no one would ever use such a sentence, but if one did it could hardly be anything but a strained, pseudo-objective way of saying that John waved *at* or pointed *to* something in his surroundings.

To take a less clumsy example, suppose we said that a torpedo's direction of movement changed with respect to a ship in its vicinity. Now, that could mean either that its direction of movement changed and we happen to choose a particular ship as a convenient reference point, yet might have chosen any number of other reference points; or it could mean that the torpedo's direction of movement changed *so as* to bring it closer (for example) to that particular ship, where no other reference point than that specific ship could convey what we meant. (I choose 'closer to' for convenience, though any specifiable relationship such as 'abreast of' would do.) This second kind of meaning is the one most plausibly conveyed by 'with respect to', and of course what it means is the active approaching of the ship as distinct from just as a matter of fact getting closer to it. That is the meaning which best fits the whole approach of Rosenblueth *et al.* (1943), but if that is so, then they are including in the specification of the behaviour of a given object something that really *follows from* what should properly be called its behaviour, that is, from the sequence of changes *in it* (sense (c), above). Of course, no one is entitled to lay down the 'proper' usage of a term, but underlying the question of usage in this case is a perfectly real distinction between the changes in something and the consequences of those changes. The uncritical common usage of 'behaviour', which is the one preferred by Rosenblueth *et al.,* treats as inseparable aspects of *one* process both the changes in the behaving object (in the case of the torpedo, the processes in its steering mechanism, resulting in a change in the direction of its motion relative to its previous direction) and the consequences of those changes (the torpedo's coming nearer to the ship). But those are obviously conceptually distinct, and the connection between them is a contingent one. To treat them as one indissoluble process, to treat 'target-seeking' as something that the missile simply *does*, is to suggest that the connection between the movements of the object's parts and the effects of the movements is much more intimate than mere contingency, and in fact that the object makes those movements because they are needed for their effects.

One begins to see the connection between the behaviouristic approach, which ignores the intrinsic nature of the behaving object, and the claim that there is a recognisable category of behaviour called 'purposive behaviour'. The connection between the two is not a necessary one, but the one way of thinking encourages the other. The more one does discover of the intrinsic structure of the object, the less room there is in it for purposiveness. Explanation by purpose consorts very oddly with the authors' professional interests. The co-author Wiener, at least, is regarded as one of the pioneers of cybernetics in a thoroughly technical way, and as such would be an authority on the 'specific structure and intrinsic organisation' of precisely those mechanisms which give the appearance of purposive behaviour while being completely mechanistic. The cyberneticist, the expert on the technology of feedback, would, one would think, be the person best qualified to sketch in a model of what is really going on when we (mistakenly) attribute purpose to machines, and, by extension, to organisms. Yet instead of reducing the concept of the goal-directedness of behaviour to that of feedback control, these authors make in the opposite direction and argue that feedback-controlled behaviour is intrinsically purposeful in some meaningful sense, and 'may be interpreted as directed to the attainment of a goal' (Rosenblueth *et al.* 1943, p. 18).

The best prophylactic against this kind of teleological thinking is to be on guard against accepting 'changes with respect to the environment' as being the stuff of which behaviour is composed, and to think of an organism's behaviour as being changes in it. These may be changes in the movements of its limbs or other parts, changes in its belief system (coming to believe some proposition; becoming aware of the presence of particular things), that complex of changes which we describe as the utterance of a sentence, and so on. Yet even this last example, 'uttering a sentence', shows how difficult an exercise this is, since it runs together into one the vocal-motor events that produce the sounds and the conveying of information that is their effect, and, as we have seen, practically all names of behavioural events do that kind of thing. But there is no earthly reason to think that psychology should be easy to do, since it is the science of easily the most intricate, adaptable, feedback-governed 'target-seeking' entities in the world. In describing human beings in that way, I am anticipating by several stages the course of my argument, and will immediately have to cope with several objections to lumping human beings in with man-made feedback systems. Nevertheless, that is the general position towards which I am working, provided that 'feedback' is understood in an enlarged sense to include cognitive processes – i.e. knowledge of where the 'goal-object' may be, the perceiving of environmental objects and the retention of information about them – and allowing that we lock on to a greater variety of targets than guided missiles do, and have a more varied repertoire of responses than just running into them and exploding. The essential point is that despite these factual differences, human organisms do not exhibit a different kind of causality from guided missiles or any other kind of physical system.

It is, of course, not to be disputed that we do phenomenally behave 'with respect to' the environment, which is to say that our bodily movements are admirably adapted to producing specifiable kinds of change in the things and people about us, but once we accept that the environmental effects are distinct from the bodily movements that cause them, then we can see that it is a scientific problem of the first importance to discover how these 'admirably adapted' movements come into being.

It seems probable that there is an array of basic actions or object-manipulations which one can in fact just do, which are in some sense pre-formed, ready to run off automatically yet not in a purely stereotyped way, being moulded through innate feedback mechanisms to the shape and positioning of the concrete physical objects concerned. One thinks of such things as chewing and swallowing, grasping, crawling and walking; more elaborate unlearned patterns in other species of animal and in insects, and so on. If there were no unlearned abilities, no ready-made responses to be put together and improved upon, then such a creature could hardly survive; it would simply take too long to learn anything – much longer than it actually does take – if one started with absolutely inchoate, random muscle contractions. But in the case of unlearned abilities the question of where the movement patterns come from and how they are fitted to the environment, although still a very real scientific question, is perhaps one for the physiologist and cyberneticist to answer, since the mechanisms must be innate. Where the abilities are species-specific and unlearned, then in many contexts it would be legitimate for the psychologist to accept them as a going concern, as a basic repertoire that the organism can perform 'just like that', as Hornsby (1980) puts it. But where the abilities are obviously acquired, then it is precisely their 'goal-directed' nature that *cannot* be taken for granted by the psychologist; the mechanisms that account for novel modes of object-manipulation are very much his concern.

If we adopt the conception of an organism's behaviour as changes occurring in the organism, we can see more clearly the formal structure of an orthodox scientific explanation of that behaviour. At time t an organism begins to exhibit a complex set of properties, behaviour B, different from those it had before t. The demand to know what caused those changes in it is a typical scientific enquiry, and the typical scientific answer is to discover both the relevant intrinsic properties of the organism and the relevant properties of something that arrived at or impinged on it at or just before t and caused the change we are calling behaviour B. For the psychologist the relevant properties of the organism will mainly be its motivational or drive state, which as we have seen must be characterised intrinsically, and its beliefs about the likely consequences of various behaviours in the situation it is in. What arrives as the external cause will typically, in fact invariably, be stimulation from the objects around the organism impinging on its sense organs, causing its perception of them, which will in turn recruit its acquired beliefs about those objects and what can be done with them relevant to relieving its drive state. ('Relieving its drive state' is a phrase that will be unpacked later.) To say that this confluence of factors will cause behaviour that is likely to reduce the drive state is just the beginning of the problem. But even to have got this far is an enormous advance in understanding beyond what is offered by saying that the organism originates its own behaviour, which is to say, *changes itself*, which I am claiming is entailed in saying its behaviour is goal-directed.

For the self-caused act, for the organism that can change itself, the orthodox model of explanation sketched in above would be inapplicable. By definition there would be no connection with the arrival of any stimulus from outside; thus the covering law model (cf. e.g. Hempel 1965) specifying that 'every organism with these properties when subject to stimulus E exhibits B' could not be filled in. There would be no antecedent event to observe that would enable the prediction or explanation of B. The organism so conceived would be one that carried the potency for self-change with it all the time. It would be impossible to explain, then, why such a change happened at one time rather than another. Any theory holding that an organism originates its own behaviour, directs itself towards a goal, will need some quite different model of explanation and prediction from the standard scientific one, and it will be part of my concern to examine some of these proposed alternatives to see what enlightenment they can hope to offer.

I said above that it may seem over-confident to declare that human beings are feedback systems whose apparently target-seeking behaviour can be accounted for in the efficient-causality terms of cybernetics. Both Woodfield (1976) and Wilson (1979) have reservations, differing in kind, about different parts of this view, Woodfield feeling that human behaviour has aspects about which cybernetics has nothing to say, and Wilson holding that cybernetic systems themselves, even inanimate ones, have a type of causality other than the merely efficient. In the following section I examine these claims, arguing that although feedback is essential to the explanation of 'goal-directed' behaviour, it exhibits only efficient causality.

Cybernetics and goal-direction

Woodfield gives a clear-cut account of the logic of feedback systems, insisting that they show only efficient causality. He says that:

... feeding back is a process of reciprocal causation, as objective as causation itself. There are two separate causal chains of events which are mediated by two separate channels: the first chain of events is the process whereby the output at t_0 brings about some change in the environment which affects the input at t_1. This channel passes outside the system. The second chain of events occurs within the system, and is the process whereby the input at t_1 determines the output at t_2. This output then feeds back again via the environment and affects the input at t_3. In many cases, these two processes go on simultaneously, but it is useful to separate them temporally for purposes of exposition (Woodfield 1976, p. 184).

Actually, for Woodfield to say that the two processes go on *simultaneously* is injudicious; it collapses the sequence too much and obscures the one-directional nature of the causal connections. One would rather say that both the input and output processes may be going on continuously and concurrently, but nevertheless there will always be some time lapse, however short, between the output at t_0 and the change in output at t_2 which (through the feedback loop) results from it, if only because the signals take some time to pass through space. This is not contrary to Woodfield's intention, since he goes on to point out that the system

. . . must contain at least two separate components, a part that is sensitive to environmental changes (sensor), and a part that can produce environmental changes (effector) . . . In between the sensor and the effector there must be a link (Woodfield 1976, p. 184).

He gives the example of a self-guided missile:

Information in the form of light, heat or radio signals is picked up by a sensor connected to a controlling device which adjusts the steering mechanism of the missile so that it points towards the source of the signals. If the target moves, or the missile veers off course, the deviation is corrected (Woodfield 1976, p. 188).

It is essential to see that the causality of feedback systems is just efficient causality (the only kind, I am contending, that there is), in order to resist the suggestion that modern technology establishes the existence of some higher type. A certain ambivalence about this is manifested by Wilson (1979), even though the large proposition to which his book is dedicated is one with which I am in complete sympathy, namely, that 'mind-directed human behaviour (action) is subject to the same categories of causal determination as other physical processes' (Wilson 1979, p. 4). In discussing feedback systems he says:

The crucial difference between linear and feedback systems is in their structure or organisation, *not* in the mode of productive connexity [i.e. causality] between system states. Specifically, feedback systems embody circuits composed of links, and *the state-changing productive connection within each link is causal* (Wilson 1979, p. 233, italics in original).

He goes on to summarise von Bertalanffy's criteria of feedback control systems, which include the following:

Causal trains within the feedback system are linear and unidirectional. *The basic feedback scheme is still the classical stimulus–response (S–R) scheme*, only the feedback loop being added so that causality becomes circular (Wilson 1979, p. 233, italics in original).

Yet on the previous page he had said that:

Even the rudimentary process of goal-directed behaviour [of a thermo-stat] described above does not conform to the basic action–reaction model of linear unidirectional causation on the billiard ball paradigm assumed by Hume (Wilson 1979, p. 232).

Although there are aspects of Hume's theory of causality that I do not embrace, especially the view that there is nothing to causal relations but constant conjunction, nevertheless it is altogether too glib to refer patronis-ingly to 'the billiard ball paradigm'. If we understand that paradigm to mean that causes and their effects must be spatially and temporally contiguous, then there is nothing simple-minded about it at all, as I have argued above (Ch. 2). Equally, it is hard to conceive of causal relations that are not linear and unidirectional. When acid is applied to litmus, then presumably some change is produced in the acid as well as in the litmus, but that is separate from the fact that the acid turns the litmus red, and the red-turning event is not bi-directional, since what that would mean (if any-thing) is that the litmus's turning red caused the acid to be applied to it – yet that bizarre type of supposition is at the nub of many conceptions of teleology. By the same token, the 'circular' causality that Wilson wants to contrast to the linear variety also reverses temporal relationships. Putting it briefly, the notion is that (for example) the running of a refrigerator's motor causes the inside temperature to fall, which affects the sensor of the thermostat, which eventually switches off the motor, which allows the temperature to rise, which causes the motor to start again, and so on. We can now visualise a circular diagram of arrows each representing a causal connection; one point on the diagram is marked 'motor running' and the arrows leave it and go round the circle until they get back to 'motor running', which is supposed to incline us to think that it is amongst *its own* causes. But that, of course, is ridiculous; any change in the running of the motor at t_2 will be the effect of (amongst other things) its having run (or not run) at some *earlier* time t_1; those events are distinct from one another and the relationship between them is a linear one.

How then is Wilson's rejection of the adequacy of 'linear unidirectional causality' for feedback systems (Wilson 1979, p. 232) to be reconciled with his agreeing (p. 233) with von Bertalanffy that 'causal trains within the system are linear and unidirectional'? The answer is that he contrasts the linear causation between the parts of the system with the circular or self-governing causation of the system as a whole. This apparently is assimilated to one of the varieties of causation in Bunge's taxonomy, which Wilson quotes earlier in the book (Wilson 1979, p. 190), in particular to the 'structural (or holistic) causation of the parts by the whole', i.e. the behaviour of a part is 'determined by the overall structure of the collection to which it belongs'. But one cannot apply the two conceptions to the same series of events. If one has said that part A causes a certain change in part B, it only makes nonsense of that statement if one goes on to say that the same sequence is really the work of the whole structure determining what happens in both A and B. One is impelled to ask, what is this entity 'the whole' which can operate on its own parts as if it were set over against them? Of course, such a notion cannot really be understood; a whole just consists of its parts as arranged and nothing else, and its behaviour (at least in the only deterministic conception of behaviour, as I have argued) consists only of the interrelated events in its parts, initiated by stimulation from its environment. It is true that the parts can only produce the effects they do in each other because they are linked together in the way they are, but there is nothing distinctive of special systems in that; every causal relation, whether we choose to regard it as occurring within a larger 'system' or not, includes the requirement of specifiable contextual features. It is true also that the whole system will be able to produce effects in its environment that its parts separately could not, but that does not mean that it does so by activating its own parts; none of this entails that whole systems, however complex, have a kind of causality different from that of their parts. Indeed, when we reflect that anything whatever is itself both a whole of parts and a part of larger wholes, we see that such a distinction could not coherently be maintained.

It is Wilson's subscribing to this 'general systems theory' conception of holistic causation which prevents him (in my assessment) from presenting his grand project as a viable scientific one. That project, since he accepts (as I do) the mind–brain identity thesis, is to exhibit the human organism as a very complex, feedback-controlled system incorporating learning circuits, memory, and so on, subject to just the same physical laws as any physical system. Unfortunately, 'physical causality' for general systems theory includes the 'holistic' conception that the whole can determine the changes in its own parts; that is to say, can change itself, which, when applied to the human organism, is no more scientifically advanced than voluntarism, and indeed Wilson is quite content to talk about 'willing' as a holistic activity of the central nervous system (Wilson 1979, p. 236). There is a kind of bi-perspectivism about general systems theory – i.e. from the molecular perspective a series of events is linearly caused, and from the molar perspective it is holistically caused – a bi-perspectivism that Wilson finds congenial when it comes to explaining how reasons can be causes. 'Reasons', he says a number of times, 'are causes seen from the inside.' As causes they are processes in the central nervous system, and he means literally that a person can have access to 'the processes of his own central nervous system unmediated through external sense', in which case they 'have the phenomenal quality that constitutes the mental world of the (privileged) observer' – i.e. they present themselves to him as the reasons he has for the direction of his actions. But to talk about seeing brain events 'from the inside' is only a question-begging metaphor. There are no internal sense organs to enable us to 'see' them, and if there were, all they would disclose would be *brain* processes seen from an unusual angle. As Honderich (1981b) says in replying to a later version of Wilson's argument (1981), he cannot coherently assert that 'there is no metaphysical or ontological duality' between the mental and the physical by proposing that the mental is merely the (mental) presentation of the (physical) brain state.

Wilson seeks to avoid this contradiction between the explicit denial and implicit assumption of duality by talking of the subject's 'immediate mode of knowing' his own brain processes. The notion of immediate knowing used in this way seeks to collapse the relation between subject and object into one self-aware state or process – i.e. to know something immediately is to be that thing, one's consciousness is its own object – or would be so if the terms subject and object had not been cancelled out in the saying. If knowing something dissolves into being it, the theorist prevents himself from talking about consciousness (or indeed anything else) at all. A closely similar position is advanced by Globus (1976) and Globus and Franklin (1980), and its obscurity is not really dispelled by Globus's appeal to the ineffable revelations of transcendental meditation, in which the self is said no longer to exist. Wilson's formula cannot brush aside the problems of showing the causal relationship between a person's beliefs about his actions and those actions themselves; however, for the present I shall postpone a more detailed discussion of these matters.

So, then, although Wilson agrees that the human organism is a feedback-controlled system, he also believes that it is a self-directing one. Woodfield, by contrast, holds that feedback systems do have only efficient causality, yet thinks that the goal-directed behaviour of human organisms (higher organisms in general) has features that are not captured by the concept of feedback, and not possessed by inanimate feedback systems; thus in their different ways neither philosopher is quite prepared to see human behaviour as subject to purely efficient causation. As we have seen, Woodfield holds that what is necessary for goal-directed behaviour is that the agent should have a desire for the goal and a belief that the behaviour in question is likely to bring it about. He doubts whether inanimate objects can be said to have these, though they may have analogues for them. Having a desire for a goal-object, he says, requires both having an internal representation of it and placing a positive value on it. Some sophisticated machines, such as the Stanford Robot, a mobile computer incorporating a television camera, can quite literally be said to have an internal representation of their 'goal' object and of objects in the environment, and if we take the built-in programs of response to stimulation by these objects as 'beliefs about how to get to the goal', then the cognitive aspect of having a goal is satisfied in some machines (though, he says, it would be hard to decide whether the setting of a thermostat at 70° is an 'internal representation' of that as its goal state). What machines lack, however, is the evaluative aspect of having a goal. They are simply constructed so that once they are set going the external stimuli emanating from the goal-object cause their parts to operate in such a way that the system converges on the goal-object. My own way of expressing it would be to say that even the most complicated feedback system, a 'target-seeking' missile or mobile robot or whatever, does not in any sense seek the target or direct itself towards the target; it is brought to the target by the physical effects of the stimuli from the target striking its sensors. As Richard Taylor (1950) said, commenting on the paper by Rosenblueth *et al.* (1943), a 'target-seeking' torpedo differs only in mechanical complexity, not in causality, from a torpedo that runs along a cable attached to the target ship. This too is pulled back on course if it becomes diverted. That would also be Woodfield's view of inanimate feedback systems. But where I differ from both Woodfield and Richard Taylor is in their exempting higher organisms – especially human beings, so I shall refer just to them – from the iron law of efficient causality. Taylor's book *Action and purpose* (1966) is dedicated to the proposition that agency is a fundamental, unanalysable property of human behaviour; he embraces agent-causality whole-heartedly. Woodfield is reluctant to press the matter so far; when he comes to the question of where our goals come from and just how they manage to energise behaviour, he tends as we have seen to slip behind the linguistic philosopher's defensive screen, saying that he is not pursuing such factual questions but just explicating meanings.

Consistent with his denial that it is possible to give a brain-state analysis of what 'having goal *G*' means for organisms (cf. Ch. 2, p. 33 above), he denies that inanimate feedback systems can be said to *want* their 'goals' or set a positive *value* on them or *try* to get them:

Satisfaction here involves a number of elements, e.g. the feeling of pleasantness upon attainment of the object, the fact that the desire normally ceases upon attainment ... When we describe a machine as having goal *G*, we describe its internal state by reference to that which satisfies it, in the quasi-semantic sense, while cancelling the implication of feeling or emotion that would be present if we had said that the machine 'wanted' *G* (Woodfield 1976, p. 194).

Feedback machines, he says, do not actually have desires or beliefs, they merely act as if they had them. If they have internal representational states, then those can be accepted as analogues of beliefs, by a mentalistic metaphor. But there is nothing in machines that is even analogous to desiring something, as human beings desire things.

As far as knowing is concerned, I suspect that it is correct to say that there are not as yet any machines, including the most modern computers, which actually know or believe anything. (I am not talking about the distinction between true and false beliefs, but only the presence or absence of cognitive processes.) Machines may act as if they perceive and believe, but it is just a matter of simulation. This can be argued to be merely an arbitrary nominal distinction, and it is not one I am deeply concerned with; I do not feel threatened by the supposition that there may in principle be manufactured entities that perceive, believe, draw conclusions, and so on. My reason for saying that present-day machines (those of which I know) do not, is that they do not seem to have *propositional* knowledge, do not react to propositional input as such. It is rather that items of input having property A are pushed through this gate, and those of them which are now found to have property B are pushed through a further gate, and those without through some other gate. Can this machine be said to know that some A are B and some A are not B? I choose to answer 'no' to that question; however, as I said, not a great deal hangs on it in this connection, though it will reappear when I am specifically discussing cognitive processes. What I am confident of is that human beings are perceiving and believing creatures, that they have masses of propositional information, and that this information affects the way they react to the things they perceive. So I seem to be in accord with Woodfield on that ground of distinction between machines and persons; persons have beliefs, machines have only analogues of them. But in the matter of desires and intentions I am at odds with him; he believes that organisms have them and machines do not, and I believe that *neither* kind of entity possesses them, because, as conceived by Woodfield and common thought, there are no such things. When I say that I want to do G, what I should say is that the early stages of the G-doing program are already running off in me, though it may yet be prevented from going through all its stages.

In the case of higher organisms it is much more difficult than in that of feedback-governed machines to understand the detailed working of the S–R loops that adjust the system's movements to the unique form of the current physical environment. Machines are designed and constructed by human beings and may be taken apart for inspection; further, their repertoire of response forms is very limited compared with that of organisms. The problem of the mechanism of adaptive behaviour will be discussed in greater depth in Chapter 6, in connection with learning; but to illustrate one way in which it *cannot* be illuminated, and to show how pervasive teleological thinking is even in explaining the muscular contractions that compose bodily actions, I want to examine one attempt by Andrew Woodfield and another by John Searle to give an allegedly causal explanation of just how intentional actions come about.

Woodfield offers a concrete account of how an embodied state of desire actually energises the muscles to produce an intentional act, and if my earlier criticisms of his concept of desire are sound, then it is incumbent on me to show either that his model does not exhibit efficient causality (i.e. could not actually work), or that what he is calling 'desire' is something quite different from what he has said it is, i.e. different from an intrinsically relational 'state' for which no substantive intrinsic properties can be given. He addresses himself to a group of cleverly constructed counter-examples to the desire-plus-belief analysis of 'S does B in order to do G'. In each counter-example the agent desires a particular goal, and has a reasonable belief about how to achieve it, and this desire–belief pair does, in fact, cause behaviour B, which in turn brings about the goal, but in a roundabout, accidental, *unintended* way. Thus, it seems an insufficient account of an intentional act to say that it was *caused by* the relevant desire–belief pair, since such a pair can cause the result unintentionally; something else must be added. This led Chisholm (1964), who provided one of the examples, to propose that the concept of intentional goal-directed action should be regarded as unanalysable or primitive.

Chisholm's example, quoted by Woodfield, is:

Suppose a man believes that if he kills his uncle he will inherit a fortune and suppose he desires to inherit a fortune; this belief and desire may agitate him and cause him to drive in such a way that he accidentally kills his uncle (Chisholm 1964, p. 616).

Woodfield, wanting to dispose of these counter-examples, believes that by filling in the details of the causal chain between desire and action he can objectively distinguish between the 'accidental' causal sequence and the intentional causal sequence; thus, the accidental cases will be shown not to be counter-examples to his elaborated account, and the theory of intentional actions as being caused by a desire–belief pair will prevail.

Woodfield assumes that any action must at least in part consist of bodily movements and that the detailed causal account will have to show how those movements come about; the crucial factor is that the agent must believe that those movements are an effective way of doing B (a view that I also hold), and this belief, conjoined with a desire to do B (believing that it will lead to G) and with a further belief that 'the time is now ripe', *must cause* the movements to occur. (This is an abbreviated paraphrase of what Woodfield says, but I think it is no less favourable to his position than to mine.) The belief that the time is ripe has two components, namely, that the outside world offers an opportunity to do B, and that there is no internal handicap. One possible internal obstacle is that S might at the moment be engaged in another activity.

Intentional behaviour is controlled by a plan in the way in which a computer's output is controlled by its programme. Before the computer can embark on a new operation, its circuits have to be cleared. It takes time for the executive components to revert to a state in which they can respond to new instructions (Woodfield 1976, p. 179).

Woodfield now begins to talk in physiological terms, pointing out that from the moment t_k at which he forms the opinion that the time is right, up to the moment t_m at which the action begins, 'S's brain receives a barrage of information from afferent nerves about the position and state of the body' (Woodfield 1976, p. 179), and eventually some of these afferent impulses 'will be "All Clear" signals, emanating from the parts of the body that are required for doing B, which "tell" the brain that the parts are in position and ready to receive instructions' (Woodfield 1976, p. 180). We should remember, however, that Woodfield has previously said that no account of the meaning of 'intention' can be given by talking about brain processes. Perhaps because of his own memory of that he goes on to ask:

> But is there any other *mental* state which intervenes between t_k and t_m, such as a volition or a decision to do B next? I don't think so. After t_k, whatever else may be going on in the agent's mind, no mental states other than the wanting and believing are needed to produce an intentional action (Woodfield 1976, p. 180).

This makes it sound as if the mental states of wanting and believing are direct efficient causes of initiation of the efferent nervous impulses that will cause the muscle contractions involved in doing B. The suggestion of the inexorable running off of causal processes is increased when Woodfield goes on to point out that it takes some time for the efferent impulses to get to the limbs, but once they have started they cannot be inhibited before initiating the movement at t_m, because any cancelling 'message' would start later and could not travel faster. Such an inhibition could happen, after a lag, he says, if the agent 'stopped wanting to do B', but if it does not, and the B-producing nerve impulses keep pouring out, then S's 'being in that state must be causally sufficient in the circumstances for the whole movement, if he is to do B intentionally' (Woodfield 1976, p. 181).

Now, all that this says, really, is that the muscular contractions that produced the B-effect must have been caused by efferent nerve impulses which were in turn caused by *the intention or desire* to do B-enacting movements, rather than being caused in some other way, if we are to say that S did B intentionally. If the efferent nerve impulses were caused in some other way, then that would not count. As Woodfield says, 'if a physiologically normal agent were brought into this state as a result of electrical stimulation of the cortex, and not as a result of wanting to do B and believing that the time is ripe, he would do B, but his action would be unintentional' (Woodfield 1976, p. 181). Or if the covetous nephew's convulsive stamping on the accelerator (suppose it to be) were caused, not by his seeing his uncle in front of the car and believing that making that movement would cause him to be run down, but by some general inchoate dysfunction of the nervous system brought on as a psychosomatic by-product of his horror at his murderous impulses (a most contrived and implausible defence, on a Freudian view of parapraxes, but let that pass), we would not say, despite the causal relation, that it was an intentional action, because it did not have the kind of causal chain that intentionality entails.

But we must see that Woodfield's account of this kind of causal chain is severely limited, or perhaps one might say, truncated. Certainly, we may agree that if B were something we say S *did* then the motor movements that brought about the B effect must have been his and they must have been caused by 'normal' processes in his motor nerves, which in turn were caused by nervous processes in the motor areas of his central nervous system, but then, for a *causal* account of his behaviour, we must ask, what caused *them*? We may again agree that if they were caused by some artificially supplied electrical stimulation, then perhaps the action would not count as S's behaviour, but the question is whether there could be *any* physical causes of the central motor nerve processes that could fit in with Woodfield's view that actions are caused by intentions or desires. The only factors that we can list as causing electrical discharges in nerve cells are physical ones. Certain biochemical factors are necessary but the predominant efficient cause of a particular neurone discharging is that one or more other neurones with which it has synaptic connections have discharged, passing excitation across the synapses and bringing about the discharge of its potential. Although there is continual activity in the nervous system, such a causal sequence from cell to cell must begin somewhere, otherwise the brain would be a perpetual motion machine, and the initiating events are to be found in those nerve cells that have connections with sensory end-organs, and which are thus caused to discharge by physical stimuli – light waves, sound waves, mechanical pressure, and so on – impinging on the sense organs. According to this model, one's behaviour, as I have contended before, is caused by the perception of environmental events, entering into the matrix of ongoing processes (including state of drive, to be defined below) in the organism. This is, of course, a simplified picture of the operation of the nervous system but its main lines are sound enough. At least in this post-Cartesian era we are not required to entertain the supposition of a non-physical mental somewhat, breaking into this causal sequence and bringing about the *physical* event of electrical discharge in nerve cells *de novo*. Nor does the 'dual-aspect' conception of mind–body relations, according to which some nervous processes have 'mental properties' which cause them to work differently from nervous processes that lack them, deserve serious consideration. It is a mere verbalism to speak of 'mental properties of nervous processes' if by that is meant localised, embodied, intrinsic properties; any imaginable properties of nerve cells and the events in them are plain physical ones. Finally, the suggestion that the nervous system is such an intricately interrelated whole that it generates its own activity by way of 'circular' or 'holistic' causation, the power which, as we saw, Wilson attributes to feedback mechanisms, and which one might choose, remembering Woodfield's own description of intention as a 'holistic state', to call 'intention', is simply to abandon any understandable conception of causality and propose that such an entity has the power of changing itself – a kind of event which, if it should ever happen, would be blankly incomprehensible.

Just which of these conceptions of the *modus operandi* of 'intention' is Woodfield's is not perfectly explicit, but that there is some extra-neural, non-efficient-causality process behind the initiation of the efferent nervous impulses in his agent seems pretty plain. He says, for example, that it takes time for the (physical) executive components 'to revert to a state in which they can respond to new instructions', but where the 'instructions' originate is unsaid. Again, it is slightly misleading of Woodfield to deny that any mental state 'such as a volition or decision to do *B* next' need intervene between forming the belief that the time is ripe and beginning the movement. The 'decision' had already been taken, it being that which set the physiological causal sequence in train, so that the question of what the 'decision' could be as a causal physiological event still obtrudes itself. All the material about the time lag due to the rate of nervous transmission, though true, is misleading in so far as it creates an image of the body as a rather rickety causal machine. The point is that, concealed behind the fleshy exterior, Woodfield's agent is lodged within his body like a pilot in his vessel, listening to the sensory feedback signals and sending instructions down the motor nerves to the lumbering muscles. If his plan of action were soundly based and if the muscles responded as ordered, then that would satisfy Woodfield's criteria for an intentional action. But, of course, if I may be forgiven for labouring the point, the problem of giving a causal explanation of the intentional actions of the whole organism has been resolved, only to reappear in the problem of giving a causal explanation of the intentional actions of the little man within.

Woodfield seeks to cap his argument by saying that:

> In terms of the hydraulic analogy beloved of motivation theorists, desire is like water in a tank connected to a network of channels. The water can be routed in various ways by opening and closing the entrances to different channels. The water exerts continuous pressure . . . (Woodfield 1976, p. 181).

– and so on. In spite of the superior tone of the opening sentence, Woodfield is embracing this model as a way of showing how desire works. I find this ironic because I too am going to launch a spirited defence of the 'beloved hydraulic analogy' in an updated form later on, for a reason precisely opposed to Woodfield's. He uses it to try to persuade us that desire, intention, and goal-direction are at home in the workaday causal world, but the entire point of the hydraulic model is to show that the apparent 'goal-seeking' aspects of behaviour can be given an efficient-causality explanation. The fluid in a hydraulic system does not seek outlets, it is pushed along tubes. When we transpose this to the living organism and say that the 'tubes' are analogues for motor nerve trunks, then what flows along them is not essentially goal-directed stuff like desire and intention but just *nervous excitation*. Then at least we have some hope of a scientific causal explanation of why it takes the paths it does.

Searle, in a paper (1979b) following hard on the heels of his 'What is an intentional state?', referred to above, addresses himself to this same issue of saying when the effects of intentions are their *intended* effects, not their accidental by-products, but does not achieve much more than showing once again that having said 'Intentionality comes from Intentional states' nothing further can be said. His approach is quite similar to Woodfield's (although he does not mention him) in that he sees that the intention must cause the actual bodily movements that produce the effect, and he does not get any closer than Woodfield does to giving a believable account of intentions as causes.

Searle distinguishes between prior intentions to act and 'intentions in action'. The former is the familiar conception, and the latter says that when I am engaged in performing an action I have at that instant an intention to perform certain specific bodily movements, and if the bodily movements occur in the form specified by this intention in action *and* as the direct effect of it, then the conditions of satisfaction of that intention in action would have been realised and the act would have been my intentional action. If there had also been a prior intention to perform the whole action, though Searle thinks there need *not* have been, then in the case of my intending to raise my arm, he says that:

> . . . the Intentional content of the prior intention can now be expressed as follows:
>
> (I have an intention in action which is a presentation of my arm going up, which causes my arm to go up, and which is caused by this prior intention.)

And thus the prior intention causes the intention in action. By transitivity of causation, the prior intention represents and causes the entire action, but the intention in action presents and causes the bodily movement (Searle 1979b, p. 267).

What caused Searle to posit this intervening link, intention in action, was his earlier reflection that a prior intention is self-referential in that it intends the action to come about as a result of *it*, not in any other way. Thus:

Suppose I intend to raise my arm. The content of my intention can't be that my arm goes up, for my arm can go up without me raising my arm. Nor can it be simply that my intention causes my arm to go up, for we saw in our discussion of the uncle example [Chisholm's] that a prior intention can cause a state of affairs represented by the intention without that state of affairs being the action that would satisfy the intention. Nor, oddly enough, can it be

(that I perform the action of raising my arm)

because I might perform the action of raising my arm in ways that had nothing to do with this prior intention. I might forget all about this intention and later raise my arm for some other independent reason. The representative content of my intention must be

(that I perform the action of raising my arm by way of carrying out *this intention*) (Searle, 1979b, p. 259).

But what all this boils down to in the long run is just to say that counter-examples such as Chisholm's can be dealt with by specifying that a certain event is the effect of my intentional action if and only if it is the direct effect of *my willed bodily movements*, but this, of course, is not to *meet* Chisholm's counter-example but precisely to admit the force of Chisholm's argument that no efficient-causality analysis of intentional action with desire-plus-belief as antecedent cause is possible, and nor is any other analysis in any other terms. 'Intentionality' is allowed by Searle to be an unanalysable term. Searle goes through the familiar move of denying that he is talking about acts of willing, because the experiences he is talking about 'are not acts at all', but his attempts to describe what he calls 'the experience of acting' show that it is just the conviction that the movements one is making are one's willed movements, which he contrasts with the compelled movements produced in Penfield's patients by his electrodes on their exposed motor cortex (Penfield 1975).

The major issue I have been concerned with in this chapter is the question of how those bodily changes, i.e. movements, in us which I call behaviour are produced, and how they are produced in such patterns that they very frequently bring about changes in our relations with the environment of the kind we call 'achieving goals'. What I have contended is that the use of terms such as 'goal-seeking', 'purpose', 'intention', and so on can produce only the merest illusion of understanding. To say these changes are self-caused is to offer a stone, not honest nourishment, to the understanding. I have flirted with the concept of feedback as explanatory, and I am sure it provides a basis on which one can build, but a good deal of elaboration and enrichment is required before it begins to offer a feasible account of the working of the human organism. It is time to see what sort of elaboration that would be.

4

Cognition and determinism

In referring above to higher organisms as feedback-controlled, multi-programmed target-seeking entities, I suggested briefly that the most distinctive of the input relationships to the programs was the cognitive relation; that is, that organisms discover facts about things in their environment, and that when these facts bear upon the means of getting to a target-object, they will modify the behaviour of the organism in a way that will bring it to the target-object more quickly and directly than would otherwise have been the case (other things being equal). However, there is a widespread tendency to think that if one says that an organism's behaviour changes in that way according to its beliefs, then one is saying that it directs its own behaviour in the light of its information, and such a concept of self-direction is precisely what a deterministic psychology must avoid.

The assumption that *cognition implies purpose* was one of the main reasons for the development of S–R learning theory, because behaviourism was certainly intent on being deterministic, and in consequence held (effectively if not explicitly) that there were no cognitive processes. Now that the pointlessness of trying to deny the reality or behavioural import of cognitive processes has become plain, and their role in learning is again a subject of study, it becomes necessary to dissociate cognition from purpose, and to show what view of the nature of cognition is required if there is to be viable empirical study of it. An examination of the fate of cognitive processes in modern learning theory, and then in artificial intelligence (AI) theorising, will allow me to show some ways of conceiving them that do *not* permit such meaningful study, and perhaps to point the way to a workable approach.

Cognitive processes and modern learning theory

Since the demise of S–R learning theory, the experimental study of learning in animals has been used mainly as a tool for generating and testing speculations about the nature and limitations of animals' cognitive processes. But the overarching cognitive theory related to this stream of research does not derive from the observations. Rather, the trend has been to take over without much reflection certain philosophical traditions about the basis of human thought, and to interpret the animal behavioural phenomena in those terms, and the most common option has been the associationist tradition stemming from the British Empiricists. The irony of this is that one of the factors in the eruption of behaviourism in the early years of the twentieth century was disillusion with the atomistic analysis of conscious content which had dominated academic psychology up to that time. One hopes that this does not develop into a repetitive 60-year cycle of two sterile atomistic associationisms, one of ideas and another of reflexes, endlessly consuming one another.

One large theme in this recent stream of research has been the question of whether it is stimulus–stimulus relations or response–stimulus relations that animals are learning, especially in the phenomenon called 'sign-tracking' (e.g. the review by Hearst in Hulse *et al.* 1978). One way of paraphrasing that question would be to ask whether the animal is learning that the conditioned stimulus (CS) of light or tone, for example, is a sign that the unconditioned stimulus (US) of food or shock, say, is about to be delivered, or that some response that it has been making is likely to be followed by the US. Variations on this would be preferred by different experimenters; for example, Morgan (1979a) seems to prefer to speak in the traditional way of associations growing up between representations of the CS and the US and/or the response, rather than the propositional forms suggested by 'learning *that*'. Others leave it ambiguous as to whether the learning of response–stimulus relations is some kind of cognitive representation of the connection, or the old-fashioned S–R connectionism, according to which the response itself becomes functionally attached to the CS by virtue of the fact that it has been followed by the US, i.e. the reinforcer, with no question of the animal recognising the connection.

Pavlovian conditioning procedures are seen as a test-bed for this issue. As is well known, what distinguishes Pavlovian procedures is that the CS will be followed by the US whether the animal makes any response in the meantime or not. Yet what is regularly found is that with pigeons, for example, when the CS is the illumination of a disc in the Skinner box and the US is the delivery of grain, the birds form the practice of approaching the lighted disc and pecking at it during the period before the grain is delivered, even though this US is not at all contingent on their doing so. This is called 'autoshaping', a variety of sign-tracking, which Hearst defines as 'behavior (e.g., eye movements, bodily orientation, approach, signal contact) that is directed toward or away from a feature of the environment (a sign) as a result of the relation between that environmental feature and another (the reinforcer, in a typical experiment)' (Hearst 1978, p. 59). Those who favour the response–reinforcement view of learning could hold that even though the reinforcer is not, in fact, contingent on the response being made it does regularly follow it (in whatever way the response may first appear); this consideration, however, seems to be ruled out by arranging conditions so that after the sign-tracking response is well established, the making of it will prevent the animal actually availing itself of the reinforcer, yet the response shows great persistence even so. A complementary procedure is to prevent the animal making any directed response while it is being given the opportunity to observe a regular relation between CS and US; it is found that the autoshaping appears much more rapidly when it is later made possible than if this pretraining had not occurred.

Such demonstrations are in favour of some version of a cognitive view of learning; that is, that the organism discovers facts, or forms hypotheses, about regularities in its environment, about sign-significate relationships, or even, as Mackintosh (1977) is bold enough to suggest, about cause–effect relationships. This is the kind of 'anomalous' finding, as Kuhn might call it, that helped to bring about the shift away from the S–R learning paradigm. If one basic premise of S–R theory was that *there are no cognitive processes*, these experimental findings could not stand as an orthodox Popperian *falsification* or disconfirmation of that premise as long as S–R theorists stood firm by their methodological dictum – one that has indeed been accepted as axiomatic by psychologists of every persuasion – that the mental processes of other organisms (including persons) are unobservable, so that there can be no intersubjective corroboration of their occurrence in any particular case. Let us call the response-prevention procedure referred to above a demonstration of 'latent learning', borrowing the term from Tolman's experiments of some 40 years ago. Then, if this were to be a falsification of the cognition-denying premise, the form of the argument would be:

> Latent learning depends on cognitive processes
> Some animals manifest latent learning
> Therefore some animals have cognitive processes.

Stimulus–response learning theorists simply rejected the major premise, denying that it could be taken as a fact of observation, a classical ideological self-preserving mechanism. Some onus was laid on them to explain how their non-cognitive system could encompass the behavioural manifestations, a project at which Hull showed great skill. His most accommodating explanatory device was the 'pure stimulus act', a habitual, implicit (i.e. unobservable) motor response that an organism is postulated to make to any stimulus element, characteristic of that element, thus functioning as if it were an act of recognition of that element, but declared to be motor, not cognitive, and serving to form internal S–R links between stimuli and overt motor responses that had never actually been reinforced in connection with those stimuli (Hull 1930, 1934, 1943, etc.). Such devices are now recognised to have no better observational status than the mental processes they were to replace, and that, combined with some obscure shift in the 'spirit of the times' has led to the experimental demonstrations of the 1970s having an effect on psychological orthodoxy denied to those of Tolman and his colleagues in the 1940s.

But at least the hard-line S–R learning theorists took very seriously a fundamentally important psychological problem that is passed over by the present-day stimulus–stimulus learning theorists for the most part, and that is the problem of how it comes about that an organism's behaviour in a given situation actually changes as a result of its previous experiences of frustration and gratification in situations of that kind. This, of course, is the most interesting and difficult part of that large phenomenon of the plasticity of behaviour relative to a goal that I have been discussing throughout. That plasticity may be partitioned under two heads: (a) the specific form of the animal's bodily movements which on any occasion seems nicely adapted to reorienting it to an environmental object in a particular way, an adaptation that characterises virtually every instance of anything we would call a response or an action; and (b) the progressive reorganisation, gradual or rapid, over a series of trials, of the sequence of component responses to a given situation which (ordinarily) seem to bring about the animal's arrival at what we are calling the goal in a more effective way – the matter of the improvement of performance which, oddly enough, McDougall thought the least important of his marks of purpose but which the S–R learning theorists rightly identified as the most difficult to explain in a deterministic way.

This is simply ignored by the majority of today's cognitive learning theorists. They just assume that when an organism discovers, or believes it has discovered, that certain events in its surroundings are relevant in one way or another to the advent of some reward or punishment, then the organism naturally alters its own behaviour in such a way as to capitalise on that discovery in the case of instrumental learning, or to express some emotive or ritual or preconsummatory response to the anticipated advent of the reinforcer in the case of Pavlovian conditioning. They are hardly alone in this; the great majority of the world's inhabitants, including the great majority of psychologists, take it as *self-evident* that when an organism has had a chance to discover a more effective way of getting something it wants or avoiding something it does not want, then it will take that way; if it does not 'profit by experience', then it is stupid or neurotic or both. But it is *not* self-evident. It is quite conceivable that an organism should cognitively discover that in situation E_1 behaviour B_1 is regularly followed by electric shock, and helplessly go on doing B_1 for ever; or that a certain arrangement of stimulus cards shows that the food is now in the right-hand alley of the T-maze, yet be entirely unable to change its existing habit of going to the left.

That this awkward gap between thoughts and the actions to which they may be relevant remains unfilled is recognised by Dickinson (1979) in his review of *Cognitive processes in animal behavior* (Hulse *et al.* 1978), but in my opinion he plays down its importance too much. He says that:

> ... the focus of interest has changed; according to the consensus view expressed in this book, behaviour is but a spade to disinter thought, and the mistake made by the traditional cognitive theorists in their battle with S–R theory was to assume that the two enterprises had a common focus. It is not so much that behaviourism is wrong and in need of replacement by a better theoretical perspective, but that an analysis which refers solely to behavioural changes has largely run its course and left untouched many of the psychological capacities of animals (Dickinson 1979, p. 553).

But this is only to concur from the other side in the dissembling defence by S–R theorists that they were not disputing the reality of cognitive processes, they just chose to confine their attention to behavioural changes contingent on reinforcement, and could peacefully coexist with cognitive psychology. The two enterprises did indeed have a common focus; they were both concerned with explaining behavioural changes (a cognitive psychology that did not concern itself with the causal role of thought in affecting behaviour would be pitifully stunted), and their modes of explanation were directly in conflict. Although S–R theory may now be not much more than an historical curiosity, it may be instructive to look briefly at its account of how changes in response come about, for example at Hull's 'Law of Primary Reinforcement', because although it was misconceived and a failure, it gives something of the flavour of what a hard-nosed, disabused, thoroughly deterministic explanation of behavioural change might be like. It shows what the difficulty is, and has a healthily unsettling effect on comfortable, commonsense notions.

One may loosely paraphrase Hull's 'Law of Primary Reinforcement' (Hull 1943, 1952) by saying that he conceived of an organism's behavioural life as two concurrent and continuous streams, one being that of afferent or sensory neural processes, and the other efferent or motor ones. They interact, but are always distinct in kind and location. At various times, whether in the laboratory or in nature, a reinforcing event is injected into this system, and that brings about a joining together in some degree of the recently preceding afferent process and its contemporaneous efferent process. This was thought of as the merest brute matter of fact, a fortunate survival-promoting accident of evolution, not at all teleological or purposive. Hull was quite prepared to conceive this joining together as being literally a physiological connection developing between those sensory neurones which were active in the sensory process concerned and the motor neurones mediating the motor one. In consequence, if the organism was later subjected to the same sensory stimulus, the nervous impulse aroused would pass over directly into the newly connected motor

nerves and thus cause the motor response to occur again. There was
absolutely no room for 'thoughts about' the meaning of the stimulus or the
outcome of the response at all.

Now, it is true that any such model-railway conception of the operation
of the nervous system is outrageously primitive and could not really
encompass the observable variability of forms of response. It is equally true
and much more important to see that the S–R notion of appropriate
explanation was based on the quite bizarre and crippling metaphysical
premise of the non-existence of mental processes – something that is
observably false and which if adhered to would make it impossible even to
say what an organism was doing – a point to which I shall shortly return.
Yet even so, even though there are mental processes that affect behaviour,
and even though the central nervous system is unimaginably complex and
sophisticated and equipped with all manner of elaborate and devious
back-up circuitry and switching mechanisms, nevertheless Hull's belief
that there must be *some* sort of connecting and reconnecting in the brain
was not at all nonsensical. If a type of external situation that used to
provoke one kind of behaviour now provokes another, then something in
the organism's brain must have changed (assuming that the path from
input to output is routed through the brain), even though neurology is still
so remotely distant from the most basic conception of what such changes
are that psychology must struggle along without it. All that can be said is
that we must keep in mind that these changes in behaviour are caused, not
goal-directed (for all the reasons given above), and try to work up a sketchy
model (yet one as life-like as possible, not a non-cognitive one) of how a
complex, multiple-target-'seeking', learning machine might work.

To return to the modern school of researchers into animal learning, they
may be complimented on having thrown off the barbarous yoke of S–R
connectionism, but that is not to say that they need feel no concern about
the mechanism of behavioural changes while they speculate about the
mental capacities of our speechless cousins. (If one were concerned with
the study of mental processes *per se*, it would seem an unnecessary
handicap to restrict oneself to dealing with non-verbal species.) Since these
experimenters have nothing but their subjects' bodily behaviour to go on as
evidence of their beliefs, they too are committed to some presupposition or
other, explicit or not, about what projects their subjects are embarked on
and how their behaviour comes to change. If it is observed that an animal
that formerly turned right at a particular junction in a maze now begins
regularly to turn left, and it is also observable that the left-hand alley is a
shorter path to the food box, then if the observer says 'The rat has discovered that the left-hand alley is a shorter path to the food box', this
conclusion is based on the prior assumption that the rat is engaged in
getting to the food box by the shortest available path, and that the new
piece of knowledge has brought about the change in behaviour at this
junction. To ignore the question of *how* the knowledge changes the

behaviour is in effect to support the purposivist position by default, i.e. to assume that the rat actively directs itself round this corner in order to get to the food box. I have been trying to show how uninformative this everyday 'explanation' is.

Nevertheless, what I am proposing will not at first sound much more enlightening. It is simply this, that it is not an organism's 'purposes' but just its *cognitions* which cause the reassembling of its behaviour segments in what we call more effective ways, and which link together as members of one response-type the various patterns of muscular movements that we make on different occasions of doing 'the same action'. It is well known that even for much-practised actions in which a high value is placed on precise similarity, such as signing one's name, no two performances will be exactly alike, yet within quite wide limits we are prepared to agree that they are instances of the same action. In all these cases the components of the action or sequence of actions are joined together by the organism's acquired beliefs about what the consequences of the movements will be.

A critic may well feel inclined to say that this is no advance in understanding at all, merely another form of words. The purposivists I am opposing say that the organism changes its own behaviour, in the light of its acquired knowledge, in such a way as to get to the goal, and I am saying that its behaviour is changed *by* its acquired knowledge in such a way as to bring it to what I only provisionally call its goal. But at least my formulation has this negative advantage, that it refuses to incorporate the mind-bemusing notion that the organism is able to change itself or not 'at will', and that it points to (instead of concealing) a gap which needs to be filled but conceivably *can* be filled in a genuinely enlightening way by empirical discoveries, presumably of a neurological kind. That is, we must take it as a fact that sufficiently evolved organisms possess some as yet unidentified coordinating nerve centres, genetically provided, which incorporate information coming through the sense organs into existing behaviour programs in such a way that those programs (which we assume by and large to have biological utility) can still run off effectively in the environmental situation to which the organism is exposed. This, of course, is allowing a very heavy burden to be carried by the phrase 'unidentified nerve centres', but at least such mechanisms are conceivable as working entities, not just metaphysical puzzles. We do not find it surprising that a computer's response to a given input should change after it has been fed new information about that input, if the new information is relevant to the program being run. It is pointless to say that the computer has been designed and programmed to operate that way and cannot step outside its programs; in whatever way it came into being, it does run through its routines and subroutines, and incorporate new information into them when it is provided, and it does so deterministically.

Or suppose someone set out to invent a reusable target-seeking missile, which did not destroy itself along with its target, but was able to profit from accumulated experience to improve its flight patterns. It is not difficult to imagine its basic requirements. It would need a device in which records of previous responses to sensory input were collected, along with a tabulation of consequent hits or misses. This would be incorporated somewhere between the sensors and the steering mechanism. On any given trial the current incoming sensory pattern would be very rapidly matched with the previously recorded ones, and the device would transmit 'messages' to the steering mechanism, bringing about the kind of response that in similar circumstances had previously been followed by hits and eliminating those which had been followed by misses. All this may be much more easily said than done, but at least one can see that a working model is a possibility.

To show how such a way of thinking applies to human beings calls for the assumption, as I said above, that there are some unlearned abilities that when set in motion run their course automatically. These will probably include the direct physical manipulation of objects, the adjustment of the detailed motions to the size and position of the objects being determined by sensorimotor feedback loops of a comparatively simple kind. A further reasonable assumption is that these unlearned abilities are likely to have survival value, and in fact later in this work I will develop in some detail the supposition that they are primitive forms of consummatory action which become progressively elaborated by the learning process. One may think of them as programs, and a developmental sketch of a familiar one may add some substance to the rather skeletal proposal above that it is cognitions that bind actions together.

Computers and feedback systems get their programs from human beings; human beings get theirs with their genes. One of these is the eating program; it is relatively simple at the beginning of life but can become indefinitely complicated later on. In the beginning it consists of this: if the infant has been deprived of food for a sufficient period, then when food is presented to it, *it eats the food.* That simple exposition of the program calls for some spelling out. Concerning the input side, the infant does not have the same understanding of what constitutes food as it will have later in life, when it gets to know something of the difference between nutritious and non-nutritious eatable substances – proteins, carbohydrates, inert substances, toxic substances, and so on. However, an infant does not swallow just anything that is put in its mouth; some things it spits out. In speaking of an infant, the concept 'food' should be replaced by 'substances of a certain taste, odour, and consistency'. Fortunately, because of its innate programming, most of the substances whose sensory qualities prompt the infant to swallow them would actually *be* food; however, because the program is not perfect and all-embracing, we need to keep infants from getting hold of bottles of kerosene, ant poison, and so on. The output side of the program, eating, at first consists of just the complicated interaction of lips, tongue, jaws and throat that constitutes sucking and swallowing. No one who has watched an infant's first effort at sucking and swallowing could seriously hold that those component movements need to be assembled by learning, it seems to me.

What does come about through learning is the elaboration of the program on both the input and the output side. These may be considered separately, but of course there must be intimate interplay between them. The effective input or stimulus aspect of the program becomes elaborated as the young organism discovers various facts about food – most importantly, where it is and what needs to be done to get it. As this happens, those other types of object which are discovered to be regularly and understandably related to food come to act, in a sense, as *surrogates* for food when the baby is hungry and actual food is not present. I say 'surrogates' in order to stress the fact that they *cause* the eating program to begin running off, whereas in the first place it was only food itself that would do so. In another way it would be better to say that the associated objects stand as *signs* of where food is, or perhaps that the stimulus 'food' has become a complex that includes the associated objects, since the young organism knows them propositionally as related to food. In any case, if an associated object causes the eating program to begin running off in the absence of actual food, the program would obviously be abortive if its motor output continued to consist only of sucking or chewing and swallowing – that is, if the response to the associated object were the same as the one to the original stimulus, food. Instrumental actions need to become incorporated into the eating program if it is to get food into the stomach. As I have been saying, the need for them does not mean that they *will* be incorporated; to retain the determinist view we must suppose the genetic provision of the coordinating nerve centres that I hypothesised above, and certainly the very early age at which some of these instrumental acts begin to be incorporated makes that a plausible supposition. Some of the integrations seem to be preformed, ready to run off as soon as the motor abilities have developed sufficiently to follow the guidance of perception. One very early elaboration of the eating program is for the baby to turn its head so as to bring its mouth to the nipple. Later comes the grasping of objects and transporting them to the mouth, and then progressively the various forms of bodily locomotion – shuffling, crawling, or walking to the food, before grasping it and putting it into the mouth.

Allowing a span of years to elapse, consider the following everyday example of the elaboration of both input and output in my eating program. I am sitting in my room at the university and gradually become hungry. I know that the nearest source of accessible foodstuffs is the cafeteria in the Students Union building. I know the geographical relatedness of my room and the cafeteria – the passage outside my door, the stairs, the exit from this building, the path beneath the plane tree, the door of the Union. Because of that information, because of my state of drive, because there are no other programs running off in me at the moment that prevail over the eating program, the sight of the door of my room causes me to get up and walk through it, the familiar passage outside is responded to as path-to-stairs-and-food rather than, say, path-to-lecture-room, and so on, until I come to the food. Each succeeding part of that path is seen by me in its relation to food (though this is not to deny that I also had the conception of the whole path before I started), and so keeps my extended eating program running.

In a way this concedes to S–R psychology that everything I do is a response to some stimulus object in my immediate environment. Even thinking about an absent friend, for instance, would be prompted in however roundabout a way by some present object. But the important difference from S–R theory is that these present stimulus objects prompt behaviour in me because of their connections in the web of my cognitions, and the action that occurs does so because of its place in the same web. To return to the food-getting example, one may think of each of the various food locations with which I am familiar as having a great number of invisible tentacles spreading through the neighbourhood, each tentacle being a path that I know of from some place to that food location, so that wherever I am when I get hungry, provided I know even in general terms the spatial relation between the place where I am and some food supply, that present stimulus situation causes me to start moving away from it in the direction of the food. Further, although it is a strained usage, what I can most informatively be said to be doing, even as I take the first steps towards the food, is *engaging in eating.* That is to make the point that it is still the same eating program which in its germinal form I acquired genetically that is running off in me, and it shows also that the language of purposivism, which would say that I am walking *in order* to get the food, is not inescapable. It is possible to express in a deterministic way the relationship between the instrumental activity and the consummatory activity that motivates it by saying that the former has become incorporated as a *part* of the latter in an extended and elaborated version of the same basic program. In saying this I am anticipating a later part of my argument which will claim that in this sense everything that an organism ever does, however sophisticated, is a version or a part of one of its *unlearned* consummatory activities, which is to say, one of its genetically determined behavioural programs. Thus, the eating programme for most adults in industrial communities must include exchanging money for the food, so that the occupations one takes up for the receipt of money also count as part of the eating program, although of course they will serve as part of other programs as well. The medium through which this elaboration works is cognition; that is, most prominently, through the formation of beliefs about the locations of the objects on which the consummatory actions are performed, and about the likely effects of actions on objects in the present environment and the relation of those effects to the getting of the goal objects. The actions are caused by (amongst other things) the organism's beliefs about their outcomes, not in any sense at all by the outcomes themselves.

The separation of cognition from purpose

Cognition and purpose do not form an inseparable pair; one can recognise the causal role of cognitive processes in the determination of behaviour without at all committing oneself to the view that cognition-guided behaviour must be purposive. The belief that the two concepts form an indissoluble compound was one ground for the S–R behaviourists' rejection of all mental processes; realising that if psychology were to be a science, then it must be deterministic, they believed that cognition had to go as well. By the same token, when S–R psychology collapsed, phenomenologists and humanists assumed that the rehabilitation of cognitive psychology automatically meant that purposivism was also vindicated. The same error of thought is perpetuated in common usage, when people say 'He did it knowingly' to mean 'He did it on purpose.' These are simply *non sequiturs*.

A causal theory of cognition must hold, not only that beliefs determine behaviour, but that their occurrence is itself determined; that is, that we are caused to have our perceptions and beliefs by, in the first place, the physical stimulation of our sense organs. Two main objections have been raised to this: (a) if our beliefs and inferences are caused, then the distinction between true and false beliefs and valid and invalid inferences disappears; and (b) perception and memory are selective; not just everything is registered and retained but only those things relevant to our interests; therefore, it is held, cognitive events are in themselves purposive acts of an agent, and cannot be thought of as 'passively' caused.

The first objection has recently been given expression by Gauld and Shotter (1977). Addressing the view that the thoughts in a process of inference form a 'causal chain', they say:

> It leads almost inevitably to 'logical psychologism', the view that logical 'laws' and the normative statements made by logicians are in effect generalizations about the mental processes of thinkers. For if valid and invalid inferences are alike determined by the antecedent beliefs of the reasoner, it is difficult to see how the two are to be distinguished except either (a) in terms of the causal laws which they exemplify, or (b) in terms of whether or not they conform to patterns of events in the outside world. Since the causal laws are bound to reflect external events, these positions inevitably coalesce. Logical 'laws' are the mental correlates of environmental regularities (Gauld & Shotter 1977, pp. 119–20).

What Gauld and Shotter mean by this last sentence is that the notion of logical laws becomes empty if we think of the beliefs that we call the 'premises' of an argument as simply *causing*, in a contingent, matter-of-fact way, another psychological event, a belief that we misleadingly call the 'conclusion of the inference'. They go on to say that we could observe such sequences occurring in any number of persons 'and fail to understand why they inferred as they did, or why they stopped when they did' (Gauld & Shotter 1977, p. 121). Presumably, what Gauld and Shotter would prefer to say in opposition to this is that people infer as they do *because* they see that the premises validly imply the conclusion. 'That someone reasons correctly', they say, 'requires, generally speaking, no further explanation than that his reasoning is correct' (Gauld & Shotter 1977, p. 121). All of this seems to presume that a person *chooses* to believe the conclusion because he has seen that the reasoning is correct, but that is an *a priori* assumption of purposivism, not necessitated by the reality of valid argument. This assimilation of rational thought to rational *action* is able to creep in only because Gauld and Shotter make the common mistake of thinking that reasoning is a kind of generative activity, that 'drawing a conclusion' is somehow more than simply seeing the *fact* that the premises imply the conclusion. But once having seen that *fact*, there is nothing more to be done; the conclusion's being implied has been *recognised*, and there is no sense in which it can be *drawn* as a separate act. Of course, it is possible to fail to see such a particular relation of facts in the world, just as it is possible to fail to see any relational fact; one can be aware of a set of facts (the premises) without being aware of their interlockingness (the *implicatum*), but that does not mean that one has failed to carry out some internal process of transformation, operating on the input of premises to generate an output of conclusion, by a process that must meet some normative standard. Gauld and Shotter think that it is a *reductio ad absurdum* to say that 'logical "laws" are the mental correlates of environmental regularities', but if one understands 'correlates of' to mean representations of or apprehensions of environmental regularities (regularities of the most general kind, not mere particular causal relationships), then it seems to me not a *reductio* but the correct view. The rules of logic are not simply conventionally agreed upon rules like those of chess, or sound heuristic principles devised by wise men, which is shown by the fact that there are constraints on tinkering about with them that one cannot ignore without finding oneself trying to play an unplayable game. Even the rules of chess are subject to the superior rules of logic; if one of the rules of chess says that when my piece lands on a square occupied by your piece, then it captures it, and another rule says that it does not, that is a game one cannot play, and in general if one moves to suspend the Law of Contradiction, then that makes all of language a 'game' one cannot play – but then one could not even say what the new rules were supposed to be.

The laws of logic, according to the view I am expressing, are statements about the categorial aspects of the structure of the universe. It is possible on occasion to misapprehend particular instantiations of them, in which case the rationalisations a person may give for his or her opinions will misrepresent some part of the structure of the universe. To say that all beliefs are *caused*, whether they are true or false or whether the rationalisations for them are valid or invalid, does not mean that the grounds for distinguishing between true and false and valid and invalid have been taken away. The only reason for saying so would be the implicit assumption that surveying the evidence (or cognising in general) is a willed act, and that if one forms a conclusion on the basis of the evidence, then that is a rational decision, a principled choice. But that assumption is no more necessary than is the assumption that if my bodily behaviour is guided by my beliefs about the situation, then I must have *decided* to act on the basis of those beliefs, rather than being caused to do so. One may be brought to (i.e. caused to) recognise the actuality of an unwelcome implication just as one may be brought to recognise any unpleasant fact. It is not through rational volition that the unwelcomeness is overcome, but rather because some stronger motive opposing the source of unpleasure is enlisted – it may, for example, be the pressure to please one's teacher, or one's psychoanalyst, or to preserve some valued personal relationship. (The critical reader will be aware that in expressing the determinist position I continually fall back into the language of goal-seeking, as in the last sentence. At present I can only ask him or her to suspend judgement until a causal account of motivation is given in a later chapter, and to suppose that it may be a human error due to the undeveloped state of the science, rather than an inescapable self-contradiction in the theory itself.)

There is, in general, a strong, overdetermined motivation to register facts and implications in the environment simply because doing so warns of dangers to come and shows where the objects necessary for gratification are to be found. This motivation, the reality principle as Freud called it, can become so overdetermined that it operates as if it had become independent of any extrinsic motivation, as if it were a spirit of pure enquiry, but that kind of motivational concept, I shall argue later, is not a viable one in a deterministic theory of motivation, since it is defined as a striving-towards, rather than as a driving mechanism, and enquiry always remains instrumental to drives defined by their biological source (cf. also Maze 1973).

The first objection to the causal theory of cognition, the objection that 'rational' thought must be purposive, is not, I am claiming, a well founded argument but an unnecessary assumption, in fact, a *petitio principii*. The second, that which claims that since cognition is *selective* it must be inherently purposive, contains a much more difficult puzzle within it, but one that is as much a problem for the purposivist as for the determinist. At first approach the directedness of cognition presents neither more nor less a problem for the determinist than does the apparent goal-directedness of bodily behaviour. It shows that internal motivational factors play a part in determining whether something will be recognised or not, but motivational factors play a part in the forming of all behaviour, and a deterministic account of them can (in principle) be given by developing an adequate theory of primary drives and their auxiliary mechanisms, as we shall see. But the general line is that when the requisite motivational state obtains and the person's sense organs are exposed to adequate physical stimulation from objects in the environment (I am referring to perception but a similar account can be given of memory and so on), then he or she will be caused to be aware of the presence of those objects. If some opposing motivational state obtains, one that would render the presence of those objects highly unpleasant, then the person may be unable to perceive them. However, both the determinist and the purposivist are faced with an often-remarked and still unresolved difficulty in trying to explain the mechanism by which the person manages not to see something unpleasant *because* it is unpleasant. It seems that one must first identify it as unwelcome in order to ignore it; must know it in order not to know it. A number of proposals, varying widely in ingenuity, have been offered by psychologists over the years, ranging from the concept of 'sensory filter', which is the merest uninformative metaphor, since in perception things are filtered out not on the basis of being too big to get through the pores but on the basis of having already (i.e. before reaching the 'filter') been recognised as unwelcome, to the more workable proposal (Hochberg 1970) that we do actually register *everything* but forget things very quickly unless they are verbally encoded, and that the process of encoding, which takes some little time, is disrupted at a physiological level by a charge of anxiety at having seen the threatening things.

Sartre

The Hochberg model has the virtue that the breaking out of anxiety on seeing a threatening situation, and its consequent disruption of the verbal encoding process, are thought of as automatic physiological effects of the threat, not as directed behaviour. Shiffrin's later (1976) proposal lacks any such deterministic mechanism. He too relies on the proposition that every-thing available to the senses is perceived, or goes into the short-term store (STS), as he says, but will be forgotten very quickly (within half a second, say) if it is not further encoded. However, he has nothing more to say about the mechanics of selective attention than this:

> In this system, selective attention is relegated entirely to the action of control processes [i.e. rehearsal and coding] in STS following the completion of the automatic stages of sensory processes . . . Most of this information dumped into STS will be lost very quickly so that the sub-ject must select certain important components for rehearsal, for coding, and for decision making. This selective process within STS is assumed to be the locus of selective attention (Shiffrin 1976, pp. 215–16).

The trouble with this, in the first place, is that the phenomenon of selective attention is supposed to be based on the control processes of rehearsal and coding, but they follow upon a *previous* process of *selecting the most important input* – an example of the question-begging sort of boot-strapping common in this field. Secondly, all the work is presented as the *subject*'s, in actively selecting what he will perceive and what forget.

A similar faith in the power of purposiveness is shown by Neisser:

When perception is treated as something we do rather than something thrust upon us, no internal mechanisms of selection are required at all . . . Organisms are active: they do some things and leave others undone . . .

Attention is nothing but perception: we choose what we will see by anticipating the structured information we will provide (Neisser 1976, p. 87).

Here again are the same two errors of thought. We may anticipate certain information as relevant, but we will still have to perceive the remainder in order to see that it is irrelevant. Further, merely conjuring with words like 'choosing' does not increase our understanding of how the apparent self-directedness of perceiving comes about, any more than it does in the case of apparently goal-seeking behaviour.

This is not to pretend that it is easy to find a deterministic account of how knowing something leads to not knowing it. I think that Hochberg was right in believing that verbalising thoughts plays an important part in what we call being conscious of them, and I shall be returning to that below. At present I am just claiming that our inability to report more than a part of what is potentially available for perception does not establish that the concept of perception is of something intrinsically purposive, so that a deterministic psychology must contradict itself if it incorporates perceptual and cognitive processes. 'Purpose' does not enlarge our understanding of these patently real happenings, for the reasons given earlier, and in this particular instance the notion that we simply *choose* not to see the things we do not like hardly makes the mechanism of perceptual defence or selective forgetting any clearer.

I have been arguing in this section, then, that the view that cognitive processes are intrinsically purposive is mistaken and unenlightening. However, the main stream of thought that currently treats cognitive processes as deterministic is that deriving from computer-simulation studies or AI. These theorists unfailingly embrace a representationist and constructivist epistemology, holding its truth to be demonstrated by the way their AI devices work. I am going on energetically to dissociate myself from that epistemology (a) because it is demonstrably self-defeating, and (b) because, paradoxically enough, in the hands of phenomenologists and existentialists, representationism and constructivism lend themselves to the view that persons in constructing their own worlds, and their own selves in those worlds, do so by an act of free choice – the most radically anti-determinist conception extant, which will be examined in detail in Chapter 5 below.

Cognition as non-representational: irrelevance of computer simulation

In allowing for the causal role of cognitive processes in a deterministic account of behaviour, they are to be conceived of as state variables (but in the form of *relational* properties, as I am about to argue) of the organism, produced by previous interactions with environmental objects, and, along with drive state and other organismic variables, determining the behavioural effects produced in the organism by subsequent environmental stimulation. (To say that behaviour is produced by environmental stimulation does not exclude stimulation arising from within the subject's own body; such proprioceptive stimulation will always have originated in bodily events other than or external to the central processes giving rise to the behaviour one is seeking to explain, and thus can be called parts of *its* environment.)

The problem in talking of cognitions or beliefs as state variables is to avoid giving the impression that one is embracing a representationist theory of knowledge, in which the state variables are internal representational entities. The view that our knowledge of external objects must be mediated by some kind of internal modelling of them is ubiquitous in psychology, and is taken as self-evident to such an extent that there is no widely understood theory of direct realism to stand as a rival. J. J. Gibson has been gradually refining his theory of direct visual (and other) perception for many years, and has given it its clearest and most uncompromising statement in a recent book (Gibson 1979), yet so entrenched has the computational–representational approach to perception become that his critics apparently cannot believe that he means what he says. His basic assertion is that what we perceive consists of places, attached objects, separate objects, substances and events (Gibson 1979, p. 240), *not* of colour, form, location, space, time and motion, and most especially not of retinal images or the complex of nervous processes initiated by them. Naturally, he does not deny that a perceived object or event must send physical energies to our sense organs, nor that object-specific physiological events must occur in the sense organs, afferent nerves and central nervous system. He is simply asserting that those physiological events *are not perceived*, are not in any sense objects of awareness to the perceiver. For Gibson (and this seems to me exactly the required position), the whole complex physiological event involving the brain and sense organs is *the perceiving of the environment*, and does not require that any of its own constituents be perceived or scanned in any way whatever – a supposition which, he contends, leads on to a ludicrous infinite regress of homunculi within homunculi.

To say that the perception of an object is direct or immediate is to say that it is not mediated by the perception of some intermediary, of some internal representing state that must then be processed or decoded to yield an indirect – i.e. 'inferred' – knowledge of the external object. Gibson sees that the postulation of such mediated knowledge defeats its own ends, in that, in its explanation of perception as mediated, it implicitly assumes the immediacy of some prior perception. That is, a perceiver can only know the meaning of an internal representation or symbol if he is already informed of the relation between the symbol and the thing symbolised – i.e. if he knows independently and directly the latter's existence (a point also made clearly by Heil 1981). As Gibson puts it: 'Knowledge of the world cannot be explained by supposing that knowledge of the world already exists. All forms of cognitive processing imply cognition so as to account for cognition' (Gibson 1979, p. 253). Another form of the argument he gives is this:

> Even the more sophisticated theory that the retinal image is transmitted as signals in the fibers of the optic nerve has the lurking implication of a little man in the brain. For these signals must be in code and therefore have to be decoded; signals are messages, and messages have to be interpreted (Gibson 1979, p. 61).

Thus, the theory of perception as being indirect, or mediated by internal representations, involves a *petitio principii*; it proposes to explain perception as the end-product of a process, but the constituent stages of this process implicitly assume that perception is already a going concern, i.e. are themselves acts of perception. This is a powerful logical criticism of the entire conceptual basis of representationism, yet Gibson's critics persist in treating the issue of direct versus indirect perception as one to be decided by empirical evidence. Typically, their arguments proceed by citing irreproachable evidence about the physiological stages involved in some act of perception, and then allowing these stages to slide surreptitiously over the dividing line between the physiological and the psychological, so that the relationship between one phase and the next is represented as being not simply a physiological–causal one, but rather as the 'extraction' – i.e. the *apprehension* – of 'information'. For example, Ullman (1980) claims that there is 'substantial evidence' for a number of distinct channels, or 'mechanisms sensitive to different ranges of size and spatial frequency' in human vision, and that a variety of phenomena in pattern detection can be explained by 'the properties of the channels and non-linear interactions between them' (Ullman 1980, p. 377). So far these statements deal only with the physiological mechanisms of the perceptual apparatus, but Ullman goes on:

> In general, the 'directness' of perceptual mechanisms may be a matter of degree, with no absolute boundary distinguishing the direct from the indirect. In the above example it appears that one can be comfortable with viewing the underlying channels as the basic mechanisms that register patterns of light more or less directly, since (a) the channels appear to be explicable in physiological terms, and (b) the detailed dissection of the channels does not appear to have significant perceptual implications (Ullman 1980, p. 377).

When he says that the patterns of light are registered 'more or less directly', he is saying that the patterns of nervous activity in the channels are isomorphic with the patterns in the lateral geniculate nucleus and the retina, and thus with the patterns of light entering the eye. The use of the term 'directly' here has absolutely nothing to do with the directness or indirectness of *perception*. But Ullman now argues that more complex 'visual modules', such as stereopsis, can be explained by using the properties of the underlying channels and their interaction, and claims that:

The conclusion from this is that a psychologically meaningful decomposition of, say, stereoscopic vision, seems possible. But if it is, then the explanation of stereoscopic vision as the immediate pickup of binocular information (Gibson 1979, Ch. 12) would not be justified (Ullman 1980, p. 377).

However, the introduction of the concept 'a psychologically meaningful decomposition' in that passage is a quite unjustified intrusion, since Ullman has been talking about merely physiological processes. A psychologically meaningful decomposition of stereoscopic vision would presumably show that it was a complex perceptual achievement depending on the performance of simpler, constituent perceptual achievements, which in this case could only mean that the activity of the nerve channels had been perceived and their 'information extracted'. How else could Ullman think that these 'findings' about the visual nerves contradict Gibson's assertion of a direct pick-up of information from the environment? In reply to such thinking one can only go on saying that events in nerve cells are not perceived by the person who has them, that they do not contain information in the sense of semantic content, and if they did there would be no internal knowing agent to extract that information. It is gratifying to find that other researchers, such as Turvey (1977) and Shaw *et al.* (1981), are pressing on with the task of showing that empirical research *cannot* establish the truth of an indirect theory of perception; of course, it cannot establish the truth of a direct one, either, since the issue is one of logical rather than empirical tenability.

The belief in the inevitability of representationism has gained enormous impetus in recent years through continuing technological advances in AI. It appears that all the perceiving devices so far constructed do, in fact, operate on representationist principles, in a certain sense. These machines are provided with a stock of templates having some sort of physical realisation; they may be called templates whether they are supposed to be of the simplest possible features to which a complex pattern can be reduced, or to be more 'global' in nature. (It is not always realised that this is just a difference in degree; no conceivable feature is actually simple, it must always have distinguishable features of its own, and thus be global.) The perceiving device works by comparing input with its stock of templates until it finds a match, which will cause it to sort that input appropriately according to its program. If these devices are simulating human perceptual processes, then (the argument goes) it is a waste of breath to argue about supposed philosophical difficulties in representationism; there cannot *be* any conceptual puzzles in it because these machines work, and work by representation. In a recent article, Heil (1981) has pointed out the fallacy of the 'existence proof' for representationism with great cogency, directing his criticism particularly against Fodor's (1975) argument that in order to learn our first natural language we must already have an innate representational system of at least as great logical complexity as the language we are to learn. For me to argue more generally that AI does not demonstrate what it claims about human perception, it is necessary to rehearse some of the standard objections to representationism as an epistemology, and to show that these so-called perceiving devices are not doing what epistemological representationism claims that human beings do.

The basic fallacy of representationism, or of the correspondence theory of truth, is neatly exemplified by Boden (1979). In summing up the mode of working of perceiving devices, she says:

> In general, the interpretative process relates picture and scene (the representational and the target domains) by way of a conceptual schema embodying the system's knowledge of the 'mapping' relation between them (Boden 1979, p. 119).

Epistemological representationism is supposed to be a way of showing how we come to know the world when we never know it or any parts of it directly; i.e. when all we ever know are images, or cues of some sort, which represent the things in the world. One reason why this theory is held to be necessary is that it sometimes happens that we are shown to have mis-perceived things, been subject to an illusion, yet, at the time, what we 'saw' was perfectly convincing; it must then have been an image, a mental picture (so the thinking runs), and since we never know that the most convincing perception may not turn out to be an illusion, then to be consistent we must say that *all* our experiences are mental pictures, some of which (the 'true' ones) correspond to reality, and some of which (the 'false' ones) do not.

Epistemic objections to representationalism [handwritten margin note]

The question, of course, is, how do we manage to *compare* the image with the reality in order to say whether it is like or not, when we are only ever able to see images, and never reality? In the passage quoted above, Boden simple brushes aside, or has not noticed, this perfectly intractable problem. She refers to 'the system's knowledge of the "mapping" relation between them', i.e. between the representational and the target domains; but that assumes that the system already has knowledge of the target domain, and therefore cannot need any apparatus of representation in order to get to know it. That is what I meant by saying above that representationism inescapably reveals itself to be unnecessary. In order to work, in order to make discourse possible, it must assume that the representation can be compared with the reality as to whether it is like or not, which means that the reality can be directly known, but if it is then we do not need the representing images – not unless we are in the business of making maps or blueprints or cryptograms, or other craft objects of that kind. As an epistemology, representationism declares itself to be superfluous.

For anyone who postulates that experience is a matter of having images, whether they are constructed out of more primitive sensa or not, it is not possible to escape this requirement that some images be declared to be 'true' or like the world and others 'false' or unlike it. However much the subjectivist declares that objective knowledge is impossible, he or she must in practice contradict that premise in saying anything. Even the statement 'objective knowledge is impossible' is offered as being objectively true, not just as the speaker's subjective imagining. And in going on to explain the reasons for subjectivism, the speaker will need to make any number of other statements about the independently existing world. In her informative survey of AI, Boden (1977) takes the subjectivist, constructivist line about the end-product of information processing.

An input that functions as a cue for one program may be meaningless 'noise' from the point of view (*sic*) ['(*sic*)' is in the original] of another program. Another way of putting this is to say that cues are not detected but constructed, that they are subjective, intentional phenomena rather than objectively definable elements in the physical world (Boden 1977, p. 397).

But if an input is discriminable then it is, in principle, objectively definable, and if it were not discriminable how could the different programs react differently to it? Boden gives an example of what she means: many of the programs she discusses are designed to identify certain shapes from incomplete line drawings, identifying a vertex, for example, when it is not actually shown, and she goes on to say that:

A microscopic examination of the pictures ... would not show the straight lines we see, but much more complex and messy structures: the lines are not objectively there *as lines* (Boden 1977, p. 183).

Certainly, the printed straight line would look messier under a microscope than it does to the naked eye, but if it were nothing *but* a mess then we would not be able to see it as anything nameable; the minute blurs that compose the printed line have a central tendency and that central tendency defines an objectively straight (enough) line. In any case, in order to give her reasons for her subjectivism, Boden must finish with some statement about the world that assumes the existence of real things that she can see, such as microscopes and the complex, messy structures they reveal.

That Boden takes perceiving machines to exemplify a general epistemological truth is shown when she says:

In the absence of any epistemological system actively imposing its constructive schemata on the input from the outside world, there would be no cues – and no perceptions, concepts, or beliefs either (Boden 1977, p. 397).

It is analytically true that in the absence of any epistemological system there would be no perceptions, concepts, or beliefs, but that does not mean that there would be no things, properties, relations, and so on to be discovered. If there were no distinguishable kinds of thing available for inspection, there would be no conceivable reason for 'imposing' a specific schema on this item of input rather than on that; in such a world anything (or nothing) goes.

Since it is a fact that perceiving machines are presented by their makers with representational templates, like a ready-made stock of innate ideas, what is it that they do with them? The first thing to say is that they neither know them, nor know anything by means of them, nor indeed know anything at all. In saying this I am not declaring that no artificial devices will ever know anything; genuine knowing machines may be built in the future, but they will be fundamentally different from the ones we are talking about. It is difficult to produce an *argument* to show that the latter do not know, because knowing is an irreducible concept and cannot be unfolded into defining constituents. Such constituents always turn out to be acts of knowledge themselves. So in trying to show that present-day 'perceiving machines' do not know, all one can do is to point out the nature of what they do and claim that it is not what knowing is.

One clue is given by a passage from Boden quoted above, when she said that an input that functions as a cue for one program may be meaningless noise from the point of view of another program. The point is that these machines cannot be said ever to 'know' anything outside their stock of innate ideas, i.e. the templates with which they have been provided. To say that anything else is meaningless noise is to say in this connection that it is not registered *as* anything at all, not even as a human listener would register static on the radio. An entity that really can know is one whose sense organs can scan the world and discriminate and register things of a kind it has never seen before, just as a human infant, coming into the world almost completely ignorant, and certainly with no articulated visual experience, must be able natively to see (cognise) kinds of thing that it has never seen before and re-cognise them when they appear again; otherwise it would live always in a world of pure particulars, which is to say, pure nothings, since they could not be collated to generate common properties unless they already *had* common properties. If we do not register the first instance of something as a kind of thing, then we could not register the second instance of it as *another* of that kind. So that is one way in which present-day perceiving machines fail to be knowing entities; they cannot discover new kinds of thing, new properties, for themselves.

Further, it is merely a metaphor to say that they know the content of their templates, or recognise instances of them in the world. When a machine is said to match an input with one of its templates, it does not do so by attending to the one and attending to the other and seeing that they have a common property; it is merely a physical matching, comparable to trying just by trial and error to fit the various shaped blocks into their appropriate apertures in a child's form board. For the machine, the matching is nothing more than the block going in, it is not an act of recognition. An input that does not fit any of the templates does not exist at all, for the machine. Such a processor cannot be said to know the difference between Xs and non-Xs, any more than a coin-sorting machine knows the difference between the acceptable coins and the lead slugs or whatever else it is that it casts out.

This points to another criterion of 'knowing'. Any feasible account of knowing takes it that the objects of knowledge are propositional, which is to say that the most logically primitive bit of information that we can grasp is the attribution of some predicate to some subject. The postulated sub-propositional atoms of input with which not only traditional association-ism but also recent stimulus–stimulus learning theory (cf. Rudy & Wagner 1975, Bolles *et al.* 1980) and modern information-processing theory supposes cognition to begin, cannot be grasped, which is precisely to say that they are not bits of information. That aspect of knowing which comes under the description of 'knowledge by acquaintance' does make it seem that the object of knowledge may be not a proposition but just a property; that is, 'I know Jane Smith' or 'I know red when I see it' are acceptable forms, and assert that one knows by acquaintance the specific property, the whatness, of being-Jane-Smith or being-red. It is true that one cannot know a propositional fact without in the same act knowing the properties that constitute its subject and predicate, and although each property can in a sense be unfolded into a proposition – 'A colleague of mine is a Swedish-speaking feminist, her name is Jane Smith'; 'Red is a warm colour, used as a danger signal' – nevertheless, it cannot be *dissolved away* into its con-stituents, otherwise we should have nothing left to talk about (since everything has constituents). But although Jane-Smith-ness and redness are identifiable properties, one cannot know either of them all by itself, just disembodied Jane-Smith-ness apart from her being and doing so-and-so at a particular time and place; no redness apart from something's being a certain shade of red, and so on. If you say to me 'Jane Smith' or 'red' with no understood context, then you have not told me *anything*; I can only under-stand (know) propositions.

Artificial intelligence studies, for the most part, by implication take it as an illusion that we directly know propositional facts, take it as something

Propositional knowledge more basic than acquaintance.

that calls for explanation in the sense of being unfolded into simpler constituent acts. But even if such constituents were understandable, which I have just denied, they could not be assembled piecemeal, as a collection of bits, to form a proposition; the relation between subject and predicate is *one* irreducible fact, and can only be grasped as such. The machines on which AI studies are run do not know propositions, but then, as I have been arguing, they do not know anything; such simulation programs are just very clever exercises in making the machines work *as if* they know propositions. To think of them as simulations of human cognitive processes is simply to lend a pseudo-objectivity to venerable epistemological blunders.

The representationist epistemology promoted by the 'computational metaphor' (Boden 1979) necessitates the concept of the intentionality of mental states, which is just a bit of metaphysical lock-picking designed to break out of the hermetic subjectivism of the representationist theory. The premise that we know *only* mental images requires some built-in escape-hatch through which we can reach out to the external objects which, according to the theory, we can never know, but which we all want to talk about, and do talk about, all the time. The postulated 'intentionality' of mental states is simply a declaration that their relation of representing or referring to something outside themselves and outside one's mind can be discovered intrinsic to the mental states themselves. As I said in comparing this cognitive intending with 'intending to do *B*', both embody the fallacy that we can discover a thing's relations just by examining the thing itself, i.e. that its relations are intrinsic to it. In a later chapter dealing with Brentano's influence on the development of the existentialist conception of Being-in-the-world, I shall be discussing intentionality as he originally proposed it in more detail. At present, I shall just say that in his endeavour to find a criterion distinguishing psychological from physical phenomena he was in a certain sense on the right line; psychological processes are, in fact, typified by a kind of relation not to be found in merely physical interactions, and that is the relation of *knowing about* or *referring to*. It is possible, it seems to me, to mount a good case that psychology's distinctive subject-matter consists of cognitive processes, and such behaviour as is determined or directed or *informed* by cognitive processes, which covers all the things that organisms do (leaving aside vegetative processes and reflexes) that inanimate objects cannot do.

By cognitive processes I mean believing, perceiving, knowing that, being conscious of, remembering, and so on; these can coherently be thought of only as *relations* into which the organism enters, or more specifically as relations between certain specific kinds of bodily process (primarily, brain-plus-sense-organ processes) and things external to those processes. I take it that this is what Gibson means when he says such things as 'Perceiving is ... a keeping-in-touch with the world, an experiencing of things rather than a having of experiences. It involves awareness-of instead of just awareness' (Gibson 1979, p. 239).

To know something is to enter into a relation *with it*, rather than to possess some token that refers to it. An objection sometimes raised against this position, direct realism, is that if it were the case, then <u>mistaken beliefs</u> would be impossible. If knowledge is a relation to an independently existing fact, then how are we to describe the situation when the fact that is believed to be the case does not actually exist? What then is the other term of the relation? This objection must be admitted to be <u>a difficult one</u>. At present, I shall just offer the partial solution that at least the materials of our false beliefs are independently existing entities and properties. If I falsely believe that I still own some half-forgotten shares in a mining company that has just found a bottomless pipe of diamonds, then there is a perfectly real cognitive relation holding between myself and the mining shares on the one hand, and myself and the property 'possessed by me' on the other (since I am aware that *some* things are possessed by me). The trouble is that I attribute the property 'possessed by me' to the mining shares when they do not have that property. Thus, I am claiming to have a cognitive relationship ('I know that . . .') to a relational situation that does not exist ('I own the shares'), and even though I do this by treating a perfectly real entity, the parcel of shares, as if it had a perfectly real type of property, being possessed by me, the question of the ontological status of the believed-in propositional object of that cognitive relation has not quite been smoothed away. <u>However, one can at least say that the claimed</u> relationship, 'knowing that', <u>simply does not obtain, rather than being</u> <u>forced to admit that it obtains between me and some merely intentional,</u> <u>mentally-existent</u> object.

Tractatus

If this remains a problem for realism, that cannot mean that representationism wins by default, for it suffers the same difficulty in an aggravated form. Its representational entities were postulated in trying to accommodate the fact of error, which is said to occur when there is nothing in the world corresponding to the representing entity. But to discover whether *that* has been the case requires that one should know (a) the intentional content of the representing entity, (b) the situation in the world, and (c) the presence or absence of fit between them, and one's judgement could be in error in either (a), (b), or (c).

The representationist (in the modern era) is likely to expostulate immediately that at least in the case of (a) we cannot be mistaken, since my having a particular intentional representation is one of the things I *do not know by observation*. That is to say, I do *know* it, but not by mere observation; I know it in some other way which, it appears, cannot be mistaken. This curious expression, *things we do not know by observation*, is used quite frequently in modern philosophy (intentions to act being especially favoured with this description; cf. Gauld & Shotter 1977, Ch. 10) and always with the impression that discussion on that point is now closed. This air of sanctity extends to the question of what this other, *non-observational* form of knowledge may be; it is difficult indeed to find a philosopher brash enough to offer an explanation. Anscombe had something to say about it in her classic *Intention* (1957), but no clear-cut line emerged. In introducing the notion she seems to be distinguishing between things one knows on the basis of evidence, these being 'known by observation', and things one knows directly ('not by observation').

> ... e.g. a man usually knows the position of his limbs without observation. It is without observation, because nothing *shews* him the position of his limbs; it is not as if he were going by a tingle in his knee, which is the sign that it is bent and not straight. Where we can speak of separately describable sensations, having which is in some sense our criterion for saying something, then we can speak of observing that thing; but that is not generally so when we know the position of our limbs (Anscombe 1957, p. 13).

Now, presumably according to this view we do not know our *sensations* by observation, at the cost of an infinite regress, but know them in the other way. Yet Anscombe goes on to say that we can still be mistaken about things known in the 'not by observation' way, which is clearly not what subsequent philosophers mean by the phrase; for them, observations can be mistaken but not this other kind of experience which I shall call self-reflexive. When I say that I observe something, that does clearly set the existence of the observed thing separate from me and from my observing it; that is, it conveys the impression that my observing it is a relation between us so that it and I are separate existences. But in the supposed self-reflexive mode of experiencing, the notion of which is an ancient one under various terminologies, subject and object are not thought of as separate existences; rather, the 'object', which in this case is always a sensation or idea or mental image or intention or feelings (that is, some mental event) is held to be mind-dependent in its being; its very existence is in *my having it*, therefore, so the argument goes, I cannot be mistaken about it. One sees why this notion of immediate self-knowledge appeals to those who hold to some version of self-determination or agency. Since my intentions to act are by definition generated by the essential indivisible me, they could not be unknown to me; it could not be necessary for me to find out about them (Gauld & Shotter 1977, pp. 165–6). But this view of self-reflexive knowledge cannot be sensibly expressed. Consider the sentence 'Its existence is dependent on my having or knowing it.' Having or knowing *what*? If I can create anything, then when I have created it, it is separate from me and I can be mistaken about its nature. The notion of the self-reflexive relation, i.e. the notion that subject and object are related-yet-identical, is just unintelligible, as I shall try to say in more detail in talking about the evolution of existentialism. So, then, the representationist way of coping with the problem of error by postulating an order of experiences about which I cannot be mistaken yet which intrinsically point to something (unknown to me) outside themselves is hardly a neat solution to that problem.

In denying that present-day perceiving machines have knowledge on the ground that what they do requires internal representations, I am, of course, not arguing that human beings' having cognitive relations transports them into some different causal or categorial realm from that of machines. Cognition is just another variety of spatiotemporal relation, and the possession of it by higher organisms is simply one of the material conditions that affect their functioning. It is just as much an efficient-cause process as the feedback loops of cybernetic systems, and does function as a feedback process, but one that employs a different medium from existing machine systems.

These observations on tenable and untenable conceptions of the apparatus of knowing were prompted by the need to elaborate my assertion that an individual's belief system stands as a complex set of state variables in part determining his reactions to environmental events or situations perceived by him. Since cognitions are not mental entities but relations, they may be spoken of as relational properties constituting a causal state variable, just as being subject to a certain gravitational pull, for example, is a state variable that can affect a thing's behaviour. But when it is a relationship peculiar to certain kinds of entity (higher organisms), one would expect to find also that those organisms had particular *intrinsic* properties in virtue of which they stood in the relations in question. Since cognitive relations (the beliefs an organism has) are so particularised and variable, then it seems reasonable to assume that any instance of such a relationship, i.e. a belief in a particular fact, would be subserved by an intrinsic state of the organism specific to that belief, and the obvious kind of intrinsic state to look for is a brain state. Having rejected the concept of mental states as subserving cognition, we substitute brain states. But in view of the mind–brain identity thesis, to which I am subscribing and giving a particular formulation, one must ask whether this is any more than a verbal substitution.

There is a fundamental conceptual difference between brain states and the putative intrinsic mental states that I am rejecting, and that is that brain states *are not intentional*, as the mental states were supposed to be. They are not representational in the cognitive or intentional sense of representation, even though each belief would have a brain state peculiar to it. Any such specific brain state would simply be whatever it physiologically is; to call upon proposals that have been made, though none of them now seems technically feasible, it may be one of Hebb's (1949) 'cell assemblies', or a 'reverberatory circuit', or some specific 'tuning' of certain neurones, but whatever it may physiologically be, it would in principle be describable in purely physiological terms without any reference to the cognitive relationship that it underlies. Having discovered what *kind* of brain state subserves cognitive relations, a neurophysiologist (if the science and its instrumentation were sufficiently advanced) might be able to discover and map large numbers of such states, identifying them by their physiological co-ordinates, say, but he would then have to *discover*, in the most empirical fact-finding way, what factual belief any one of them subserved. This would be a task of formidable practical difficulty – presumably, one would have to begin by asking the person what he or she was thinking of when a particular 'cell assembly' was activated, but then one would have to wonder how trustworthy his introspection was – but it would be inescapable if one wanted to pursue that branch of neurophysiology, because it is logically impossible that a physical entity such as a 'cell assembly' (or whatever physiological state it may be) could have intrinsic to it, and thus discoverable by inspecting it, its relation to something external to it, the fact believed in. Boden hesitated before embracing that spurious solution to the mind–brain issue, saying 'A neural model of something is not to be thought of as a *copy* of it', but only for a moment, as she went on: 'To identify or describe the neural processes concerned *as* models is itself to ascribe meaning, or intentionality, to them' (Boden 1977, p. 429). But the question is begged by describing the neural substrate as a model; that derives from her desire to assimilate organismic cognitive processes to the working of artificial perception-devices, which as we have agreed do have internal models of external objects, but, as we have also seen, do not have cognitive relations. The connection between the brain state and the external fact the knowledge of which it subserves, and the perception of which caused it to be laid down, is just that of cause and effect, not of representation.

For a person's beliefs, conscious and unconscious, to play a part in the determination of behaviour, the brain states underlying them must somehow become involved in determining the course of the nervous impulses that will eventually give rise to motor processes. However, extant models of 'information retrieval' all depend on the assumption that the meaning of brain traces can somehow be read off from them, and so are quite inappropriate if the foregoing arguments are correct. The contents of the memory store are regularly conceived of as entities that can be, if not retrieved and brought spatially forward, at least located and *scanned* by some inner agency which in this way reads off their representational content, and presumably forms an opinion of the state of the external world and what might be done in it. Rozeboom pointed out in 1965 that most talk of information retrieval is more appropriate to bringing things from the storage bin to the workshop than to cognitive operations. One might ask, what are the entities made of that are brought forward? How does the searcher know where to look? Above all, who occupies the workshop? Yet the same sort of thinking is still extant, and progress in memory theory is looked for only with regard to deciding the most effective strategies for searching this imaginary filing system – i.e. whether it should best be by directed or non-directed search processes, serial versus parallel processing, content-addressable storage, or whatever (cf. e.g. Westcourt & Atkinson 1976). But the brain does not contain items whose referential content can be read out, and the assumption that one brain state needs to be scanned by *another* before it can play a part in the direction of behaviour is not necessitated by anything but the mistaken premise that if I remember something I must be *conscious* that I remember it. The implications of the fact that the relationship 'being conscious of' is an external relation lead to a quite different understanding of 'conscious experience' from the conventional one.

So, then, when I say that a person's beliefs constitute a set of state variables that in part determine his or her behaviour, I mean that the person has a large collection of brain states specific to those beliefs, but of these brain states we know nothing directly and so their existence is of no practical use in explaining his or her behaviour. However, those brain states should not be called the person's *beliefs*, since the beliefs are the relational properties subserved by the brain states, their other terms being the facts believed in, and we can be aware of the existence of those relations with a workable, if variable, degree of confidence from observations of the person's behaviour, from listening to what he or she says, and so on. Consider, for example, my (fictitious) colleague Dr Jane Smith. One thing I have good reason to believe about her is that she has at least a sound reading knowledge of the Swedish language (which I have not) because a couple of years ago she told me she was taking lessons in Swedish because she wanted to read Swedenborg in the original; a number of times since then I have peeped over her shoulder in the library and seen that she was apparently taking notes from books that looked as if they were printed in Swedish; a few months ago she gave a paper about Swedenborg in the course of which she contended that an extant English translation was in error on a certain point; I was most impressed with this scholarly industry and said so to other members of the department, who agreed with me. Thus, I believe that she knows a great many facts about the words and phrases that Swedes use to refer to specific aspects of the world and about how these are related to English words and phrases. Further, I can be said to have known this about her through a considerable period during much of which I was not engaged in thinking 'Jane Smith knows Swedish' or even doing what would ordinarily be called thinking about Jane Smith at all. Suppose I had come across a passage quoted in Swedish in an English-language book I was reading and said helplessly to another colleague 'How can I find out what this means?'; he would be quite likely to give me an odd look and say, quite truly, 'You know Jane reads Swedish' when I had for a moment *forgotten* that she knew it (because of a little brush we had yesterday about Freud on the psychology of women). But there is no need to go to such a level of abstraction as my knowledge of another person's knowledge of a second language; cognition is ubiquitous in behaviour at every level. For instance, if when I have recovered from my fit of amnesia I telephone Jane to ask for her help, then I am assuming without even thinking of it that she knows what a telephone is, knows how to answer it, has some idea how the sound gets into the ear-piece, and so on. If I had not had those unconscious beliefs about her beliefs, I would not have telephoned.

Some philosophers cavil at the desire-plus-belief model for the explanation of 'goal-directed' behaviour because they dispute the ubiquity of means–end beliefs in the determination of behaviour. Wright, for example, in commenting on Woodfield's analysis, gives a number of instances of goal-directed behaviour in circumstances 'which rule out the conscious entertaining of means and ends' (Wright 1978, p. 224). Similarly, Hornsby, referring to the mouth movements someone makes in saying 'Grass is green' claims that 'he does not make these movements with his mouth because he believes that they are a means of saying that grass is green. For most probably he does not have any interesting beliefs about how he moves his mouth when he says that or says anything else' (Hornsby 1980, p. 81). But these objections seem to depend on the notion that the means-end beliefs must be consciously rehearsed in order to be at work, or at least that they could be verbalised on demand. But that is not necessary; a belief can determine behaviour without becoming conscious, as I am about to show, and especially in the case of beliefs about how to perform much-practised actions, as in speaking one's native tongue, they may be long past the possibility of verbalisation. Yet in learning a foreign tongue that employs sounds not included in one's own, the need to know what movements to make manifests itself again, as it must have done (inarticulately) when one was acquiring the first language. To say that we do not consciously know how to do something is not to say that we do not know how to do it, nor that we do not need to know. That causal requirement can only be waived, it seems to me, in the case of unlearned or innate abilities (which Wright also exempts).

To protect from over-hasty criticism my assertion that behaviour is at almost every point shaped by the organism's beliefs about what movements will produce what effects, and to elaborate more generally the nature of cognition from the realist view, I turn to examine the distinction between conscious and unconscious beliefs.

Conscious and unconscious cognitions

Although the notion that there can be unconscious mental processes has long been a respectable one in psychology, it is still difficult to grasp the fact that one can be aware of something, can contemplate anew a fact that one has known for a long time, and have one's behaviour affected by that knowledge, without having to be aware in any degree that those mental processes are occurring. The view that we must be conscious of our own mental processes has become ingrained into our usage of most cognitive words, though it is not actually entailed by them, and could not be. 'Contemplate' seems to carry that aura of self-consciousness with it more than 'to be aware of' does, and a word such as 'excogitate' even more so. As an undergraduate I once heard my professor of philosophy say 'I was just excogitating my next lecture', which called up for me the most vivid impression of powerful, directed and *conscious* mental activity; but what I am proposing now is that running through the implications of a train of thought not only does not presuppose a purpose (as I argued above with reference to Gauld & Shotter 1977), but also does not entail that we be conscious of doing it, although we may become so. That applies *a fortiori* to less complicated cognitive happenings, such as perceiving a particular fact, or remembering one.

The majority of mental acts (and perhaps all of them, if there are no intendings) are the becoming conscious of something, yet *every mental act is in the first instance unconscious*. To say that it may become conscious is only to say that it may become the object of a *further* act of awareness, and it cannot become conscious in any other way. To say that I was consciously aware that Jane knew Swedish means (properly) only that (a) I was aware of the fact that she knew Swedish, and (b) I was *also* aware of (a). The content of the first act was 'Jane knows Swedish' and the content of the second was 'I know that Jane knows Swedish'. This, of course, does *not* lead to a vicious infinite regress, which is a frequent too-ready response to it. It could be the beginning of an infinite *series* of 'I know that I know . . .' acts, but that does not show that there is anything logically wrong with the underlying concept, any more than the fact that one could in principle go on counting successively by ones for ever shows that there is anything logically wrong with the series of integers. It is precisely the opposing view, the view that awareness is immediately self-aware, as if in being conscious of something I must *in the same act* be aware that I am conscious of it, which leads to a vicious infinite regress. What it proposes is that ' I know *p*' entails 'I know that I know *p*'. But since that is to say that the expression 'I know' must be replaced by a compound expression 'I know that I know' which includes *itself*, then, according to the same rule, the substitution must be made again within that compound expression, yielding 'I know that I know that I know', and so on without end. To say that this is vicious is to say that no one step in the series is complete and understandable in itself, but instantly declines into the next, and so on without ceasing, which is not the case when I say that knowing that I know *p* is a *separate* act from knowing *p*, and one which may or may *not* occur.

If my knowing *p* does become the object of my attention, i.e. if something such as someone else's query makes me aware that I know it, then it is a conscious belief *at that time*. When my believing *p* is not being contemplated by me, then it is preconscious or unconscious. Such a change does not mean that my belief that *p* is the case undergoes any change in its nature at all. Consciousness is not an intrinsic or one-place property that a belief or mental event may have or not have; it is a relationship in which one awareness is the object of another within the same mental life.

The ontological status of perseverating unconscious beliefs is difficult to conceive. A number of times I have contended that one cannot really form a notion of mental entities, whether lodged in the memory store or elsewhere, and it is difficult also to form an idea of an enduring mental process. Freud often speaks of the dynamically unconscious thoughts as being continually active, giving rise to dreams and various kinds of psychopathology, and necessitating the continual expenditure of energy to maintain the repression. One point about this last notion is that it exacerbates the problem discussed above in connection with perceptual defence, since it seems that the repressing ego would have to remain continuously aware of the repressed thoughts in order to keep them from consciousness, yet the upshot is supposed to be that it remains unaware of them. Thus the rapid one-shot disruption of the verbal encoding process (Hochberg 1970) would hardly be adequate. Further, it can hardly be that one is unconsciously endlessly reiterating, wordlessly though it may be, beliefs about what one's parents had done to one in childhood, about the awful consequences of incestuous and parricidal lusts, and so on. In saying this I do not intend to ridicule the general descriptive notion of repression or of unconscious beliefs, without which a great deal of mental life would be incapable of explanation. I am simply trying to show how difficult it is to give substance to the idea of an enduring *mental* something constituting the substance of my enduring belief that p is the case when I am not thinking 'p is the case'. There is nothing conceptually odd about enduring *brain* states, each one set up when a belief is first acquired and lasting until something disrupts it, if that should ever happen. Whether one would then be inclined to say that the relationship between each such state and the event the perception of which caused it continues as an actual psychological fact ('believing that'), or just provides the potential for it, I find hard to decide. But in neurological terms one would need to distinguish between such a brain state's simply being there, and its occasionally playing some active role in determining a course of behaviour to which the situation that had given rise to it (the fact believed) was relevant.

If we reject the assumption that the brain trace must be scanned by some information-collecting control centre (an homunculus disguised by AI jargon) so that its 'content' may be put to work, how does it come to be active, how does the person's knowledge become effective when relevant? One can get an impression of how intricate the neural mechanisms must be, and of the context-related variability of their operation, by reflecting that there could not be one separate neural trace for each proposition known, because any one subject-term will be known as having simultaneously many predicates and as being itself the predicate of other subjects; each of its predicates will in turn be the subject of other predicates, and so on. Thus, I perceive a quotation in a foreign language in my book, a closer look reveals some unfamiliar letters, this afferent perceptual process somehow arrives at my general-information-about-languages store (for simplicity of expression and because nothing is known about the actual neurology I revert to 'information retrieval' talk) where it matches with what little I know about Swedish; because I am engaged in finding out what is in the book it shuttles to 'speakers of Swedish' but they need also to be not ill disposed towards me since I must ask them a favour; one of the items in my 'Jane Smith' node is 'Jane is annoyed with me' which (and this is very mysterious) prevents the input from arriving at 'Jane reads Swedish' or at least prevents it being verbalised (monitored); the new perceptual input from seeing our mutual colleague gets into the pattern because he is a potential source of information about translators; his verbalisation 'You know Jane reads Swedish' causes a re-entry into the 'Jane Smith' node with additional complications, and so on. If I had been in a different drive state, for example if I had fallen into the harbour at a lonely spot and were in danger of drowning, and Jane appeared, then the Jane-Smith-percept would have arrived at the intersection of the 'Jane Smith' node and the (not highly selective) 'things-that-can-save-one-from-drowning' node, rapidly identifying her as a possible saviour and resulting in my escape-from-drowning program addressing a desperate appeal to her.

One of the reasons I reject the concept of the 'scanner' is that none of these processes need be conscious. In neither case would it be necessary that I know that I had those beliefs about Jane in order for them to be activated and affect my behaviour. If my belief that she reads Swedish had been directly activated, its sole content would have been 'Jane reads Swedish', not 'I remember that Jane reads Swedish'. The latter event could occur, and in the instance in question very likely would have, since my colleague had prompted me and given me an odd look; there is a widespread and constant social pressure to act in what is considered a rational manner and this results in us monitoring and verbalising a good deal of our behaviour, which might be expressed by saying that our acquired social-acceptance programs interfere with our more immediately impulsive ones. Though I may seem at present to be postulating 'programs' *ad libitum*, just as purposivists postulate purposes, my later discussion of the bases of motivation will show what is required to justify such attributions. The fact that self-monitoring may occur and affect the course of one's behaviour does not entail that we are *purposive* rule-following creatures as Harré and others have argued in recent years (Harré & Secord 1972, Harré 1979); our awareness of social rules is simply awareness of positive and negative consequences of particular behaviours, and so is just one more case of cognitions affecting our instrumental and consummatory acts.

The position is that an experienced organism will be in possession of a fund of information as to the general nature and potentialities for action of most of the things with which it comes into contact, and in consequence the afferent perceptual processes arising from things perceived here and now will, if the present objects are perceived as having properties relevant to what the organism is doing, be shuttled off into motor channels other than those they would have taken if the neural 'information' traces in the intermediary brain tracts had been other than they are; that is, if the organism had in the past acquired different information.

One sees that the traditional puzzles about the causal relationship between 'mind' and brain just disappear when one takes the relational view of mental processes. The question of whether there is an epiphenomenalist, one-way causal relation, brain events causing mental events but not vice versa since the physical system is supposed to be closed, or of whether, indeed, there is interaction, with 'non-physical' events managing somehow to interfere with physical ones, really only arises when mental events are thought of as substantive. Thus, in a recent recrudescence of this needless debate, Puccetti and Dykes (1978) point out that there are no discernible differences in the microstructure of the tactile, visual, and auditory sensory projection areas of the cortex, yet their stimulation yields different kinds of experience, and conclude:

An essentially homogenous sensory cortex could subserve diverse psychological functions if it does this by *causing* our experiences rather than constituting them (Puccetti & Dykes 1978, p. 343).

That is, they take it that this apparent fact of neurology conflicts with the mind–brain identity thesis and shows that there must be a causal relation between the separate entities, mind and brain. They elaborate this into an interactionist position:

Hearing is indeed *caused* by what goes on in area 41 of our brains, and this in turn probably acts upon other neural mechanisms to bring about appropriate auditory behaviour, but the subjective experience cannot simply be reduced to brain events (Puccetti & Dykes 1978, p. 343).

In his commentary D. M. Armstrong points out that the alleged homogeneity of brain processes would be just as difficult a problem for Puccetti and Dykes's interactionism as for the identity theory if, as their argument assumes, different effects must have different causes; different mental effects would need different brain causes. But the important point of criticism is that Puccetti and Dykes think of 'subjective experiences' as substantive, and only in that way could they think of their effect on brain processes, i.e. the fact, as they say, that the experience of hearing acts upon other neural mechanisms. Once we get rid of substantive 'subjective experiences' and the self-defeating subjectivist epistemology that goes along with them, we can see that the experience of hearing is simply the hearing of a sound-producing event in the world; as with all our experiencings, it is an external relationship. The direction of relationship is not from brain to 'mind' or 'mind' to brain, it is (in perception) from the world to the organism. An event to which my senses are exposed (a tree falls nearby) causes me to perceive it. That is a psychological description, but what has happened can also be described in physical–physiological terms referring to vibrations of the air affecting my hearing mechanisms and thus the auditory area of the brain. (That whole complex is the hearing; the hearing is not something extra that occurs after the sequence reaches the auditory cortical area.) This physical–physiological event results in a lasting brain trace having a specific relation to the tree's having fallen; the relation between the brain trace and the external event can be spoken of as my knowing the external event, or at least as my being in a condition such that I can remember (though not necessarily consciously remember) that event if it becomes relevant to anything I am doing, i.e. if I see something else as related to it. There are not two orders of being, the mental and the physical, presenting the problem of the causal relations between them; there is just the one spatiotemporal order and the relation of 'knowing that' is a distinctive kind of relationship occurring in that spatiotemporal order between organisms and things around them. It is, in fact, a particular kind of causal action by which the environment continually affects the organism's behaviour, which behaviour, of course, further affects the environment, and so on, resulting in, among other things, further cognitive acquisitions. Cognition is a way in which physically present objects can affect the organism's behaviour by virtue of the organism's knowledge of their relations to things that are not present, including their relations to future states that could be made to follow from them. The fact that it is neurophysiological processes which subserve or sustain the organism's cognitive relations does not negate the fact that the latter are of that distinctive kind that we call *mental*, that is, are the registering of propositional happenings.

All this seems to me an adequate account of that 'mental efficacy' which Honderich (1981a) finds deplorably lacking in extant versions of the mind–brain identity thesis. The existence of cognitive processes understood in this way simply does affect the organism's responses to its environment. If, however, Honderich's demand that *his* efficacy be recognised, that *he* not be left on the sidelines while his body does the work, is not satisfied by allowing that the movements of his body, programmed through his acquired beliefs and prompted by his drive states, can affect his environment in predictable ways, then I confess I can do no more for him.

My discussion has returned once more to what is distinctive of organismic behaviour, given that it is not goal-seeking – that is, to its being directed by cognitive relations. If that is so, and if we are to have a science of organismic behaviour, then it is necessary to believe that the cognitive relations in which other organisms stand – their beliefs – can be empirically discovered, allowing that errors of observation may occur but can be kept within reasonable bounds. Yet it is accepted virtually as axiomatic by most philosophers and psychologists that the mental processes of other organisms, including of course other persons, are unobservable. If that were so, and one had to hypothesise the existence of these hidden mental processes on the basis of external behavioural evidence, and then seek to explain the latter by the former, that would be a gross case of unconstrained and uninformative *ad hoc* theorising. But before going on to defend the observability of others' mental processes, I must first say something about the observability of one's own, in order to tidy up what I have been saying about the distinction between conscious and unconscious beliefs.

If everything that we know must derive in the long run from information obtained through our senses, then what are the sense organs I use when I say I am observing my own mental processes? I have, in fact, just been thinking about the weather outside, which is decidedly cold; I shall call that thought, act A. What I am writing prompted me to pay attention to act A to use it as an example; I shall call that attending act B, its object, of course, being the occurrence of act A. Each of A and B involves a brain event, the formation of the trace (whatever its physiological nature may be) caused by the apprehension of its object. Can trace B be said to know trace A? That is, to know it in its neurological realisation, directly? This seems to me impossible. It is obviously possible for one brain event to *cause* another, but that does not mean that the effect knows the cause. In general, the nearest I could come to direct knowledge of my brain states would be by the use of some electronic brain scanner, and even then I would only know something about the pattern of nervous impulses in some part of the brain and need not know at all what their relationship of believing-that was to a fact external to themselves. As I said earlier, that relationship cannot be intrinsic to the brain state, and therefore beliefs cannot be read off from brain states without a laboriously compiled code-book, the compilation of which has not even begun.

There can be so such thing as direct internal access to one's own brain states, and no such thing as one brain state's knowing another, because there are no sense organs there to yield such information. There are no sensory mechanisms to provide proprioceptive feedback from one part of the brain to another comparable to those which provide feedback from the muscles, joints, and so on, to the brain. (This, by the way, makes nonsense of the still repeated proposal from some mind–brain identity theorists that we could get rid of the concept 'anger', for instance, by teaching children to say 'My brain area so-and-so is active' rather than 'I am angry'. That would just be teaching them a clumsy synonym for 'angry'.)

Trace B, then, cannot directly know trace A. What is claimed is that trace B underlies the knowledge that the organism that I call 'I' also performed act A, i.e. became aware of the state of the weather. Is the relation of knowing, of which act A is constituted, directly discernible in itself, as for example the relation of being-on-top-of is directly discernible? Again one must answer no. It only becomes discernible when given flesh in the form of my actions. Yet I, as distinct from other persons, seem able to be aware of my act A while I am just sitting here, not acting on it at all.

However, I think it is not actually the case that I can be aware of it without in a certain sense acting on it. This still bears on the question of what sense organs I could be using. Without pretending that I am arriving at this view by logical inference, what I am proposing is that when I silently pay attention to my own thoughts I do so by implicitly verbalising them, or using some other set of motor processes to symbolise them, where 'implicitly' means performing a tiny and schematically condensed version of the possible overt recital or other overt motor representation of their content. In a similar way, when I become aware of what I am about to do ('planning' to do), there is running off in me a minute, condensed, anticipatory rehearsal of the action-type. These implicit motor performances, however slight, would generate proprioceptive sensations through demonstrable sense organs excited by the motor elements involved, and that is the type of sense channel through which I have access to what I am thinking and planning to do. I do not have to recite my thoughts *aloud* so that they pass through my auditory channel, but at least I must give them a motor representation that I can perceive through the proprioceptive channel. That is a type of access which, just as a matter of physical impossibility, no one else can have to my mental life, though they may have modes of access to it that for psychopathological reasons, say, are denied to me.

An objection that might be brought against this account of knowing one's mental acts only by knowing a verbalisation of them is similar to the one that I brought against representationism, and would hold that I can only understand the verbalisation if I had previously been able to see the relation between the words used and the thought that they verbalise – i.e. had been able to apprehend the thought directly. But the verbalisation of act A is simply 'The weather is cold', and I have often heard that verbalisation used by other persons to refer to the objective fact observable by me as well as by them that the weather is cold. When I hear others use it I am made aware of something in their mental life, that is that they have noticed the coldness, and when something causes me to verbalise it to myself (suppose I am going to warn someone to prepare for winter), then I am made aware that I too have noticed it. To say that I understand language is to say that I have learned that people use certain expressions to *refer* to facts of nature, and the notion of referring entails that they *know of* the facts to which they are referring. The interesting point about this is that my apprehension of other people's knowing must be prior to my apprehension of my own knowing (if the latter depends on verbalisation), though not, of course, prior to my knowing in general. Certainly, *my apprehension of others as knowers is presupposed by my learning of language.* I shall return to this radical consideration shortly, in connection with our knowledge of other persons' mental processes.

The foregoing is my best effort to give substance to Freud's view that thoughts become conscious by becoming associated with verbal images (e.g. Freud 1900, Ch. 7). A person could, in fact, be possessed of a given belief over a long period of time, during which some of his acts may have been explicable only by supposing him to have that belief, yet if it were debarred from the subroutine of becoming verbally encoded, then he could not have known by any sort of privileged access that he had it. He may eventually have been forced to the conclusion that he had it, but only in the way that an external observer may have formed the opinion that he did, by coming to see that some of his acts were quite irrational except on the world-view posited in the unconscious belief. Those acts and the supposition underlying them would present themselves to him with much the same otherness as the acts of other persons, the feeling that for Freud marks manifestations from the id. But as to the mechanism by which a belief could be debarred from the verbal encoding subroutine, unless it be by the repeated evocation of anxiety and its disruption of encoding as in the Hochberg model (see above), each time some perception activated the relevant brain trace, I fear I have nothing to offer.

Knowledge of the mental processes of other persons

If there is no such thing as immediate non-observational self-awareness, but the knowledge of one's own beliefs and the direction of one's own behaviour comes only through the activation of proprioceptive sense receptors, then we see at a stroke that knowing one's own mental acts is in a broad sense on the same epistemological footing (i.e. knowledge by means of the senses) as the knowing of other persons' mental processes (with the qualification that for them we must use senses other than the proprioceptive). Neither may be as yet completely perspicuous, but at least the unbridgeable gap posited by the supposed difference between mere observation and immediate self-consciousness is seen not to be real. Admittedly, we cannot have the awareness of other persons' minute motor performances that we can have of our own, but we can see what they do and hear what they say, and the knowing in proprioception is not of a different kind from the knowing in visual and auditory perception; it is just knowing through a different channel. The important point is that in seeing what people do and hearing what they say, we are not seeing mere movement and hearing mere sounds, which we must then try to relate speculatively to inner mental processes; we are seeing movements and hearing sounds as informed by their makers' beliefs.

A psychology that studies cognitive processes and their role in behaviour must hold that they are observable, yet as I said there is a long-standing tradition that the only mental processes with which one is acquainted are one's own, and that if others do have any, they are not observable by oneself.

The latter belief is so deeply ingrained that it is difficult not to take it as an awkward fact of life which, if we are to study cognitive processes as a general phenomenon, we must find our way around by relying on indirect evidence. It has a certain *a priori* plausibility. In talking to people I can see the movements of their eyes and faces and hands, I can hear the sounds they utter, but I cannot *see their thoughts*. Those are 'inside', if anywhere. Yet most of our daily life is unreflectingly predicated on the belief that we can know at least something of what others think; it is easily the most important and ubiquitous aspect of our social intercourse. What are the data on which we rely?

A frequent answer has been that one infers the existence of others' mental processes by analogy with one's own. The argument is that, knowing our own mental happenings, we observe the correlation between them and aspects of our own behaviour, which we take to be intimately related, perhaps causally related, to them. Consequently, when we see similar kinds of behaviour in other persons then, according to this view, we infer that they are having the same sorts of mental happening that accompany those behaviours in us. But such an inference, being merely inductive, would have much less than perfect reliability. Others' behaviour is interpreted by analogy with one's own as being the external effect of certain inner causes, but as has been pointed out by, for example, Malcolm (1958), if one has never been able to observe that those others have any such 'inner' processes, then it may be the case that their behaviour is caused in some way quite different from one's own. Thus, if mental processes are 'inner', there are no good grounds for asserting that anyone other than oneself has them at all.

There has been a great deal of critical discussion for and against this 'argument by analogy', but there has been little serious challenge to the premise that both makes the analogical argument necessary and shows that its conclusions are shaky, namely, that the phenomena referred to in the conclusion (others' mental processes) are unobservable. It is true that Hyslop and Jackson, in a strongly argued defence of the analogy, claiming that it has just as good standing as inductive analogical arguments in the natural sciences and that an unreasonable standard of reliability is being demanded of it by some philosophers, do say that 'it is not at all clear that it is impossible to be directly aware of another's mental state' (Hyslop & Jackson 1972, p. 168). But they leave this aside almost immediately, saying that 'being directly aware of someone else's pain would not, in itself, tell me that that person was in pain, because I should still require grounds for supposing that what I was aware of *was* someone else's pain (as well as my own). These grounds would have to lie in that person's behavior (or brain states, etc.)' (Hyslop & Jackson 1972, p. 168). That is, we would be back in the position of having to argue by analogy. But it seems to me strange to say that I could be directly aware of someone else's pain and not know that that person was in pain; it seems a direct self-contradiction, and one can only understand Hyslop and Jackson's (1972) saying it if they mean that to be directly aware of someone else's pain is to *have* that person's pain. But that is not necessary and, in fact, cannot be understood; it is analytically impossible to have someone else's pain, though that is not because of anything peculiarly private or sealed off about other persons' mental happenings; it is also analytically impossible to do someone else's breathing, or flex someone else's muscles, but that does not mean that I cannot know that a person does or has these things. What I am claiming is that we can observe other persons' mental processes with a reasonable degree of certainty (admitting that *no* observations are certain), and that, therefore, it is not necessary to rely on the argument by analogy. And if it should turn out that I cannot establish this proposition by arguments that compel belief, nevertheless I can show that every one of us, however positivistic his or her notion of observables, makes the *assumption* that it is possible to see what others are thinking, in the process of saying what they are doing.

The belief that it is *in principle* impossible to observe another's thoughts is a consequence of that conception of mental processes which I have been rejecting, namely, that their objects are entities of a shadowy non-physical nature whose existence is constituted by the subject's having or knowing them, i.e. they exist only in 'their' relation to the subject, so by definition they cannot stand in that relation of being the object of knowledge to any other subject. But, as I have argued, the objects of mental acts are not constituted even in part by standing in that relation; they are states of affairs that exist independently of their being known and which therefore can in principle be observed by anyone with an adequate opportunity to do so. Therefore, since it is in principle possible for me to be independently acquainted with some fact that you too are acquainted with, since you do not create it by being aware of it, then at least that objection to the possibility of my knowing the cognitive relation between you and the objects of your knowledge has been removed.

Of course, I cannot physically observe your cognitive relation to something as I can observe your spatial relation to it ('standing within 5 ft of it'). Your knowing something only becomes apparent to me (leaving aside for the moment the special matter of your talking to me about it) when it becomes embodied, as it were, in your behaviour with regard to the thing in question. ('Embodied' may be only a metaphor, but the metaphorical relation is close and intimate.) We identify another's beliefs in identifying the causal texture of his or her movements in relation to the environment. Suppose we are watching someone who has said he will make a cup of coffee if he can find the coffee jar. He opens the cupboard and directs his gaze inside. We see that he thinks the coffee may be in that cupboard, or so I am claiming. He reacts to the sight of the closed cupboard door *as if* it concealed the coffee jar. Examples of this kind could, of course, be multiplied indefinitely, since what I am saying applies to everything that can be called behaviour. The effect of coming to see the beliefs implicit in a person's behaviour is most striking when we come upon someone going through a complicated series of actions the point of which we cannot at first see at all. While waiting for a bus I watched a documentary film on television in a shop window, so that I could not hear the commentary. It was of an Australian aboriginal living in the traditional way, filmed in his desert environment, a perennially harsh, ungenerous one. He began digging in the sand in what seemed to me a randomly chosen spot and went on and on until he was standing in a pit up to his chest. Then he began on a collateral shaft, his movements became faster and more urgent, he plunged his arms into the sand and came up with a burrowing animal a bit larger than a large rat; I confess I still do not know what it was, but to him, as subsequent clips showed, it was edible prey. His behaviour was immediately understandable. Certain signs on the surface had caused him to begin digging there because he believed they indicated the presence of this animal, and that is the mark of behaviour guided by cognition; it is a reaction to some present object in terms of its relation to something else that is not present or not discernible. The objection may be made that by my own admission I could not for a long time *see* the aboriginal's knowledge of the animal's presence implicit in his behaviour; he may have been digging for water or to earn the TV producer's fee; however, my reply is that my inability was due to my ignorance of the fauna in that area, and the recognition of the actions' specific meaning occurred in retrospect. At least I could see him digging for something, not just randomly striking at the sand with his wooden implement. When his actions led to an event, catching the animal, after which the digging was not resumed, and which his manner suggested was in some sense consummatory (a sense I shall try to explicate in determinist terms in a later chapter), then I could see that the whole sequence was the catching of an animal, informed by his knowledge of where the animal was likely to be. Naturally, I am not claiming that perceptions of the kind I believe I had made even approach infallibility, nor that they can be made in instantaneous time slices, but then, that would be too much to ask for perceptions of the overall character of any sequential processes in nature, even non-organismic ones.

Further, I can of course be misled. My friend who seemed to be looking in the cupboard for the coffee jar may not have expected to find it there, may merely have been pretending to look for it because he did not want to go to the trouble of making a cup of coffee for me at the time. But objections of this kind rest on the presupposition that it is possible to find out what he *was* in fact doing, otherwise the whole issue would devolve into a formless scepticism, and the notion of what another person was doing would lose all content. And *to say what someone is doing is to say what that person thinks he or she is doing.* To say my friend opened the cupboard door is to deny that its opening was an accidental consequence of the movements of his hand. It is to claim that his movements were guided by his perception of the position of the door and his (probably unverbalised) belief that those movements would get it open. The difference between opening a door and accidentally knocking it open is one we can see as reliably as we can see a lot of less controversial differences. It is fruitless to be sceptical about such an assumption, because we cannot talk intelligibly about an organism's behaviour without making it. Even the purposivist, in saying that the co-ordination of the man's movements into the act of opening the door was the result of his purposing to open the door, is not relieved of the necessity of saying that he made those movements because he believed they would achieve the goal. To say that purposive behaviour could occur without the agent's having to know anything about the means–end relations involved in it would leave us in hopeless mystification in trying to understand how the organism does what it does. In contrast to that it seems thoroughly empirical to maintain the cognitive–determinist position, despite any remaining uneasiness over the observability of cognitive processes in others.

Even the attempt to infer another person's mental processes by analogy with one's own could not get under way without describing that other's behaviour in terms that make this implicit cognitive attribution. To talk of observing 'bodily manifestations' would not suffice. As I have already suggested, one could not begin by saying 'If I had opened the cupboard door in that way, I would have been looking for something inside' because that assumes the man had *opened* the door instead of accidentally knocking it open, which is already to say that his movements came about because he believed they would get the door open. The analogist would be pushed back to something like this: 'If I had moved my arm and hand in that way, I would have been opening the door'; but immediately we can ask him, in *what* way, and he will not, for the same reason, be able to say 'in such a way as to seize the knob and pull'. To avoid the suggestion of cognitive co-ordination, the analogist would have to arrive at an extremely detailed and laborious account of the sequence of contractions of the man's muscles, and items of that kind; would not in fact be able to say anything about what the *person* did but only what the person's muscles did; and though it may be just possible to say in this grassroots, positivistic way what had happened on a single occasion, the analogist, like the S–R theorist, would be committed to the most extreme particularism, because it is unlikely that anyone uses just the same pattern of muscular contractions on *any* two occasions of opening the same cupboard door even if trying to do so, and certainly not if one uses sometimes the left hand and sometimes the right, and consequently the analogist could not talk about *kinds* of action at all.

But perhaps the strangest thing about the proposition that human beings cannot be acquainted with one another's mental processes is that if it were true, then it would have made the generation of language impossible. Language is inescapably social. Even though the first few words may have originated in non-linguistic grunts of effort or moans of hunger or what-ever, there was no *language* until it came to be recognised and agreed that particular sounds could and would be used to *refer* to particular aspects of the world – to draw people's attention to things and make them understand something – whatever ambiguities may have needed and will always need to be resolved. But this presupposes that the members of the community knew one another as perceiving creatures, because the concept of *referring* is essentially cognitive. To say that one thing is used to symbolise another means that the audience must understand what the user is thinking of. The alternative view would be a Skinnerian one, holding that 'words' were merely habitual motor responses to stimulus objects, which might indeed be capitalised upon by a hearer to predict what further responses the utterer was likely to make, but which were not *used* by the utterer to refer to anything, and could not be used by him in novel combinations to convey information to the hearer about things he had never seen. Of course, it is possible any day to observe groups of living creatures amongst whom sounds do have merely that habitual stimulus and response role and who do succeed to some extent in manipulating one another's behaviour by them, and that is to say, groups of most species other than man, but one difference between those species and ours is that we have language and they do not. From the Skinnerian view language does not exist; but what is not commonly seen is that from the view that we could never be directly acquainted with others' mental processes it could not exist either. And, of course, the special thing about language is that, being existent, it is a uniquely rich, sensitive, and articulated means of discovering other persons' beliefs about the world and their bearing on their behaviour – far more so than the observation of non-verbal behaviour, though that is not to be despised, as I have been arguing.

I use the expression 'beliefs about the world' for what is discovered about other persons in this way, rather than their 'private world-view', 'phenomenological environment', 'subjective reality', or cognate phrases, in order to stress once again that psychology can study the role of cognitive processes in determining behaviour without resorting to a subjectivist epistemology. For a realist it is sufficient to say that some of any person's beliefs about the world will be true and some will be false, not that one creates an internal world. Subjectivist epistemologies include phenomenology, which has become fashionable again, and which I shall be discussing in some detail in my next chapter. Phenomenology sometimes appears nowadays under the title of 'hermeneutics', though hermeneutics is not committed to it. Hermeneutics was originally the science of the interpretation of ancient texts, in which the linguistic conventions, literary images, and so on are much more open to misunderstanding than with contemporary documents, because of the paucity of information about the cultural context in which they were used. By analogy, modern hermeneutical psychology, at its best, seeks to discover the significance of social customs and rituals – the whole complex network of symbolic rewards used within a culture to regulate interpersonal relations. All this is just as objective as the relation between a text and the world events to which it refers. The meanings are not 'private'; if an individual gave an idiosyncratic meaning to a gesture he would not be understood. Gauld and Shotter (1977) give the example that in one traditional culture, the Foulah of Africa, if a woman turns her back on a man and bends over, it is a compliment, but amongst the Kikuyu and East End Londoners it is an insult. This is objectively discoverable without any special faculty of intuition; it is an interesting sociological fact and could well be a handy thing for a traveller to know. But in some usages, Boden's for example, 'hermeneutics' refers to the putative discovery of the *internal* constructive schemata by which persons are held to 'impose meaning' on the input from their environment (Boden 1977, p. 397). But the only way in which one can 'impose meaning' on something is to agree that a certain sound or mark or gesture shall be used to stand for something else in the world, where both symbol and symbolised are objective entities. The notion that one needs to impose meaning on the whole world in order to make anything of it is one that cannot be sensibly expressed; there would be no discriminable things *there* to start work on. One does not impose meanings on situations; one forms beliefs (some true, some false) about what sorts of situation they *are*, what is going on, what the actors are trying to do to one another, what the outcome is likely to be. The cognitive relationships that a person has to his environment are, in principle, objectively discoverable by others. There is no need to attempt the impossible task of entering into another's mind-dependent, subjective reality, because no such reality exists.

The argument so far

The central theme of the discussion has been to examine the internalist 'desire or intention plus belief' approach to the explanation of apparently goal-directed behaviour. Accepting this as an attempt at causal explanation, I contended that desires and intentions are not eligible candidates for the intrinsic properties requisite for efficient-cause explanations, because they are conceived as having a relational tendency-towards-something intrinsic to their nature – something that I claimed cannot be. But there is real content, nevertheless, to the notion of motivational states, and some acceptable substantive account of them must be found if the internalist explanation is to work. The general outline of such an account and the difficulty of filling it in will be the subject of a later chapter.

Turning to the causal role of beliefs, I insisted that cognitive processes are not tied to purposivism and that an adequate science of organismic behaviour must be a cognitive determinist one. This led to the issue of the observability of mental processes, and to my contention that one cannot usefully say what an organism is doing without implicitly assuming that one can see what the organism believes the results of its movements will be.

In pursuing these arguments I have tried to demonstrate by example, though some may say I have simply assumed, first that efficient-cause explanation is the only adequate way of explaining events, and secondly, that nothing can have its relations intrinsic to itself. Yet there are European philosophic traditions, especially those related to phenomenology, that are quite at ease with the concept of intrinsic relations; which insist that the self in particular is intrinsically relational in its being and cannot possibly be thought of in any other way; and which claim that by adopting a certain attitude of mind, a presuppositionless openness to this mode of psychological being, one can understand how its phases develop one from another, although nothing of efficient or any other causality is involved in this.

In the following chapter I shall be examining some strands in the development of phenomenology and existentialism, and something of their influence in modern psychological thought, to see whether these thinkers can communicate their insights to us in a way that can be understood, or whether they must be regarded as ineffable, revelatory.

5

The constitution of the 'self'

The mode of being of phenomenal objects

As the 1970s progressed, and the internal creakings that heralded the collapse of S–R behaviourism became clearer, psychologists again began a self-conscious search for the distinguishing characteristics of their subject-matter and the methods appropriate to its study (cf. e.g. many papers in *American Psychologist*, 1974). If it was still to be the science of behaviour, it was certainly not to be that of merely motor behaviour; cognition had to play a part in it somewhere. Within the study of cognition two contrasting trends emerged: the more noticeable and academically respectable was analytic, objectivist, experimental, typified perhaps by the computer simulation studies I have commented on; the other, stubbornly asserting itself from the periphery and associated much more with clinical and social psychology than with laboratory experimentalism, was the holistic and subjectivist world-view of phenomenology.

Phenomenology insists that the world of phenomenal appearances is at least as real as the world of neutral objective facts, stripped (by the natural sciences) of their significance as objects that ordinary human perception can grasp, or so it is said. Phenomenologists seem to agree (Giorgi 1975, Bolton 1979) that the natural sciences have their rightful subject-matter, but that this does not include the kinds of thing we can apprehend in every-day experience; presumably, natural science reduces everything to collections of atoms and physical vibrations of one kind and another, and has nothing to say about tables and chairs and men and women. The latter group are considered to be amongst the *meanings* with which human apprehension endows the collections of basic particles. What is conveyed by their use of the word 'meaning' often seems inexpressible; I suggested in the preceding chapter that the only things that can meaningfully be said to have meaning are linguistic expressions or symbolic gestures, but for the phenomenologist it is rather that 'having meaning' is just *being of some kind*, having recognisable properties in common with other members of a class, being a kind of thing that a person can immediately intuit. The difficulty with that notion is that it assumes there must also be meaningless things, things that have no distinguishable properties, yet which pheno-menologists presumably must know in order to differentiate them from meaningful ones.

However, for phenomenology it is human perception which endows objects with experienced properties; perception is a constitutive activity; a person's experiential world is constituted by him. Phenomenology is distinguished from ordinary introspection in that it is less interested in the particular nature of what one perceives at a given time, or as Bolton says 'whether the subject uses imagery in problem-solving or feels depressed' (Bolton 1979, p. 160). Its focus is rather upon the essential nature of the constructive activity itself – it is 'a critical reflection upon experience in order to discover its necessary structure' (Bolton 1979, p. 160). It is not just a special field of psychology but is propaedeutic to psychology in general. Bolton contends that:

> . . . since it is consciousness that constitutes objectivity, the discipline which investigates the essential nature of that constitution, namely phenomenology, is the necessary foundation for that which investigates consciousness as part of the objective world, namely psychology (Bolton 1979, p. 161).

In some hands its range embraces even more. If in experiencing I endow my environment with meaning-for-me, then in some sense I am constitut-ing my *self*, since my psychological existence consists of transactions with my experienced world (cf. Merleau-Ponty 1963). It is by taking this step, which I shall be considering in more detail shortly, that phenomenology becomes existentialism, a general account of the nature of existence, not just of perceptual processes. In existentialism's basic principle that man freely creates himself, we find an extreme form of the demand that psychology not be subject to the explanatory categories of the natural sciences. Phenomenology found the defining property of psychology in the fact that human beings are experiencing creatures, and the objects studied by the natural sciences are not. But this is felt not to be just a difference in the kind of process studied; it is held to entail also a difference in logical categories. What characterises the natural sciences is the assumption of mechanical, efficient causation – that every event has a prior cause and that to discover it is to explain the event. But none of the processes studied in those sciences, so the argument runs, have the uniquely generative power of constitutive perception. To this, causality does not apply, and for the same reason does not apply to the self-creativity of being human. One must try to see whether from this standpoint outside natural science categories more enlightening insights are possible than from within them.

Among the thinkers who have striven to incorporate the doctrines of existentialism into psychology and psychiatry, those best known to the Western world are the Swiss psychiatrists Binswanger and Boss, and although Binswanger's conceptions are in some ways indiosyncratic I propose to take them up for detailed examination a little further on because they are perhaps the more explicitly formulated of the two, and in any case they exhibit what I regard as the flaw basic to all existentialist thinking, in not being able to constrain the ubiquity of choosing one's being, and in consequently not being able to give any account of that being.

Binswanger claims to have derived his leading concepts from the work of Heidegger, the German philosopher who is considered the most important academic contributor to philosophical existentialism in the 20th century. Quickly sketching in some main lines of intellectual influence, we might note that Heidegger had studied under Husserl, the leader of the modern phenomenological school in philosophy, and Husserl had been a student of Brentano, the Austrian philosopher and psychologist who had proposed that the proper subject-matter of psychology is mental acts. This was in opposition to the prevailing Wundtian empiricist orthodoxy that mental life consisted solely of trains of content – a 'heap or collection of different perceptions', as Hume had it, or clusters of sensations and ideas for Wundt – and that notions of mental acts were prescientific and animistic.

Husserl came to reject some of Brentano's leading ideas (particularly some implications of the concept of immanent objectivity), and Heidegger in his turn rejected the transcendental idealism at which Husserl finally arrived. But it may be useful to begin an account of this movement with Brentano, since his Aristotelian notion of the intentionality of conscious-ness was preserved as a fundamental concept throughout this succession, and makes its appearance (enlarged in scope) in Binswanger's psychology as the concept of 'Being-in-the world' (taken over directly from Heidegger). Being-in-the-world is the special mode of being that distinguishes spirit or self from merely physical objects, just as for Brentano intentionality marked off mental from physical phenomena. Being-in-the-world is intended to convey the notion of an essentially relational way of being; it is to say that spirit or self consists of nothing but relatedness to its environ-ment – i.e. that it has no intrinsic properties. It is not an entity that can be considered apart from its environment; nor can one speak properly of *the* environment apart from a particular individual's environment, since one constitutes one's existential or functional or meaningful environment by selecting some of the myriad possibilities of the world and excluding others. Such a self-constituting experiential world, the unitary psycho-logical entity of person-in-environment, Binswanger calls a *Dasein*, borrowing the term directly from Heidegger. I will postpone a critical account of these concepts until I come to consider the explanatory role with which Binswanger endows them. He seeks to find an explanatory framework for the vicissitudes of personal existence in the universal formal structural aspects of *Dasein*. He argues that these universals are realised in different ways in the *Dasein* of different individuals. He refers to this as the person's 'world-design' and claims that a proper explication of it is essential in rendering that person's behaviour intelligible; however, I shall argue that whatever promise this approach may hold is rendered void by existentialism's second founding concept, this being our freedom to choose our being, our potential ability to recreate our *Dasein* at any moment by an act of will.

Of course, the view that the world we are acquainted with is a world of appearances, impressions, ideas – an 'experiential world' – rather than a world of objective existences, is hardly a modern invention. Rather it is a perennial tendency of human thought, even though the absurdity of the solipsism to which it seems to lead has so frequently been pointed out. But one might treat Brentano as the originator of the particular trend of thought with which we are concerned here, if only because his work directly instigated Husserl's 'phenomenological method', which existential psychology claims as its distinctive methodology.

The relevant leading concepts in Brentano's work are, first, the intentionality that distinguishes mental phenomena – remembering that for Brentano 'mental phenomena' are mental *acts* – and, secondly, the intentional inexistence of their objects. For him, intentionality means being necessarily related to or directed upon some object, and is characteristic not only of believing but of all mental acts. In an often-quoted passage in his *Psychology from an empirical standpoint*, Brentano, after critically surveying a number of attempts to define the mental, says:

> Every mental phenomenon is characterized by what the Scholastics of the Middle Ages called the intentional (or mental) inexistence of an object, and what we might call, though not wholly unambiguously, reference to a content, direction towards an object (which is not to be understood here as meaning a thing), or immanent objectivity. Every mental phenomenon includes something as object within itself, although they do not all do so in the same way. In presentation something is presented, in judgement something is affirmed or denied, in love loved, in hate hated, in desire desired and so on.
>
> This intentional inexistence is characteristic exclusively of mental phenomena. No physical phenomenon exhibits anything like it. We can, therefore, define mental phenomena by saying that they are those phenomena which contain an object intentionally within themselves (Brentano 1874, 1973 edn, pp. 88–9).

Spiegelberg considers the stress on 'reference to an object' one of Brentano's most important and original contributions (despite Brentano's modestly giving credit to Aristotle), and says that Brentano here 'for the first time uncovered a structure which was to become one of the basic patterns for all phenomenological analysis' (Spiegelberg 1960, p. 41). It is plain that it was an influential concept, but the implications of what Brentano was saying are not immediately apparent. Obviously, he was saying that mental acts are relational in nature, but sometimes it seems that this being-essentially-relational extends to the objects of those acts, since (at this stage in Brentano's thought at least, though he later retracted this, cf. Farber 1943, p. 12) he held that the object of a mental act need not have objective existence external to that act; presumably then it can be constituted by the act. Thus, in the passage just quoted he says that the object 'is not to be understood here as meaning a thing', and he elaborates on this in his 'Supplementary Remarks', saying that mental reference is distinguished from other relations in that in this case 'the terminus of the so-called relation does not need to exist in reality at all' (which I pointed out above as a problem for a realist account of error). Brentano goes on: 'If someone thinks of something, the one who is thinking must certainly exist, but the object of his thinking need not exist at all ... So the only thing which is required by mental reference is the person thinking' (Brentano 1874, 1973 edn, p. 272).

This gives us some notion of what he means by the 'intentional inexistence' or 'immanent objectivity' of the objects of thought, which apparently characterises all thought's objects whether they are such things as centaurs, which we believe not to exist, or the book before us, which we do believe to exist in the world, as well as in being the object of our thought. The centaur of which we think would be credited with this Platonic sort of intentional existence, just as a perfect circle would, though there may be no worldly instances of them to be found.

It is this ambiguous ontological status of the object which in Brentano's thinking actually distinguishes mental acts or relations from physical ones. Merely to say that they are necessarily directed towards an object, i.e. that as relations they must have an object, cannot do so. 'In love something is loved, in hate hated ...' Can one not say that in kicking something is kicked, in eating, eaten? Perhaps it could be argued that these are in part mental acts too, since as we saw in the preceding chapter kicking something as distinct from accidentally striking one's foot against it entails the foreseeing of consequences, which falls in the class of mental events. But even to say that the pen is lying on something requires an object. In lying on, something is lain on. Thus, the mere fact that mental relations require objects does not distinguish them from physical relations. Although it was an advance on Brentano's part to see that mentality is to be understood as consisting of acts rather than entities, nevertheless the important point is that mental relations are of *a kind peculiar to organisms* and are not to be found occurring between inanimate objects. In fact, in thinking that it is the ontological status of their objects which distinguishes mental relations (rather than the nature of the relation itself), Brentano readmits the possibility of mental entities, of mental phenomena as 'content'. It is hard to escape the conclusion that for him an intentional object is thought of as having an intrinsically relational existence, that is, as mind-dependent in its being, despite the fact that Brentano and the later phenomenologists insist on claiming some sort of objectivity ('immanent objectivity', which, however, is nothing but a contradiction in terms) for such phenomena.

A correlative question is whether, for Brentano, the *subject* term of the relation, the knowing entity, has a substantive nature of its own, or is also constituted by or of the relationships of perceiving, loving, judging, etc. (To say that mentality consists only of certain kinds of relations and not of mental entities, which is what I take the mind–brain identity thesis to assert, does not mean that the knowing entity has no intrinsic properties; it allows, of course, that it has physiological properties.) The ontological status (a) of the subject term and (b) of the object term, and the question of whether they are conceptually independent of one another, will provide the framework for my discussion of each of this sequence of thinkers.

Brentano's position with regard to the subject term is not clear. In his introductory discussion of the nature of psychology he defends Aristotle's discussion of it as 'the science of the soul', but is hesitant to commit himself on the question of the soul's substantive nature. According to his editor and interpreter, Oscar Kraus, Brentano considered the soul a substance in the sense of an entity in which other things subsist (presentations, wishes, etc.) but which does not itself subsist in anything: 'the ultimate subject'. It cannot itself be the *object* of such apprehensions, though its *acts* are known immediately (in 'inner perception'). But a pure subject (if that is what Brentano intends) could not be thought of as having any intrinsic nature at all, since to think of it so would be to constitute it an object. Certainly, the later thinkers in this succession. Heidegger and Binswanger, are quite explicit that the psychological self has no intrinsic nature, but consists only in relatedness, that is, in Being-in-the-world. The relevance of that to my main theme is that it is intimately connected with their rejection of determinism and their insistence on the freedom of choice. To treat something as having any *nature* is to suggest that its processes are bound or determined by that nature. Although it is true that I have a number of times earlier contended that there are no intrinsic mental properties, that does not mean that I am admitting the possibility of a purely relationally-constituted psychical somewhat that is the author of my acts; I am, of course, arguing that a human being is a purely physiological organism, with distinctive modes of functioning but of a deterministic kind. The existentialists find an exactly opposed solution.

Husserl and the phenomenological world

Brentano's concept of intentional inexistence prompted Husserl's development of his phenomenological method (cf. Spiegelberg 1960). Although the objects of our beliefs may not exist in the external world, still, Brentano and Husserl and all the phenomenologists take it as self-evidently true that they exist in a mental world. This experiential world is what phenomenology takes as its subject-matter. It seeks the universal structural forms and process laws of that subjective world.

The first step of Husserl's phenomenological method is known as 'bracketing off'. This means to suspend entirely the question of whether what occurs in experience exists outside it as well.

We put out of action the general thesis which belongs to the essence of the natural standpoint, we place in brackets whatever it includes respecting the nature of Being (Husserl 1913, 1931 edn, p. 110).

The 'natural standpoint' that is suspended assumes that we inhabit a world of independently existing objects with which we can be acquainted. Husserl indicates the similarity between his bracketing off and Descartes' method of attempting to doubt everything whatever, but claims that his intention is different. Descartes wanted to arrive at the existence of something that was unarguably the case, i.e. to discover an indisputable existent, and in the course of this he discarded from attention everything whose existence he could doubt; 'one can say that his universal attempt at doubt is just an attempt at universal denial' (Husserl 1913, 1931 edn, p. 109). That is not Husserl's concern; he continues to pay attention to the bracketed phenomenal world; his method simply bars him from using 'any judgement that concerns spatio-temporal existence' (Husserl 1913, 1931 edn, p. 111).

The effect of this is to direct his attention in the first place to the nature of mental processes (perception, understanding, and so on) rather than to the nature of their intentional objects. He seeks through contemplation and analysis to discover the absolutely universal formal structure of pure consciousness. This is to be sharply distinguished, he says, from the study of *psychological* processes in perception. By comparison, those phenomenologists within psychology, the Gestaltists, were concerned more with particular empirical findings, with the ways in which manipulation of such variables as proximity, contour, etc. would alter the way in which a given display is perceived. Husserl strives continually to free himself from the standpoint of empirical science; he is not interested in this perception and that perception but with the essential nature of the consciousness of anything, of consciousness *per se*.

That the conception of this enterprise owes a good deal to Kant's critique of pure reason is plain enough, but Husserl and later on Heidegger insist that their enquiry is altogether more comprehensive and more fundamental than Kant's. Kant they see as dealing only with the operations of the understanding as it engages in the natural sciences, whereas they consider that to be only one department or mode of experience. 'Experience' includes the phenomena of valuing and willing, and, perhaps most important of all for Husserl, of intuiting.

Husserl accuses Kant of not having shaken off the taint of psychologism, and of course Kant left open the possibility that the categories were just constitutive processes of the understanding, so that conceivably creatures whose intellect was of a different structure from ours might constitute their phenomenal world using different categories. (As we shall see, this suggestion was caught up in a very literal way by Binswanger to explain the mental life of neurotics.) Yet the whole force of Kant's work is to show by a detailed unfolding of the implicit assumptions of our thought that an experience that does not incorporate his categories is *not* conceivable, so that in a sense it is self-contradictory, or at best just a mere verbal exercise, even to speculate about its possibility. He endeavours to show what is necessarily entailed in our thinking of anything: for example, we cannot think of anything except as being spatial, for to think of anything requires that it be distinguishable from its environment and thus *in* some environment, and also in some spatial relationship to oneself. For much the same reason we necessarily think of or perceive things as temporal, for without this *a priori* foundation 'we could not represent to ourselves that things exist together at one and the same time, or at different times, that is, contemporaneously, or in succession' (Kant 1781, 1943 edn, p. 28). Again, anything that does not exhibit the categories of quality and quantity – i.e. is not of any kind and does not exist in any quantity – is inconceivable, and so on.

If we leave aside Kant's view that the categories are the outcome of innate constitutive operations of the mind, and see them rather as inseparable not from knowing anything but from *being* anything, then the unfolding of the categories might at least relieve psychology of the burden of pursuing certain metaphysical speculations as if they were issues that could be resolved by experimental research. Some researchers take as an empirical question how we manage to perceive spatial relations, how we manage to see segregated objects or to recognise common properties, and the assumption underlying their approach to these problems is that we must begin with the awareness of 'sense-data' that are not spatial, not organised, and not 'meaningful' (Neisser 1967, 1976). Yet, any example of these supposedly pre-cognitive sense-data that one could specify, in language, would inevitably turn out to be a *kind* of thing, distinguishable by quality and contour from its environment, located in that environment, and having the entire complement of categorial aspects, since anything else is *inconceivable*, and if inconceivable, cannot exist as an item of information (or anything else).

Some of Husserl's analyses, in *The idea of phenomenology* (1950), for example, of the necessary categorial structure of perception rival Kant's for perceptiveness and close argument. But there is also a liberal admixture of another ingredient, a mystical kind of *a priorism* or intuitionism to which the Western empirical tradition is inimical, and which seems to have become distinctive of the phenomenological 'method'. In Husserl this begins with his taking over of Descartes' *cogito ergo sum* and putting it to

[margin handwritten note: Must have properties or must be recognized to have properties] an extended and rather different use. It is not only that I cannot doubt that I doubt, but that any mental act that I have is indubitable in its nature though not in its reference, thus:

> Howsoever I perceive, imagine, judge, infer, howsoever these acts may be certain or uncertain, whether or not they have objects that exist, as far as the perceiving itself is concerned, it is absolutely clear and certain that I am perceiving this or that, and as far as the judgement is concerned, that I am judging of this or that, etc. (Husserl 1950, 1970 edn, p. 23).

Of course, Husserl means something more than the truism that if I am perceiving I am perceiving; he means that I am, or can be, immediately reflexively aware of my mental acts. To know my perceiving is not in his view to have a second mental act with a previous perceiving as its object, it is to enjoy immediately the perceiving as it happens, in the one act. For Husserl this does not *inevitably* happen, though how he can avoid that, if the two acts are *one*, is not clear. If our mental processes are overlaid with abstract intellectualising, then that will militate against this pure intuition, or immediate 'seeing', he says. But the phenomenological method re-establishes our openness to phenomena. This method, as pointed out above, begins with the bracketing off of the question of objective reality, and directing the attention to the present field of consciousness. The second step is the 'eidetic reduction', which consists of disregarding the accidental individual properties of this particular perception so as to intuit in it, by 'immediate grasping', the universal essence of perception-in-general. The description of this second step can hardly be regarded as a set of instructions for how to do it; it is really just an injunction to do it, and indeed the concept of 'immediate grasping' cannot be further analysed. It is precisely this which disqualifies it from being called a *method* of enquiry in any sense comparable to the experimental method, for example. One cannot test its steps, since there are none, nor challenge its findings. When one achieves a *genuine* intuition, Husserl claims, one sees immediately that it is self-evidently true, and this applies not merely to the apprehension of particulars but to that of universal essences and universal truths. Husserl was (understandably) never able adequately to express what he meant by 'the total phenomenological attitude', being compelled finally to say that it called for 'a complete personal transformation which might be compared to a religious conversion' (see Spiegelberg 1960, pp. 135–6).

At first in Husserl's exposition it seems that the essences so revealed are limited to those of mental processes, i.e. the essence of perception, of imagination, of judgement, of inference, etc. Here there are valuable contributions to the explication of the categories, as I said before, and in that connection the concept of self-evidence has some force. Some statements about the inescapability of specific categories are necessarily or analytically true. But Husserl goes on to attribute self-evidence also to intuitions of what are plainly empirical matters. This failure to see that the categorial aspects of knowledge are on a quite different footing from empirical regularities becomes an increasing tendency in phenomenological and existential literature. It is present in a gross way in Binswanger's existential psychiatric theories, and as I shall argue shortly it results in his explanatory scheme being question-begging and theoretically sterile.

A clear-cut example of this slurring over from the self-evidence of categorial matters to the supposed self-evidence of particular empirical contents of consciousness is to be found in Lecture IV of *The idea of phenomenology:*

> I have a particular intuition of redness, or rather several such intuitions. I stick strictly to the pure immanence [i.e. to what is in the mental act]; I am careful to perform the phenomenological reduction. I snip off any further significance of redness, any way in which it may be viewed as something transcendent, e.g., as the redness of a piece of blotting paper on my table, etc. And now I fully grasp in pure 'seeing' the *meaning* of the concept of redness in general, redness *in specie* . . . If we really did this in pure 'seeing', could we then still intelligibly doubt what redness is in general, what is meant by this expression, what it may be in its very essence? (Husserl 1950, 1970 edn, pp. 44–5).

It would be fruitless to dispute with Husserl that in this way he might get a perfectly clear and distinct idea of what *he* means by redness, but it is hardly clear how this could be of use to him in knowing what other people mean by it, or indeed how it could be of any use whatever. But the method is sometimes put to more questionable and question-begging uses when, for example, it is held to reveal what the essence of *being human* is, which may be held to show not only why people act as they do but how they *ought* to act, if they are to be held truly human, in the view of the particular phenomenologist whose intuition has revealed this essence.

Husserl himself found a special employment for the 'method' in *Ideas* (1913), and in the *Cartesian meditations* (1929). It is intended to solve the problem inherent in the method itself, that is, how to leap the gap from pure subjectivity to knowledge of other minds, and to communication with them. The solution is simply that the essence of our concept of objectively existing things is that they are 'intersubjective identical things', and of such an order of thing he says that:

> Its constitution is related to an indefinite plurality of subjects that stand in a relation of 'mutual understanding'. The intersubjective world is the correlate of the intersubjective experience, mediated, that is, through 'empathy' (Husserl 1913, 1931 edn, p. 420).

That is to say, through 'empathy' we *know* that we are talking to one another about a shared intersubjective world and are thus mutually *constituting* that intersubjective world. Our conception of objects could not be as it is if it were not for that. But actual discourse as an historical event has *empirical* prerequisites, namely, other cognitive beings and a shared language, and the existence of these empirical entities is *not* yielded by a categorial analysis of cognition, as Husserl is trying to suggest. I argued above that the existence of language presupposes our perception of others as perceiving creatures, but I was addressing myself to the empirical issue of our knowledge of others' mental processes. I was adopting the realist position (as I argued one must) that there is a world there for them to perceive. Husserl is asking the epistemological question of whether we can know that there is a world of independently existing objects, and claiming that we can feel reassured of it by sharing others' perceptions of things as intersubjective. But, of course, this is question-begging; other persons are independently existing objects, and their existence is *assumed* by the argument.

'Empathy' has an ambiguous status in Husserl's writings, and its status has remained unimproved in the various versions of it that his successors are still offering today. The phenomenologist, wanting to believe both that other egos exist, and that each ego including one's own is acquainted only with its own world of phenomenal experience, must posit some special, but in the long run inconceivable, kind of cognitive operation that leaps over this barrier and enters into another's phenomenological field. This communion is essential to the conviction that other minds objectively exist. More mundanely, in existential psychology it is considered necessary, if we are to understand another's behaviour, to apprehend that other's phenomenal world-design, to share his or her Being-in-the-world. This intractable epistemological problem accounts in large measure for the repeated appearance of notions of empathy or *Verstehen* in existentialism and phenomenology, but some such concept is also called for by the rejection of the natural science approach, by the stress on the idiographic and the denial of the nomothetic (Allport 1937), which so often characterises such psychologies. When the uniqueness of the individual is elevated to such a pitch that no general law or even any general description can accurately be applied to any person, then it is plain that workaday empirical methods of accumulating information about such creatures are inappropriate and fruitless. Another's inexpressible personal quiddity can only be intuited, with that special kind of revelation of essence that the phenomenological method claims to provide. (It must be pointed out once again that if consciousness is constitutive, as phenomenology claims, these attributions of special personal essences can have no claim to objectivity.) Since this unrealistic conception of uniqueness, which actually deprives one of a vocabulary with which to talk about persons, derives basically from the conviction that each of us is a self-determining agent, not the creature of causal laws, then this grasping for a special mode of understanding of the life histories of such agents must be taken as a recognition that a *science* of self-determining agents is impossible – but whatever the method provides seems not intersubjectively communicable.

Self-awareness and self-creation

Before leaving Husserl we might note a precise anticipation of a strain of thinking that is an important constituent of existentialism, though it is rarely explicitly stated, and that is that the fact that we are self-aware somehow implies that we create our own being. For Husserl the transition between the two notions is mediated by his view that the mind in its cognitive activity constitutes its intentional objects. Further, since one is always, in his view, aware of oneself in relation to one's intentional objects, the perceiver's immediate awareness of his own subjectivity is essential to his awareness of anything. Consequently:

> The ego is himself *existent for himself* in continuous evidence; thus, in himself, he is continuously constituting himself as existing (Husserl 1929, 1973 edn, p. 66).

To be aware of oneself is to create oneself. That assertion can present even the semblance of argument only in a theory in which awareness is a constitutive activity. Some of Husserl's successors have had an equivocal attitude to his transcendental subjectivism, but they have regularly felt that *somehow* the fact of self-consciousness brings self-creation in its train. Whatever its origin, whether intellectual, theological, or emotional, the conviction that persons choose their own being is fundamental to existentialism, and the problem for existential psychologists and psychiatrists has been to see how they could flesh out the stark absoluteness of that principle in any way that would give an understandable account of what a human being *is*. The requisite psychological content, at least in the work of Binswanger, derives in large measure from an elaboration of strands in Heidegger's thought. Heidegger provided the most direct philosophical influence on Binswanger, though he appeals also to Husserl's authority.

Because of the accretion of 'intuition' to Husserl's phenomenological method, that method claimed to generate a self-evident knowledge of various *kinds of thing* as distinct from the *categorial* aspects that are, in fact, inseparable from awareness. That tendency increases in Heidegger and is greatly exaggerated in Binswanger. Binswanger, indeed, still speaks of the categories as being formal, structural properties of *Dasein*, yet he treats them also as being individual and personal! As we shall see below, they have in his psychology much the same explanatory role as the detested instinctual drives have in Freud's.

From Heidegger's work I select only those parts which have been important in the development of existential psychology. The most relevant of those is his concept of *Dasein*, with its special mode of existence, that of Being-in-the-world. *Dasein* may be translated literally as 'being-there', but at Heidegger's hands it has acquired so many special connotations that it is usually considered better to treat it as a technical term of his own with no straightforward English translation.

A *Dasein* is a particular human existence, where that is conceived of as a self-illuminated *life-world*, to borrow a term from Husserl's later writings. Husserl had puzzled over the intrinsic nature of the ego, wanting to say both that it existed only as the pure subject of its acts (suggesting that it has no intrinsic nature over and above those acts) and yet that it is the '*active and affected*' subject of consciousness, standing as the subject-pole which is related through the processes of consciousness to all object-poles (which suggests that it does have some intrinsic nature: cf. the fourth of the *Cartesian meditations*). But in Heidegger's *Dasein* there is, by declaration at least, no such duality of poles; they dissolve into one another to form one experiential totality, a realm of self-sustaining consciousness. The being of *Dasein* may be called Being-in-the-world, but it would be a mistake to speak as if *Dasein* were a psychological entity with an intrinsic or essential nature that exists in that special way. (Something of that nature is implied in the debased usage of the expression 'Man's being-in-the-world' in much current psychological writing, where it means little more than 'Man is a social animal' or some sentiment of that kind.) It seems rather that the two terms are almost interchangeable; a *Dasein* is a Being-in-the-world and nothing else. Heidegger expressly denies that what we might call the self has any intrinsic properties whatever, as in this passage from his major work, *Being and time:*

> *The essence of Dasein lies in its existence.* Accordingly those character-istics which can be exhibited in this entity are not 'properties' present-at-hand of some entity which 'looks' so and so and is itself present-at-hand; they are in each case possible ways for it to be, and are no more than that ... So when we designate this entity with the term 'Dasein', we are expressing not its 'what' (as if it were a table, house or tree) but its Being (Heidegger 1957, 1967 edn, p. 67).

To be 'present-at-hand' is the kind of being that mere physical objects have – what Sartre (whose work has much in common with Heidegger's) would call the 'in-itself' as distinct from the 'for-itself'. The 'for-itself' for Sartre is that which is aware of itself and responds to itself, which for him too is to say *creates* itself, and that is true also for Heidegger's *Dasein*.

If *Dasein* has no present-at-hand properties, no intrinsic properties, then its entire nature consists in relatedness-to-its-world; however, 'its world' in turn is in an important sense constituted by relatedness to *Dasein* – an end-less circuit of mutual creation. (Perhaps, as I sugggested above, it would be neater, if no less obscure, to say that the two are one, that they dissolve into one another – but then they could not be related to one another.) We are not passive recorders of whatever happens to be at hand, in Heidegger's view. Without *Dasein* the world is not non-existent, but is a meaningless chaos; *Dasein* seizes on some things as relevant to its projects and makes them stand forth meaningfully, giving them 'intelligibility' in terms of their function. It does not create existences, nor, he says, is truth subjective; rather, *Dasein* endows existences with meaning, i.e. as being useful or hindering to its concerns. But this escape from subjectivism is more by declaration than by consistent argument. To say that the world exists objectively but only as a meaningless jumble is hardly an adequate account of objectivity; further, it would be impossible for *Dasein* to *select* anything from this jumble, because 'meaningless' things could not be distinguished one from another, nor one be more useful than another. To 'endow' such nothings with meaning would be pure subjectivism.

For Heidegger the expression 'concern' designates 'the Being of a possible way of Being-in-the-world' (Heidegger 1957, 1967 edn, p. 83). There is an infinitude of possible ways of Being-in-the-world, and to engage in a particular concern is to realise one of them. But for Heidegger particular concerns have their significance only in terms of that over-arching Care (*Sorge*) which is concerned with *authentic* Being. Care is not a particular psychological condition that we may fall into, as in being 'care-worn'. (Binswanger misinterpreted it in that way, and so caused Heidegger to divorce his philosophy from psychological existentialism.) Care is essential to our Being as such. Heidegger calls it an 'ontological structural concept'; that is, it is roughly comparable to a Kantian category but is a category of *Dasein*, a structural aspect without which *Dasein* would be inconceivable.

> Dasein is an entity for which, in its Being, that Being is an issue ... In each case Dasein has already compared itself, in its Being, with a possibility of itself. Being-free *for* one's ownmost potentiality-for-Being, and therewith for the possibility of authenticity and inauthenticity, is shown, with a primordial, elemental concreteness, in anxiety (Heidegger 1957, 1967 edn, p. 236).

Anxiety is a particular manifestation of Care, which is another name for the fact that our Being is at every moment *an issue* for us. When he says that 'in its Being, that Being is an issue', it has the ring of those classic phrases, turning back upon themselves, with which people have tried to unfold analytic truths, but its claim to that status is very questionable. It is to say that *how* we shall Be (what sort of person we shall be, how we shall act) is inescapably and at every moment a *moral* issue for us, and that can only be so if we are continually *responsible* for our Being, that is, if we are con- tinually creating it, and that is certainly Heidegger's intention. 'Being' is to be read very much as an active verb, not as the mere neutral fact of existence. It is a self-creation that we are actively doing, *continually*, even when, as is so often the case, we are in the condition Heidegger calls Being-fallen, which is to say, being limited in our Being, or failing to realise our potentialities. That is *inauthentic* Being, which typically comes about by resigning our responsibility in favour of simply doing what 'One' does, in favour of submitting to 'the Man', that Man being the faceless embodiment of social convention.

This brings us directly to the conceptual crisis of existentialism. Whatever the appeal of those remarks as comments on the human condition, they involve an antinomy. In Heidegger's view we *cannot* actually resign our responsibility, since it is inseparable from our Being. Even in a state of Being-fallen we are continually choosing to remain in that state, he asserts. But can what one chooses to be, be inauthentic? If when we choose to be such-and-such it is *our* choice, then being so – whatever it may be, anything and everything we do – is by definition authentic. If the Being of *Dasein* is *in its essence* self-chosen Being, then the expression 'inauthentic Being' has no referent. It is simply a contradiction in terms. Since we have no intrinsic nature, since our Being is just this principle of self-choosing, then we are identical with what we do. There can be no distinction between how we behave, how we present ourselves to the world or to our own consciousness, and our 'true' selves, from this view.

To be forced to such a conclusion is, of course, most unfortunate for existentialism, whose central message is that to be inauthentic is to lose one's human stature. But it would be still more unfortunate for psychology if the concept of inauthenticity were to be dismissed as a merely metaphysical one, inseparable from existentialism. Surely the experience of having acted inauthentically, of having been false to one's own self, is something that all but the most complacent of persons has had. Polonius's admonition to Laertes has meaning, even though we may think it came from a sententious old moralist. To be true to oneself is not merely a moral concept. Inauthenticity does refer to some actual psychological condition, and to say what it is without postulating a metaphysical distinction between actual being and 'true' or essential being is an empirical question, the answer to which in my opinion would deal with the fact that a person can come to accept an imposed morality and consequently suffer a division of the personality into repressed and repressing forces (Maze 1973).

But within the existentialist framework the *pervasiveness* of existential choice would make such an empirical enquiry quite pointless, if the concept were consistently adhered to. In order to show this, and to bring out the further self-defeating effects of the related notion that the self has no intrinsic properties, I want to examine in some detail the attempt by Binswanger, as an existential psychiatrist, to give a psychological explanation of neurotic inauthenticity within the conceptual framework of *Dasein* and *Sorge*. Binswanger acquired those concepts directly from Heidegger's writings, but, as I have said, Heidegger found his understanding and employment of them very much at variance with his own.

Binswanger, being professionally concerned with individual differences between 'experiential worlds', coined the expression 'world-design' to emphasise the conception that each person constructs or designs his own *Dasein* with its special variations, and the variations he speaks of are supposed to be in its formal structural properties, or, briefly, in its categories. An individual's world-design has a fundamental role in determining his life history. Binswanger says that 'in the mental diseases we face modifications of the fundamental or essential structure and of the structural links of being-in-the-world as transcendence' (Binswanger 1946, 1958 edn, p. 194). (By 'as transcendence' he means that he is speaking of the fundamental structure of the *Dasein* rather than its particular content.) He says further:

> Knowledge of the structure or basic constitution of existence provides us with a systematic clue for the practical existential analytic investigation at hand. We know, now, what to focus on in the exploration of a psychosis, and how to proceed. We know that we have to ascertain the kind of spatialization and temporalization, of lighting and colouring; the texture, or materiality and motility, of the world-design toward which the given form of existence or its individual configuration casts itself (Binswanger 1946, 1958 edn, p. 200).

'Spatialization', 'temporalization', and so on recall the Kantian and Husserlian categories. The reason for that is that Binswanger needs some rationally based and universal framework for his analysis or classification of world-designs; accordingly, he says that the universal formal structure of Being-in-the-world 'places a norm at our disposal and so enables us to determine deviations from this norm in the manner of the exact sciences' (Binswanger 1946, 1958 edn, p. 201). That would enable him to avoid the complete arbitrariness that seems to follow from his central idea that each person creates a world-design as an act of free choice from an infinitely various manifold of possibilities.

Admittedly, the classical categories could provide a convenient descriptive scheme for some aspects of a person's fantasies. Ellenberger says that 'categorical phenomenology' means that the phenomenologist 'attempts to reconstruct the inner world of his patients through an analysis of their manner of experiencing time, space, causality, materiality, and other "categories" (in the philosophical sense of the word)' (Ellenberger 1958, p. 101). Thus, under the heading of causality, for example, he says that:

> ... determinism predominates in the subjective experience of the melancholic and chance in the experience of the manic. The manic lives in a world of complete irresponsibility where he is bound neither by the

past nor by the future, where everything happens through sheer chance (Ellenberger 1958, p. 115).

But in Binswanger's employment of the method we find that disturbances in the categories are being given a causal, dynamic role in the explanation of psychopathology. This appears, for example, in his account of his patient Ellen West, whose most conspicuous symptom was an excessive anxiety over and repugnance for becoming fat. Yet, she liked to eat, and the extreme restrictions she placed on her own diet were at the cost of a constant tormenting struggle. Binswanger also finds in her some of the symptoms of what psychoanalysis would call the 'anal character', as he points out; namely, 'tremendous defiance and self-willedness and a great punctiliousness in the filling up of her time'. He goes on to compare the existential analytic interpretation of anal-eroticisim with the psycho-analytic one.

The main feature of anal-eroticism is tenaciously keeping-to-oneself or not-giving-away. It is a very important insight of psychoanalysis, with which existential analysis completely agrees, that such a basic trait is not tied to the mind–body distinction, but transcends it. But here the agreement stops. Here too existential analysis asks first of all what world-design is basic to anality. In regard to the case of Ellen West the answer is particularly easy: in this world-design the multiplicity and multiformity of the world are reduced to the forms of the hole. The form of being in such a world is that of being confined or oppressed; the self which designs such a world is an 'empty' self, concerned only with the filling of the emptiness. Consequently a decided anality is concurrent with a decided orality, with a greed for 'incorporating' . . . The 'category' which dominates equally this world-design, the being-in-it and the self which designs it, is only and solely that of emptiness and fullness (Binswanger 1944, 1958 edn, p. 317).

The psychoanalytic claim that anality is in some sense a basic explanatory concept derives from the postulation of a genetically provided physiological mechanism; that is, the anal erotogenic zone as an ancillary of the sex drive. But if 'anal' behaviour is, as Binswanger is contending, just one derivative realisation of a world-design based on the concept of 'the hole', then, we must ask, from what does the latter derive its force? Why should it be accepted as explanatory, anality being merely derived from it?

It is a nice question why Binswanger puts the term 'category' in the foregoing quotation in quotation marks. The presumptive answer is that he wants to borrow the universality and necessity of the Kantian categories without committing himself to the claim that emptiness–fullness really has that status. And, of course, he could not plausibly make that claim. Perhaps if one raised the notion of emptiness to its highest power, and tried to contemplate an absolute void in space, then that could be regarded as an attempt to dispute the universality of the categories of Spatiality or Continuity or Materiality, and that would imply a fundamental reason for rejecting the concept of the absolute Hole, of total emptiness, thus agreeing that fullness is omnipresent. But Binswanger is talking about something much more mundane. The categories have nothing to say about whether one's stomach must be full or empty *of food*, or whether any container should be filled with any specified substance.

Binswanger makes many attempts to link the merely contingent with the categorial: for example, in his paper 'The existential analysis school of thought' he says that '"Filling" is the *a priori* or transcendental tie that allows us to combine faeces and money through a common denominator' (Binswanger 1946, 1958 edn, p. 210). There is nothing *a priori* or transcendental about the fact that one could use either faeces or money to fill a receptacle. More generally, since the categories apply to just *everything*, they cannot constitute a common denominator for some limited selection of things.

His attempt to establish the explanatory role of the categories as determinants of particular life histories receives its most explicit formulation in a later paper, 'Introduction to *Schizophrenie*' (1957). This begins, in the analysis of schizophrenia, with the notion of a breakdown in the consistency of natural experience. His account of this consistency is an ambiguous one; at first it sounds like a matter of psychological complacency – 'our sense of being in harmony with things and circumstances, with others . . . and with ourselves' (Binswanger 1957, 1963 edn, p. 251). This is manifested 'in our *letting* beings – all beings – *be* as they are in themselves'. But if that means being perfectly happy with everything in the world, it is hardly a plausible account of mental health; further, the term 'consistency', which refers to *logical* relations, is not an apt one to describe it. However, we find almost at once that 'consistency of experience' does not mean unqualified complacency, since 'a revolutionary spirit who seeks to overthrow the things of the world actually resides in undisturbed immediacy among them, otherwise he could not overthrow them'. Evidently 'letting things *be*' does not mean liking them or putting up with them, but rather, not trying to deny their existence. The patients whose cases Binswanger reviews in the book in question are, of course, desperately unhappy with the way things are – Ellen West with her bodily nature, Jürg Zünd with the proletarian harshness of his life when he longs for aristocratic graciousness, the young hysterical woman with the impermanence of all relationships, especially of hers with her mother. But the expression 'inconsistency of experience' is not applicable to such feelings. To wish for something one cannot achieve is not in itself to suffer any inconsistency of experience, even when the inability to achieve it comes from one's own internal conflicts. 'I cannot control my eating' does not contradict, or is not in any sense inconsistent with, 'I want to be thin'. Of course, if one has a desire to eat, a desire that is available to consciousness, and yet one insists 'I have no desire to eat', then there would be some point in talking of an inconsistency of experience, as there is whenever a person tries to deny the reality of something of the existence of which he is actually aware. But even self-deception is not sufficient for what Binswanger intends by 'inconsistency of experience'.

With his repeated references to categories and the existential *a priori*, it seems that in talking of experiential inconsistency Binswanger is trying to suggest not that his patients are deceiving themselves, but that they have somehow got their categories *wrong*, that they are constructing a logically incoherent *Dasein*, so that the very possibility of experience (i.e. of their psychological *existence*) is in danger. This comes out most clearly in his account of the young woman patient for whom the category of continuity had assumed an overriding importance. This had first manifested itself at the age of five when the heel of her shoe had become jammed in her ice-skate and had been pulled off from her shoe, this incident having caused her to faint. In Binswanger's analysis that comparatively trivial misfortune was not the cause of her emotional disturbance, but then nor was the fear of separation from her mother, which she also manifested, nor yet the birth-trauma which (he suggests) a Freudian might think was symbolised by the breaking of the heel. Rather it was that she had based her world-design, as he explicitly says, 'on the category of continuity', which required that any actual 'discontinuity', in the sense of *physical separation*, could not be incorporated into her experiential world, for fear of the whole *Dasein* being destroyed.

> Just as the *a priori* or transcendental [i.e. Kantian] forms of the human mind make experience only into what experience is, so the form of that world-design had first to produce the condition of the possibility for the ice-skating incident in order for it to be experienced as traumatic.
>
> It should be mentioned that this case is not at all an isolated one. We know that anxiety can be tied to various types of disruption of continuity; *e.g.*, it may appear as horror at the sight of a loose button hanging on a thread or of a break in the thread of saliva. Whatever the life-historical events are to which these anxieties refer, we are always dealing here with the same depletion of being-in-the-world, narrowed down to include only the category of continuity (Binswanger 1946, 1958 edn, p. 205).

The disruptions instanced here, of the button thread and of the saliva, are simply particular physical separations, not some unimaginable failure of the Kantian category of continuity at all (as he is suggesting), yet even so, discontinuity will not serve him as the common denominator of what is feared. It would be quite impossible to keep any suggestion of physical separation out of one's life; every time one picks something up and puts it down again physical separation is being exemplified. It is difficult to imagine that his patients are thrown into a fit of anxiety on every such occasion. It could only be special types of disruption that upset them, and the most plausible expectation is that these have a symbolic relation to some actual trauma they have suffered, or with which they have been threatened.

Binswanger is here plainly borrowing the authority of Kant's view that the categories are logically necessary to *all* awareness and, therefore, cannot be called into question without self-contradiction, in order to endow what is just a particular psychological assertion (that this child had a neurotic need to guard against the possible disruption of certain specifiable relationships) with some sort of fundamental explanatory power, a kind of self-evidential status, as if it would be unreasonable to ask for any further explanation of it. In that connection the categories have a function in Binswanger's psychological theory similar to that which the instinctual drives have in classical psychoanalytic theory. For psychoanalysis, when a neurotic behaviour has been revealed as a distorted expression of an instinctual drive, then its motivational origin is taken as adequately explained. If one accepts the concept of instinctual drive, then it would be unreasonable to ask why an instinctual drive should press for discharge. It would be like asking why the liquid in a container presses against the sides of the container. But there is an important difference between psycho-analysis and Binswanger's existential analysis in the type of explanatory status claimed for their concepts. The psychoanalytic assertion that we have a fixed set of instinctual drives and that all our behaviour derives from their operation is basically just an empirical biological assertion, or even a schematic physiological one (as I shall argue in the following chapter). That is, it is a contingent proposition, and it would be a quite proper empirical question to ask how the species came to have just those drives and none other. But Binswanger continually suggests that his explanatory concepts, the categories, have a logically necessary status, not a contingent one. Thus, the 'category of continuity' is assimilated to the spatiotemporal unity that Kant insists is a precondition of our seeing things as related to one another – in general, of being aware of any fact at all, which means, being conscious at all, and for phenomenology and existentialism, being conscious is equated with having psychological existence. But Kant, of course, does not mean that we must desperately set ourselves to maintain that spatiotemporal unity for fear our world will collapse and our psycho-logical existence be terminated. For him, since it is literally inconceivable that we could have a thought whose content did not involve spatio-temporal unity, we could not actually conceive of its absence so as to be afraid of losing it.

But in Binswanger's conception, the patient *can* envisage the disintegra-tion of his or her entire universe, and from that the pathology follows. The pathology is the struggle of the *Dasein* to regain its categories. Binswanger (1957) refers to the *imperative* that experiential consistency be restored.

From what does that imperative derive? It is as if he were saying that if the categories are infringed, then the possibility of consciousness (thus, the existence of the *Dasein*) is endangered; therefore the defective *Dasein* must return to an observance of the categories. But on any proper understanding of the categories, the notion of consciousness deviating from them, so that it can find it imperative to return to them, is absurd. The categories cannot vary between individuals, and cannot play the dynamic role Binswanger assigns to them.

But as his discussion proceeds in the 'Introduction to *Schizophrenie*' we find it drifting away from the categories as an explanatory device, and assuming the basic form of existentialist orthodoxy. The role of the categories becomes subordinated to the overriding one of the Will. The various constitutive disorders of the *Dasein* are reduced to the conflict between will and fate (that is, between freedom and determinism). For Ellen West, becoming fat expresses subjection to fate or nature; being slender is the successful assertion of her will. Again, Binswanger says that for Jürg Zünd, '"belonging" or social existence is burdened with the role of overcoming the experiential split between the existential alternatives of life and death, ideal and reality, nature (or fate) and will' (Binswanger 1957, 1963 edn, p. 257).

Since in Ellen West's *Dasein* bodiliness is 'perversely' burdened with the role of representing fate, and since the very Being of *Dasein*, as we saw above, is to will itself at every moment, then the willed control of her eating is equated with the continuance of her Being. If she cannot succeed in this exercise of her will, she will cease to exist as a person. Any limitation on one's freedom to choose means that one's Being has been invaded by non-Being. The history of an individual life will be the history of this struggle to *be* (one might say, to be freely or authentically, but that would be a redundancy), and of the success or failure of the person's confrontation with the opponents of freedom that he or she encounters – in general, with the 'thrownness' of life, the particular set of conditions under which one is thrown into existence. These include such things as one's bodily constitution, social class of origin, even, some say, addictions to drugs or alcohol.

Can such a schema, the struggle for authenticity against thrownness, offer an informative account of why an individual life took the course it did? Despite its attractive literary quality, its value as psychological theory is severely limited. The tension in existential thought between freedom and thrownness has often been remarked. Only some aspects of the *Dasein* are experienced as thrown, and the others as willed, but the problem of finding some criterion of that distinction, in order to make sense of the struggle between will and fate, is compounded by the fact that the thrown can be changed into the willed at any time, simply by willing to be as one actually is. (That suggests a strict limitation on our power to will to be otherwise than we at present are.) Heidegger even has it that one path to authenticity is *to will one's past*, which, if it is to be taken literally, appears a fairly pointless exercise; the past is beyond our reach and will remain unchanged. Of course, there is a considerable element of psychological truth wrapped up in that notion, as there is in much of what the existentialists have to say about ethics and the trials of existence. We often blame history or the economic system or the spitefulness of others for misfortunes that are really due to our own sloth or timidity or narcissism, and it must be a gain in mental health to recognise one's own responsibility (in that factual sense of responsibility) where it exists. But it is not so obvious that we can achieve such insight just by willing to do so.

Existentialism, then, cannot provide a specification of what aspects of *Dasein* constitute its thrownness, because of the will's power to negate their thrown status. That power must render vacuous any existential account of kinds of psychological disorder (or of any kind of behaviour in general) in a life history – how they develop and what course they take. To give an explanation of the functioning of anything calls for an account of its structure, of how its parts interact, of what intrusions into it make it start working in an abnormal manner, and so on. As we saw, Binswanger tried to do that by explicating the ontological (categorial) structure of *Dasein*, but, even if he could have given a coherent description of a *Dasein* with disordered categories, we would find that the disorder was, according to existentialist theory, the result of an original act of will, elevating some one category to an undue importance, and that it could be remedied at any time by a further act of will, renouncing the former extravagant commitment – that is, if the person could muster up the will to will. Binswanger attributes the failure to make such a restorative act to the *Dasein*, this perpetually self-willed entity, having become 'worn away (as though by friction)' (Binswanger 1957, 1963 edn, p. 258) – a thoroughly uninformative metaphor. Whatever the will may be, it is not an organ whose substance can be worn away. We must conclude, then, that he has not given an intelligible account of how a disorder comes about, what is disordered, or how it might be remedied.

The indivisibility of the 'self'

The inability of existentialist thought to generate any useful or, indeed, intelligible psychological theory is not restricted to Binswanger, but in my opinion is general and inescapable. It derives from existentialism's refusal to regard the 'self' as a mechanism composed of parts (which is to say that it is not *composed* of anything) and its complementary insistence that the self is a unitary principle of agency whose sole project is to assert that agency.

To make this point, one may draw some comparisons between existentialism and psychoanalytic psychology, the latter being the most explicitly determinist and pluralist theory of psychological structure. The fundamental difference between the two theories is that psychoanalysis concerns itself with the vicissitudes of the *instincts* on their paths towards their various gratifications, whereas existentialism is concerned with the vicissitudes of the *self* in its struggle to be, to defend its Being against non-Being.

This is exemplified in Laing's case history of his patient Mrs R (Laing 1960, p. 56 ff.). Her leading symptom was her agoraphobia, her dread of being alone in the street. He comments on her childhood feeling that her parents were too engrossed in each other to take much notice of her; her intense desire to be loved and wanted; her sense of fulfilment when as a young woman she was called back to the family household to nurse her mother in a fatal illness; the collapse of her marriage and her eventual decision to live with her father as his housekeeper in his London flat. Laing goes on to say that psychoanalytic theory

> ... might attempt to show this woman as unconsciously libidinally bound to her father; with, consequently, unconscious guilt and unconscious need and/or fear of punishment. Her failure to develop lasting libidinal relationships away from her father would seem to support the first view, along with her decision to live with him, to take her mother's place, as it were, and the fact that she spent most of her day, as a woman of twenty-eight, actually thinking about him. Her ... anxiety at her mother's death would be anxiety at her unconscious wish for her mother's death coming true. And so on (Laing 1960, p. 59).

But in opposition to the psychoanalytic view, Laing contends that:

> The pivotal point around which all her life is centred is her *lack of ontological autonomy*. If she is not in the actual presence of another person who knows her, or if she cannot succeed in evoking this person's presence in his absence, her sense of her own identity fades away from her. Her panic is at the fading away of her being ... In order to exist she needs someone else to believe in her existence ... How inevitable, given this basic premise of her existence, that when her existence was not recognized she should be suffused with anxiety. For her, *esse* is *percipi*; to be seen, that is, not as an anonymous passer-by or casual acquaintance ... If she was seen *as* an anonymity, *as* no one who especially mattered or as a *thing*, then she *was* no one in particular (Laing 1960, pp. 59–60).

By her 'lack of ontological autonomy' or, as he more frequently says, her ontological insecurity, he means that she anxiously doubts the continuance of her existence as a sentient living person, as distinct from a merely physical object. Laing goes on:

> One cannot transpose her central problem into 'the unconscious'. If one discovers that she has an unconscious phantasy of being a prostitute, this

does not explain her anxiety about street-walking, or her preoccupation with women who fall in the street and are not helped to get on their feet again. The conscious phantasy is, on the contrary, to be explained by and understood in terms of the central issue implicating her self-being, her being-for-herself. Her fear of being alone is not a 'defence' against incestuous libidinal phantasies or masturbation. She had incestuous phantasies. *These phantasies were a defence against the dread of being alone . . . her sexual life and phantasies were efforts, not primarily to gain gratification, but to seek first ontological security* (Laing 1960, p. 60).

This postulation of the preservation, or actualisation, of self-being as the fundamental goal of all striving runs through most existentialist writings, and can be taken as a general principle of motivation in their theory, not just a symptom characteristic of schizophrenia. Persons in a reasonable state of psychological health, if one may use that term, are much more confident of their ontological security than are those with schizophrenia, but that does not mean that it is not the focus of their concern. Our interactions with other persons are sometimes experienced as contributions to, but more often as attempts to subtract from, our Being.

What is this non-being (or inauthenticity or *mauvais foi*) that we are said to fear? Of course, writers such as Laing and Sartre manage to call up for us an image or feeling of *something* that we know to be a real threat, some kind of soul-sickness against which we struggle, but always the question is whether their concepts can be rendered, not necessarily into orthodox psychological concepts, but at least into something that we can conceive of in a coherent, graspable way.

For Laing and Sartre non-being is explicitly not to be thought of as *death*, mundane death; it is, therefore, a particular condition or quality of life, and as such cannot be called non-being without doing violence to the most basic rule of logic. The expression 'non-being' literally gives us absolutely no information about what this condition may be. As one picks one's way through Sartre's clever maze of antinomies in his account of bad faith, it becomes clear that for him non-being means that one has become congealed into anything at all that ordinary language would specify as a way of *being*: that is, to accept that one *is* a waiter or a grocer or a pederast, or to claim that one is possessed by sadness or sincerity, or, in a word, to attribute to oneself *any intrinsic properties whatever*. To have such properties is the mode of being of the in-itself, whereas, as we have seen, the being of the self is essentially for-itself, which evidently quite excludes any in-itselfness --that is, excludes the self from having any intrinsic nature at all. This exclusion derives from two sources. First, there is the time-honoured (if question-begging) argument that whenever I attribute some property to myself, then since it is the *object* of my contemplation it cannot belong to the *subject* of that act of contemplation; that is, to contemplate 'my' properties paradoxically entails that they are *not* mine. Thus, Sartre says:

A person frees himself from himself by the very act by which he makes himself an object for himself. To draw up a perpetual inventory of what one is means constantly to redeny oneself and to take refuge in a sphere where one is no longer anything but a pure, free regard (Sartre 1943, 1956 edn, p. 65).

But the argument simply *assumes* that whatever is aware cannot be the object of (another) act of awareness. As I argued above, a mental act may become conscious when one is prompted to become aware of it in a second act. It is true that the first act cannot be aware of itself as it is occurring, but that does not mean that the *subject* (this person) cannot be aware of facts about himself or herself–i.e. it does not mean that he or she is purely a subject.

The second source of the denial of intrinsic properties to the self is the premise that personal existence essentially and continuously wills itself. Concerning the notion that one may be, for example, a waiter in a café, Sartre says that:

What I attempt to realize is a being-in-itself of the café waiter, as if it were not just in my power to confer their value and their urgency upon my duties and the rights of my position, as if it were not my free choice to get up each morning at five o'clock or to remain in bed, even though it meant getting fired (Sartre 1943, 1956 edn, p. 60).

One is not, then, according to this theory, a creature of a particular kind; rather, at each moment one wills, and may will not, to go on acting as if one were.

In the same way he denies the explanatory validity of the kind of motivational theory characteristic of psychoanalysis.

In introspection I try to determine exactly what I am, to make up my mind to be my true self without delay – even though it means consequently to set about searching for ways to change myself. But what does this mean if not that I am constituting myself as a thing? Shall I determine the ensemble of purposes and motivations which have pushed me to do this or that action? But this is already to postulate a causal determinism which constitutes the flow of my states of consciousness as a succession of physical states. Shall I uncover in myself 'drives', even though it be to affirm them in shame? But is this not deliberately to forget that these drives are realized *with my consent*, that they are not forces of nature but that I lend them their efficacy by a perpetually renewed decision concerning their value? (Sartre 1943, 1956 edn, p. 63).

There could hardly be a more explicit rejection of Freud's basic conception that we are 'lived by' our instincts. Freud intends us to understand that the mental apparatus is *composed of* instinctual drives, with their various *how?*

'Where id was, ego shall be'

modes of interaction, points of fixation, cathexes, and so on, and that there is not some 'I', some self, over and above the instinctual drives, which decides whether those drives will be allowed expression, or whether they will continue to exist. For Freud the question, what might this superior entity be composed of, is self-evidently unanswerable, being based on an incomprehensible conception of motivation, as we shall see in the next chapter. One might put the matter in this way, that if this supervalent 'I' makes perpetually renewed decisions concerning the value of the drives, as Sartre says (above), it must make those decisions on the basis of *its own* interests, i.e. must itself be a motive or set of motives of just the same order as those about which it is 'deciding'.

If we address the same question to Sartre, what is the composition of this entity that gives or withholds consent to the drives, he too will regard it as unanswerable, but his notion of why it is a misconceived question is just the opposite of Freud's. For Sartre the self is not an 'entity' at all, and is precisely to be thought of as not composed of anything. It is simply a principle of agency, of perpetual self-creation – but not, we notice, the *results* of that creation. The 'self' that I create is not *myself*. That would mean, as he said above, that 'I am constituting myself as a thing', which is by definition impossible, since I am a non-thing, a for-itself having no intrinsic nature. What description, then, shall we give of the self that creates? What differences can we specify between one self and another? What useful information can we give about their ways of working? The answer to all these questions, I suggest, is: nothing. To begin to answer them is to contradict the fundamental postulate of existence as freedom. The existentialist alternative to explanation by cause has, both literally and figuratively, no substance whatever.

Of course, the mind–brain identity thesis is also based on the rejection of substantive mental 'entities', but then it does not go on speaking of 'them' as if they existed and acted, as existentialism does. For central state materialism, the 'self', if the term is still to be used, is simply a biological organism that is capable of registering its own existence as a functioning physical entity amongst others. Wilkes (1980, 1981) shows persuasively how our increasing knowledge of the brain's working, and especially of the odd psychological by-products when its working fails to be completely coordinated, goes against the traditional conception of self or person as one and indivisible. To be more specific, in my view the history of a person's mental life will be the history of her or his biologically determined drives as they work towards consummation, collecting information and arguing their own justification as they do so. These drives are brain structures with ancillary sensory and motor mechanisms, as I shall argue in the following chapter. Having clarified the concept of drive, thus giving substance to the 'desire plus belief' account of goal-directed behaviour, I shall be in a position to add something further to a materialist conception of the constitution of the 'self' in my final chapter.

6
Drives and consummatory actions

The necessity of the drive concept

A large proportion of academic psychology occupies itself with what may broadly be called instrumental aspects of behaviour; that is, with the mechanisms of perception, with the development of skills, with the analysis of intellectual abilities and disabilities, and so on. All these, of course, are perfectly legitimate and important areas of study, but the question in the background is, for what are these skills employed? It may be important to understand, say, a person's mechanisms of access to his or her 'internal lexicon' while talking or listening, and why the wrong word may sometimes be selected, but one would also like to know what communication he or she is trying to make, and why? What effects are to be produced in the hearer, and to what end? The basic psychological question remains, why did this person act so? The large forms of the kinds of answer that have been offered are what I have been discussing.

Given that a science of behaviour, as with any science that deserves the name, will reject teleological explanation for the sorts of reason canvassed earlier, then the causes of behavioural events, as of any event, are to be found in the conjunction of external stimulation and the relevant internal states of the organism. As we saw, the 'internalist' approach defended by Woodfield sums up the internal states as a desire for a certain goal and the belief that a certain behaviour is likely to promote it. I have argued that, even given an unopposed desire for G, it is not self-evident that the belief 'B promotes G' should give rise to the *behaviour B*, once we reject the idea that a person simply *decides* to act on the basis of the belief. One can only posit that beliefs are state variables and modify the course of existing behaviour patterns (Ch. 4 above), which leaves open the question of where those behaviour patterns come from and what sustains them.

What of the other part of the couple, the desire for G? How does it stand as a causal state variable? Certainly, some motivating process is necessary, as well as the cognitive one, because identically the same belief 'B promotes G' could as well result in the avoidance of B as in the performance of it, if the person had turned against doing whatever action the letter G denotes.

Factual beliefs alone do not imply policy. I argued that some account of motive states needs to be given other than 'desire for G', because the latter is relationally defined and so cannot be an intrinsic state internal to the organism – the kind of causal variable we are seeking. What is needed, I contended in the Introduction, is rather the conception of driving mechanisms or 'biological engines' which could conceivably be given an intrinsic description, which is to say, the kind of thing that could conceivably be *found* as physiological entities, and whose operation would be such as to render causally understandable the form and the cyclical or periodic nature of 'goal-seeking' behaviour.

However, there is a good deal of opposition from certain psychological quarters to the concept of primary drives; not only from existentialists and their academically more orthodox cousins, purposive humanists such as Gauld and Shotter (1977) and many others, but from behaviouristically inclined determinists as well. Since I have said all I can about the deficits of purposivism, I shall leave it aside and turn to the latter.

The behaviourist opposition to the drive concept, recently expressed, for example, by Morgan (1979b), is difficult to understand. It may be historically conditioned, a remnant of the traditional S–R conviction that a theory of specific drives entails the notion of *directed* or goal-seeking energies (hunger seeks food, thirst seeks water) and so must be rejected along with all forms of purposivism. But this is a groundless suspicion; it is like rejecting the concept of car engines on the ground that they must be understood as striving to turn the crankshaft.

Again, it may be an historical preservation of the operationist conception of scientific propriety, i.e. that every theoretical term should be defined in the way a dispositional property is defined, solely in terms of input–output relations, and that it is pre-scientific to allow any notion of thinghood to linger about them (cf. Maze 1954). Morgan comments on N. E. Miller's exposition of the drive concept, and it is worth quoting this at length because it reveals the operationist mode of thought and its limitations. Miller's exposition is operationist, and Morgan criticises it as bad operationism, and neither seems to recognise that any other mode of conceptualising drives is possible.

> Miller argued that a drive could summarize economically the relationship between a number of different inputs and outputs. To quote one of his examples, an animal can be given a thirst drive by depriving it of water, giving it dry food, or by an intraperitoneal injection of hypertonic saline. The effect on its behaviour will be to make it drink more, to press a lever more vigorously for water, to reduce its food intake, or to drink water adulterated with a bitter-tasting quinine. To explain these findings without postulating a single intervening variable we should need a large number of separate causal connections, the argument runs, and the drive construct is conceptually more economical. This reasoning is unobjec-

tionable on the level of pure logic, but logic by itself cannot tell us how the world really is. It may be conceptually simpler to postulate a drive than to imagine many independent causal connections: but this does not in any way prove that there is such a *thing* as 'drive', or that there are 'drive centres' in the brain (Morgan 1979b, p. 240).

Morgan's italicisation of '*thing*' and his putting quotation marks around 'drive' shows that he is inclined to accuse Miller of hypostatisation, of reifying what are merely input–output relations into a substance, on the model of the 'dormitive virtue of opium' fallacy. But 'drive' is not etymologically or conceptually in the class of dispositional concepts such as 'solubility', for example. It is true that the input–output relations do not 'prove' the existence of a specialised structure that mediates them as a separate functional group, but if the correlations referred to by Miller should hold over a wide range, then (whether this is Miller's intention or not) there is no magical thinking in forming the provisional hypothesis that there may be such a structure, having a certain (schematic) kind of physical realisation that one would expect eventually to be *demonstrated*, a structure or mechanism that is made to work by the input conditions and which then produces some selection of the output behaviours depending on the external factors.

Morgan seems prepared to opt for 'many independent causal connections' between input and output variables (though they are *not* actually functionally independent), without being concerned about whatever internal structures mediate them. Admittedly, such a functional analytic approach is legitimate, but to denigrate the complementary structural research by suggesting that if one tries to fill in the black box one is guilty of pre-scientific thinking shows a misguided view of the scientific enterprise. Structural research has, in fact, given rise to most of the great advances in science; one thinks of the structure of molecules, the discovery of genes, the identification of viruses, and so on. Further, advocates of the 'many independent causal connections' approach – i.e. the many separate input–output relations approach – rather underestimate the number of such relations they would have to discover and list, when one thinks, for example, of the very large range of incidental environmental factors (all the input factors that could give rise to various illnesses, to think of only one possibility, remembering also that according to this conception of method we should not speak of the *illness* as an internal state variable, either) that could crop up from time to time and upset the correlations between normal inputs and the output of drinking behaviour.

Nevertheless, Morgan and his colleagues have given experimental demonstrations that do show that a certain stereotyped conception of drives and their effects on behaviour needs modification, and that stereotyped conception is one which, paradoxically enough, has been too much affected by the 'operational definition' orthodoxy. Miller's definition of thirst is typical in that it mistakenly attempts too monolithic and rigid a specification of the behaviour pattern that the postulated drive is said to energise, because operational definition demands, quite without justification, a detailed and exhaustive specification of the behavioural effects that are supposed to flow from the postulated construct. It is unjustified in that there can literally be no end to the effects, the behavioural effects, that any mechanism (whether organic or not) can have in different external situations. No material entity is to be dissolved away into a list of its causal manifestations. (This is the theme of Charles Taylor's (1964) excellent unfolding of Tolman's misguided attempt to give a behavioural definition of 'The rat expects food at location L.')

The particular factor that Morgan and others have demonstrated is the surprising degree to which, even in experimental animals such as the rat, instrumental activities such as the lever-pressing in Miller's definition can become functionally divorced from the consummatory behaviours to which they were originally instrumental. For example, Morgan *et al.* (1977) trained rats to get from a start box to a goal box through a cylindrical alley, which was obstructed by a rubber ball that the rats had to roll backwards into the start box before they could pass through. During training the rats were deprived of food and found food in the goal box. Then for the experimental procedure either they were still kept hungry but found no food in the goal box (extinction) or were thoroughly satiated with food before each 12-trial session. Performance of the instrumental ball-removal behaviour was depressed by both extinction and satiation, but not abolished, remaining at a surprisingly high level for the satiated rats, who were not eating the food they found when they did get into the goal box. Morgan (1979a) refers also to a number of studies by other experimenters to the same general effect, namely, that instrumental responses can persist when the motivating condition that originally prompted their acquisition has been removed. This seems to depend to a large extent on the specific nature of the external stimulus (CS) to which the response has been attached, on the nature of the instrumental task, or a combination of both. Morgan says that:

> ... it is the dissociations that are interesting in these experiments, whether they be between instrumental responding to different CSs or between instrumental and consummatory responses. Attention to this aspect of dissociation will help to avoid academic disputes about the real meanings of 'satiation', which is indeed revealed by the data to be not very meaningful as a unitary concept (Morgan 1979a, pp. 188–9).

However, this scepticism about the 'unitary' nature of satiation is justified only if the concept is given a reductionist behavioural definition of the general 'if–then' form: 'If the deprivation that led to the acquisition of the responses is removed, all the acquired responses will disappear.' But if by satiation one means rather that the drive-structure that originally activated the behaviours in question has been rendered quiescent, that *concept* remains perfectly coherent, and the question of why some of those behaviours still persist is an empirical one. In relation to that empirical question, all that Morgan has to offer is the concept of habit; that is, the persistent behaviours continue without the drive state because the animal has formed the habit of making them. He says:

> The idea that habit itself can be a motive has received very little attention in animal learning, despite the strong evidence for its importance in people (Allport 1937; James 1891, pp. 549–599) (Morgan 1979a, p. 187).

If habit can be a motive, then words lose their meaning. 'Habit' is a pre-digested, question-begging concept which is mainly used to *deny* that the behaviour is motivated: 'I don't mean it; it's just a habit.' Morgan's appeal to the authority of James and Allport is less than conclusive; hardly any of their evidence is more than anecdotal and, indeed, there could hardly be 'evidence for the importance of' such a concept; 'habit' is not an identifiable experimental variable, it is a *construction* placed upon what is observable. To say that behaviour that was formerly extrinsically motivated has now become merely habitual is to claim that no other extrinsic motivation has become implicated in its perpetuation. Most of Allport's (1937) 'evidence' consists of invented homely examples about, for example, the person who as a child worked at her piano playing only in order to win her parents' approval, but now that her parents are dead she goes on with the piano; or the ex-sailor who had taken up seafaring only in order to earn his living, yet still, having become wealthy, yearns to return to the sea. For this Allport prefers the term 'functional autonomy' rather than 'habit', but there is not much to choose between the two; both just assert that the instrumental behaviour has become functionally autonomous of the primary drive that originally instigated it, *and of all others*. But it is not difficult to suppose that as a person becomes more intimately acquainted with music, then it (with, say, its resolution of tensions which many hearers experience as psychological tensions) engages other, existing primary drives (rather than generates a brand new motive for itself alone); nor that the varied experiences offered by the seafaring life do the same. For laboratory animals, Liddell in a famous paper of many years ago (1944) quoted evidence suggesting that a much wider range of motives is engaged by their experimental tasks than those supposed to be aroused by the experimental reinforcements used, especially since the latter are often trivial; even 'to please their handler' seemed to be a plausible one, in Liddell's view. This may sound like hypothesis-saving on my part, i.e. 'supposing' that primary drives other than the original one may have been recruited, thus maintaining the behaviour after its original basis had been removed, but later in this chapter I shall be indicating techniques of investigation that might, if the practical difficulties could be overcome, confirm or disconfirm such a supposition.

The conception of primary drives or 'biological engines' which I am shortly going to put forward is not to be confused with the notion of disembodied forces or energies, nor is it merely an 'intervening variable' summarising relationships between input variables such as deprivation and reinforcement schedules on the one hand and output variables such as strength and frequency of correlated responses on the other. It is as literally the concept of an engine as the concept of a car engine is. The value of detailed observations such as those of Morgan is that they prompt one to recognise the great plasticity of organismic behaviour; for example, that one behaviour can be serving as a vehicle for several drives simultaneously, that one drive may have many alternative outlets, that the behaviour so driven is highly though not indefinitely modifiable by experience, and that it may often become in the practical sense *irrational* in that it persists despite lack of success because it is based on false beliefs that for some reason have become inflexible.

The need for a theory of primary drives is revealed by commonly occurring yet unspoken presuppositions about the origins of behaviour. Even the behaviourist tradition has an implicit specific primary drive concept, although it has been denying the need for one for many years. The official stance has been deliberately anti-theoretical, the merest positivism; the question, what it is to be a reinforcer, is declared not to be a proper one. In 1959 Chomsky, in his celebrated denunciation of Skinner's *Verbal behavior* (1957), had claimed that reinforcement, as Skinner uses the concept, was the slimmest verbal disguise for 'doing what one likes'. Belatedly replying, MacCorquodale (1970) declared that:

> . . . the fault, if any, is in nature, not in our theories. Reinforcers seem in fact to have only one universal property: they reinforce (MacCorquodale 1970, p. 87).

That has remained behaviourist orthodoxy even for latter-day 'stimulus–stimulus' learning theorists. Reinforcers have been assimilated to the concept of stimulus, the unconditioned stimulus, and the suggestion is that they are to be identified in a completely empirical manner, as if the experimenter applied randomly selected stimuli to the experimental subject one after the other, waiting to find one that modifies the subject's behaviour in the desired manner. But, of course, in practice they do not follow any such procedure; they proceed as if they already have a theory of primary drives and what gratifies them. Whatever positive reinforcer they have decided to use, they see that the animal is brought into the laboratory having been previously deprived of that reinforcer for a suitable period of time. The distinction regularly drawn between primary and secondary reinforcement, or first-order and second-order conditioning, implies a distinction between what is inherently motivating for the animal (a primary reinforcer), and what is motivating only because it has been identified by the animal as a stage on the path to a primary reinforcer (i.e. a secondary reinforcer). Once again, if we believe that functions depend on structures as in the case of dispositional properties, we will expect that an event can function as a primary reinforcer only because of its effect on some specific structure in the organism – not because it is 'inherently desirable' just in itself, or because the organism has a representation of it as having positive 'hedonic aspects' (Morgan 1979a, p. 197).

Turning back to the mental philosophers who speak of goals rather than reinforcers, we find that the goal concept presents a similar problem, namely, how to distinguish between subsidiary or derived goals, and the basic goals from which they derive. This, too, demands a theory of drives. Woodfield points out that the externalist or behaviour-defined theory of goal-direction calls for the concept of basic goal. The externalist, he says, claims that 'if an action-type is a goal, there must be a story tracing a connection back to a basic goal, which makes intelligible why the organism has it' (Woodfield 1976, p. 153). This seems to me quite a rational train of thought, though Woodfield sees it as a weakness; at least, he thinks his own internalist theory is free from this necessity, although as we shall see it is not. Any teleological description of behaviour explains an action by saying that it occurred in order to make something else possible, and for organisms this something else will also be an action rather than some impersonal state of affairs, as action-theorists are generally agreed. (Even if someone said 'I do *B* in order that peace may reign', one would think that his goal was to do the things made possible by peace, or to enjoy the contemplation of his fellows living in peace. Similarly, a goal cannot be just a physical object, though we often speak as if it were; one's object is not food, but in the ordinary case to eat food, and it is a point in favour of the externalist view to make this plain.) But if this further action that the first one makes possible is something quite peculiar, not in any way recognisably adapted to a useful biological function, then either it will itself in turn be subject to explanation as making possible some still further action, until this sequence arrives at one that does fit in with our conception of what it seems 'natural' to do, or else this peculiar act must simply be left to stand as the brutest of facts, not calling for further explanation – as if it were just something this individual creature happens to do, and that is all that can be said. It is obvious that the latter stand negates any possibility of generalising from one individual of the species to another, and in effect takes away all point from the question 'Why did *S* do *B*?', since it would always be as plausible to say about *B* that it was just something *S* was inclined to do, as to say it about anything that followed from *B*. So, then, there is nothing paradoxical about the externalists' feeling that they need to specify basic goals, ends-in-themselves, in order to make their sequential explanations intelligible, because without some such terminus none of the links in the chain would really increase one's understanding of the behaviour at all. But the externalist theory, restricting itself to behavioural observations, offers no possibility of finding objective criteria distinguishing end-activities from means-activities. The criteria they propose are that a basic goal-activity shall be (a) biologically useful and (b) common to the species. These have the familiar problems that, first, they include some behaviours that we would not hold to be goals, for example, dying, which is common and can be held to be biologically useful for the species, relieving it of useless mouths; and secondly, they exclude others that give the appearance of being consummatory yet whose biological usefulness is obscure, as Woodfield points out. Basically, the difficulty is in the concept of 'biologically useful' itself, which is as non-objective and value-laden as that of health. The nearest approach to objective specification of what is biologically useful has been the one Woodfield adopts, namely, those behaviours which (in normal circumstances) contribute to the survival of (a) the individual or (b) the species. But these often conflict, so that an activity might be included by one criterion and excluded by the other (the standard case being those insects whose mating means death). Further, in that *mere* survival leaves out any question of the quality of life, and allows that an organism's or species' behaviours might preserve it in a state of utter misery, it is not an account of the biologically useful that would conform to everybody's preference, so that it is only a pretence of objective, non-evaluative definition. Admittedly, any long-surviving species may be assumed to have innate behaviour-mechanisms at least some of which preserve its members from dangers and deprivations, but I concur with Woodfield that these are not coextensive with what is ordinarily understood by the concept of goal. Both introspectively and by external observation, certain behaviours *appear* consummatory, whether they consistently contribute to survival or not, but neither introspection nor external observation provides a reliable differentiation. It is quite possible in introspection to feel gratified yet to deceive oneself as to the character of the behaviour that led to the feeling, i.e. as to the true description under which it was consummatory; and as concerns the observable stream of another organism's behaviour, it simply goes on and on; whatever the organism does will have consequences, even if it is only to go to sleep, so it may actually have been those consequences, or *their* consequences, which were consummatory. Perhaps it eats only in order to sleep, or sleeps only in order to wake.

Although Woodfield's criticisms of the externalists' methodology for identifying basic goals are sound, it is another question whether his version of internalism finds a satisfactory way of avoiding the same interminable declension of subsidiary goals. All that he does, in sum, is to refuse to embark on that succession, but this avoids the need to make something intelligible of a bizarre predilection. For him, to have G as a goal is to be in the internal state of wanting to do G. In his concluding chapter he goes into a lengthy digression about why one might desire G, beginning by saying that it is 'much the same as a belief that to do G would be a good idea' (Woodfield 1976, p. 203). But after a page and a half of explaining that 'good' does not mean virtuous or intrinsically valuable, and so on, he comes full circle and says that 'All that is meant here by "S believes that G would be good to do" is that S wants to do G' (Woodfield 1976, p. 204). That is, S may want whatever he likes. The analyticity in that last sentence is quite intentional on my part, and I suspect that Woodfield's desire to avoid analyticity was the only reason for his pointless detour through the concept of seeing something as good to do. But to succeed in avoiding it, to give an intelligible explanation of why a person should have a particular goal, he too needs some account of basic desires, and therefore cannot simply refuse to pay attention to the subsidiation of wants.

Woodfield classes Anscombe with the externalists, but that seems inappropriate; she speaks in terms of internal wantings just as he does, and her connection with the externalists lies only in that she recognises the subsidiation of desires and the need for their terminating in something 'inherently desirable'. She makes it plain that she is not referring to moral desirability (Anscombe 1957, p. 75) but rather to states or activities that just as a matter of fact are desired by all human beings, or perhaps by all members of a particular class (all Nazis, in one of her better known examples). Apparently, she wants to think of these supposed facts as psychological laws, but perhaps because of the difficulty of finding anything that actually is desired by every one (or even every member of a designated class) she tends to move towards the concept of the intrinsically desirable – which is only to say that if people do not in fact desire this goal, they they *should* do so, because it is objectively 'best' for them. Because of this she does not always manage to avoid tautological definition; for example:

A collection of bits of bone three inches long, if it is a man's object, is something we want to hear the praise of before we can understand it as an object; it would be affectation to say 'One can want anything and I *happen* to want this', and in fact a collector does not talk like that; no one talks like that except in irritation and to make an end of tedious questioning. But when a man aims at health or pleasure, then the enquiry 'What's the good of it?' is not a sensible one (Anscombe 1957, p. 75).

Although one may sympathise with this attempt to save desirability explanations from triviality, nevertheless, if it is not a sensible question to ask what is the good of health or pleasure, that is only for the same reason that it is not sensible to ask why a rose is a rose. (Of course, it is also usually not sensible to *assert* that a rose is a rose.) If someone attempts to give health an objective physiological specification, then it will simply not be true that everyone wants that specific state, and it is only an unsupported moral statement (having no force as an assertion about motivation) to say that they should do so, or would do so if they knew what was good for them (cf. Maze 1973). 'Health', then, is a bodily state defined as the state one happens to want, and that is why it is not sensible to ask why one wants it. 'Pleasure', too, most commonly means only the experience of getting what one wants. Hedonistic theories may begin by speaking of pleasure as a particular state of feeling that one may desire, but since they typically want to claim that it is the *only* object of pursuit instead of one amongst many (bread, wine, pleasure, a book of verse, and so on), then in order to deal with apparent exceptions to the universal rule (such as moral or physical masochism, perhaps) they revert to the relativistic definition, saying that to this masochistic person, physical pain or self-denial is a pleasure. But then, to say that *of course* one seeks pleasure is only to say, tautologically, that of course one seeks to get what one wants. This may serve Anscombe's purpose of finding a self-explanatory premise for a practical syllogism, but as a theory of motivation it is useless.

Previously, Anscombe had said that 'No one needs to surround the pleasures of food and drink with such explanations' (Anscombe 1957, p. 75); that is, with the explanation that they derive their pleasure from something else. What would serve a theory of motivation better, as a beginning, would be to say that no one needs to surround the *pursuit* of food and drink with such explanations, nor with the useless supererogatory statement that consuming them gives pleasure. In the ordinary course of conversation, and in the ordinary course of academic psychology for that matter, when an explanatory chain arrives at 'in order to get food' people feel that no further questions need be asked. 'Why does this man work at such an unpleasant job?' 'It is the only way he can get food.' We may question whether there is nothing else he could do, but we do not ordinarily question why he wants to eat. However, that is only because the explanatory chain has arrived at one of our implicitly held list of primary drives, and not because it is in any way self-evident or beyond question that eating is a basic human activity. Further, even though it may approach universality so closely that we are prepared to say unreflectingly about each new human being that he or she will strive to eat, nevertheless it is still a legitimate scientific question to ask how that comes to be so. It is certainly not sufficient to say that people *need* to eat, that if they do not eat they will die; in the absence of the necessary food-getting machinery (or if it becomes defective) they simply will die. Some may be prepared to set aside as merely physiological the question of what that machinery may be, since we know *a priori* that if people have an eating program, then they must have eating machinery; however, although the records of child-protection societies show every year a large number of cases of cruelty by parents to their children, it would seem altogether too complacent to say in the same sense that those parents must have a child-beating drive.

Some implicit, not spelled out theory of primary drives is virtually universal, yet there is a marked failure on the part of many action-theorists to feel that it needs spelling out, or even to ask what the formal properties of a primary drive might be. The matter is sometimes consigned to the inarticulate notion 'human nature'. For example, Pettit says that when we specify the aspects under which an action appealed to the agent this

> ... is explanatory because it refers us to dispositions which we are ready to ascribe to any human being. We hold to a background model of human desire in which it is entirely unsurprising, for example, that someone should be moved by the prospect of enjoyment, monetary reward or benefit to his friends (Pettit 1979, p. 6).

In similar vein Gauld and Shotter say:

> We do not need a psychologist to tell us why a mother stops her child from running into a busy road or why the child tugs her mother to the toyshop window. Our understanding of these actions is, in a real though limited sense, complete (Gauld & Shotter 1977, p. 80).

The trouble with this attitude which finds certain actions 'entirely un-surprising' or 'completely understood' is its selectivity, its concealed moralism. The natural and unsurprising actions regularly turn out to be worthy, prosocial or conventionally pleasant ones, as in the examples above. But what of the person who is moved only to envy by the prospect of benefit to his friends, or the mother who turns a child out to run wild, or the child who tugs its mother to watch it set fire to a kitten? Are they to be dismissed as simply freaks? *Not like us* (when in fact they may well be quite like us)? Similar ways of thinking are to be found in the works of humanists like Maslow and neo-Freudians like Fromm, solemnified in textbooks of personality theory. Maslow, for example, advances this as one of the basic propositions of a self-actualisation psychology:

> A neurosis is not part of the inner core but rather a defence against it or an evasion of it, as well as a distorted expression of it (under the aegis of fear) ... If the sadist or exploiter or pervert says, 'Why shouldn't *I* express myself?' (e.g., by killing), or, 'Why shouldn't *I* actualize myself?' the answer to them is that such expression is a denial of, and not an expression of, instinctoid tendencies (or inner core) (Maslow 1962, p. 230).

Fromm, likewise, holds that there is a biological basis for the 'biophilia' or love of life which he posits by analogy with Freud's Life Instinct, but not for its opposite, 'necrophilia', which turns out to be a distorted by-product of biophilia which has been denied its natural expression.

We see that there is a widespread and understandable tendency to ground explanations of human behaviour on some half-formed conception of universal basic goals, but in the absence of any objective criteria for deciding what is basic there can only be a prejudiced and arbitrary *intuition* of what every proper human being will find intrinsically desirable. This is inescapable when the basic goals are thought of as objects of elective pursuit rather than as actions the performance of which is driven. Their basicity lies in their being *intrinsically* desirable, desirable in their own nature, but there can be no such thing, because that would mean that the relationship of *being desired* – by what? the human race? the deity? – is discoverable as one of the properties of the thing or activity itself, rather than as a relationship between it and a desirer. But as we have seen, that cannot be; nothing has its relations intrinsic to itself, and whoever claims to be able to discover them is imposing on us (cf. Maze 1973).

Another disability of the concept of basic goal is that it encourages a sliding back and forth between the concept of basic *drive* and that of basic *need*. It is possible to list basic needs in a fairly objective way, if we think of these as supplies in the absence of which the organism cannot long survive – water, various kinds of food, air, and so on. A drive, by contrast, is a mechanism that drives behaviours that may *or may not* procure some of those necessary supplies. In organisms that do tend to survive there is likely to be a large overlap between the list of needs and the list of drives, but there may well be drives, or rather innate driven behaviours, that do not procure any supplies needed for life, and yet which are engaged in just as compulsively as those which do. The concept of drive, then, must include not only that of an internal mechanism which when activated impels the organism to action, but also that of *the innately provided specific actions which it impels, and whose performance is a necessary condition of the termination of the drive state.* These driven, specific, consummatory actions are the reality underlying the conception of basic goals typical of a species. The methodological problem, however, is that we cannot proceed from a behavioural identification of consummatory behaviours to the list of driving mechanisms because, as we have seen, their consummatory nature cannot be objectively identified, and even if it could, there is certainly no necessary one-to-one relationship between drives and specific actions. To assume that there was would be to postulate as many driving forces as there are actions one chooses to regard as consummatory – a perfectly useless, non-explanatory procedure and exactly the one that has given the concept of instinctual drive such a bad name in psychology. It was because of his understanding of this methodological point that Freud posited that drives must be specified by identification of their somatic *source*, rather than by their *aim*.

A model of instinctual drives and their ancillary mechanisms

Freud's metapsychology, though unfinished, was the one great systematic attempt in modern psychology to outline a deterministic, physiologically based theory of motivation and extend it to embrace all of human behaviour, bodily and mental. The attempt to specify drives by source rather than by aim was the foundation of it, though the great technical difficulties of doing so led him occasionally to think that in practice one might provisionally put up with something less. Thus, in 'Instincts and their vicissitudes' he says:

> Although instincts are wholly determined by their origin in a somatic source, in mental life we know them only by their aims. An exact knowledge of the sources of an instinct is not invariably necessary for purposes of psychological investigation; sometimes its source may be inferred from its aim (Freud 1915, p. 123).

But in the same paper he goes on:

> What instincts should we suppose there are, and how many? There is obviously a wide opportunity here for arbitrary choice. No objection can be made to anyone's employing the concept of an instinct of play or of destruction or of gregariousness, when the subject-matter demands it and the limitations of psychological analysis allow of it. Nevertheless we should not neglect to ask ourselves whether instinctual motives like these, which are so highly specialized on the one hand, do not admit of further dissection in accordance with the *sources* of the instinct, so that only primal instincts – those which cannot be further dissected – can lay claim to importance (Freud 1915, pp. 123–4).

Identification of the source, then, is to be the final criterion of the existence of an independent instinctual drive. Even in the later stages of his thinking, after the reclassification into Life and Death instincts (Freud 1920, Wollheim 1971) which seem so obviously to be specified by aim, he did not entirely lose sight of this principle. One of his arguments for the existence of the Death instinct rests on the premise of natural death – the premise that even if no damage came to us from the external world we would eventually die – and he insists that the organism must have as part of its genetic equipment something that we might now call a self-destruct mechanism. Freud did not pretend to suggest what that might consist of, but he did at least draw an analogy with the catabolic processes intrinsic to each of the cells composing the organism.

It is, of course, virtually impossible to conceive of the Life and Death instincts as physiologically based primary drives with a deterministic mode of functioning; not only are they specified as strivings towards goals but those goals themselves, especially those of the Life instinct, are formulated so vaguely and globally that no specific consummatory action would seem adequate to them. Eros and Thanatos merely indicate in a literary, descriptive way certain large trends of human behaviour, and as motivational constructs their explanatory value is nil. Because of that, many commentators, seizing on those constructs as the final formulation of Freud's instinct theory, have declared that the instinct theory in general is a metaphysical invention with nothing to offer to science, and that the whole structure of psychoanalysis comes tumbling down with it. That is an over-simplification not to be taken seriously, since no scientific theory with empirical content, as psychoanalysis is, depends on just one conceptual linchpin, as a metaphysical system might. In any case, people's final views are not necessarily their best, and need not be taken as cancelling and devaluing all their earlier ones, as if they were a last will and testament negating all previous versions. What I am going on to contend is that Freud's ideas of specific independent instinctual drives, which permeated his thought in the years before *Beyond the pleasure principle* and are by no means entirely discarded from many of the papers that follow it, provide a thoroughly empirically scientific, testable explanation of human behaviour, and that his descriptions of them as physiological entities can readily be recast into a form consistent with the principles developed in the neurosciences of more recent times.

A typical example of Freud's thinking about the physiological bases of behaviour is to be found in his *Three essays on the theory of sexuality*. In the first edition (1905), addressing the question of the basis of sexuality, he says:

> It may be supposed that, as a result of an appropriate stimulation of erotogenic zones, or in other circumstances that are accompanied by an onset of sexual excitation, some substance that is disseminated generally throughout the organism becomes decomposed and the products of its decomposition give rise to a specific stimulus which acts on the reproductive organs or upon a spinal centre related to them (Freud 1905, p. 216 n).

In a later edition (1920) this is modified to the postulation of

> ... special chemical substances that are produced in the interstitial portion of the sex-glands; these are then taken up in the blood stream and cause particular parts of the central nervous system to be charged with sexual tension (Freud 1905, 1920 edn, p. 215).

Apart from the concept of 'tension', which will shortly occupy me in some detail, this is still perfectly respectable physiological theorising today. Freud's distinctive contribution, the recognition of oral and anal as well as phallic *aims* in sexuality, is incorporated into the model through his postulation of their sources in the primary erotogenic zones of mouth, anus, and genitals; the concept of such zones is essentially a physiological one, assuming as one possibility the presence of specialised tactile nerve endings in those areas, though remaining schematic and undemonstrated. The erotogenic zones have a dual role in that stimulation of them is one of the sources of sexual excitation, yet if that stimulation is carried beyond a certain pitch it brings about sexual gratification, i.e. the discharge of excitation. This is often pointed to as an inconsistency in Freud's theory, that the same stimulation can both generate sexual excitation and discharge it, but the sequence of events is actually more complicated than that. In the mature organism the paradigm case is that the excitation reaches a critical level at which orgasm occurs, and it is actually that which brings about its discharge. Furthermore, there is typically a change in attitude during the cycle; if it were initiated by passively received erotogenic stimulation there will come a point at which the person seeks to transform (as Freud puts it) a passive experience into an active one; that is, he or she begins to act upon some external object in such a way as to maximise the erotic stimulation of the favoured zone. If the oral zone is favoured, then the action may well be that of sucking, for instance; for other zones similarly directly stimulating actions; in general, there is a limited range of basic forms of action that provide optimal stimulation for the erotogenic zones, and these constitute the *specific actions* best adapted to the termination of the sexual tension (though in the case of this specific drive those basic actions are almost indefinitely modifiable by experience).

It is this aspect of Freud's theory of the instinctual drives, i.e. the tension reduction brought about by the performance of the specific or consummatory actions, which promises to give an objective basis for concepts like 'basic goal' or 'the inherently desirable'. After he had suspended his attempt to give a specifically physiological account of the instinctual drives, he turned to more metaphorical formulations couched in behavioural or psychological terms, and we find the image of an accumulation of tension in some notional kind of reservoir, one for each instinctual drive. The tension exerts increasing pressure on the barriers to the outlets from the reservoir, until it eventually forces its way through and rushes out of one of these outlets. The 'outlets' are the specific actions, constitutionally provided (in the form, we might now say, of 'wiring diagrams' in the motor nerve system), and effective for the discharge of a particular tension. (This, of course, is the general form of the 'hydraulic' model adopted by Woodfield for his account of how desire flows out into action (1976, p. 181), but the fluid Freud thought of was nervous energy flowing along pre-formed anatomical paths, not a disembodied goal-seeking tendency like desire.) In Freud's model, the tension drives the behaviour until the behaviour exhausts the tension, or until the level of tension in the reservoir falls so low that the restraining forces can reassert themselves.

Although the notions of tensions and of reservoir need recasting, at least we can see that this is a deterministic principle, not a teleological one. The organism does not seek tension reduction, it is caused to act by the tension. It does not stop because it has achieved its aim, but simply because the energy that was driving the behaviour has been dissipated. Such a model promises a thoroughly empirical basis for a deterministic science of human beings and their ways of working. It offers some factual content for 'human nature'. Persons can no longer be thought of either as determining their own nature and sources of pleasure, nor on the other hand as characterised only by conditionability. 'Reinforcement' would no longer be understood just as the application of some stimulus: positive reinforcement is the performance of a specific consummatory action and negative reinforcement the prevention of one. Further, as the saying has it, human nature will out, in that the instinctual drives cannot be conditioned out of existence, nor renounced, either, though some of their aims may be, at a cost.

However, Freud's hydraulic model, as well as similar ones advanced since his time by ethologists such as Tinbergen and Lorenz, has often been ridiculed on the ground, as it is sometimes expressed, that 'there are no flush toilets in the nervous system', and the question to be addressed is whether its formal aspects can be accommodated to what is known of nervous functioning.

In his one serious attempt to develop a detailed mechanistic account of the nervous processes underlying behaviour, i.e. in 'Project for a scientific psychology' composed in 1895, Freud's conception of the general nature of a drive mechanism is different from that of a reservoir of accumulated tension. In the Project the concept of instinctual drive is formulated as *stimuli* of 'endogenous origin', that is, originating in the cells of the body, and it is the continuing delivery of this stimulation or input to the central nervous system which accounts for the sustained, driven aspect of behaviour, rather than an accumulation of tension. The latter metaphorical concept appeared only after he had realised that he would not be able to make a success of his neurological model because neurology was not sufficiently advanced to fill in crucial gaps in it.

Freud, of course, was very conversant with the current neurophysiology, having commenced his professional life in that field, and he made full employment of its concepts in the Project. The continuous electrical activity endogenous to the nervous system itself was not recognised at the time, and Freud and his contemporaries thought of the nervous system as being devoid of energy until the sensory nerve endings were stimulated, giving rise to excitation or 'quantity' as he called it, and the primary function of the nervous system was thought to be to rid itself of this excitation, in the first place by 'giving it off through a connecting path to the muscular mechanisms' (Freud 1895, p. 296). The differentiation and relation between sensory nerves and motor nerves was incorporated in the notion of the reflex arc – quantity comes in at the sensory end and is passed out at the motor end. Thus, ideally, the nervous system divests itself of quantity and returns to a state of energy-less quiescence.

Freud argued, however, that as well as this primary function of discharging tension a secondary nervous function must develop in order to cope with those stimuli which 'have their origin in the cells of the body and give rise to the major needs: hunger, respiration, sexuality' (Freud 1895, p. 297). The organism cannot withdraw from endogenous stimuli as it ordinarily can from external ones (by a muscular movement). He says: 'They only cease subject to particular conditions, which must be realized in the external world' (Freud 1895, p. 297). That is, a specific action must be performed if the endogenous drive stimuli are to be terminated, and it will ordinarily be an action upon some object in the world, which must be found before the action can be performed. (The paradigm case is that eating is the specific action required to terminate hunger, and this cannot be done until food is obtained.) Work must be done in order to bring about the conditions in which a specific action will be possible, and Freud formed the view that some part of the nervous system must accumulate nervous energy (quantity) which it will employ in performing the work demanded for the cessation of instinctual stimuli. He says:

> In consequence, the nervous system is obliged to abandon its original trend to inertia ... It must put up with [maintaining] a store of $Q\overset{,}{\eta}$ [quantity] sufficient to meet the demand for a specific action (Freud 1895, p. 297).

Of course, the trend to inertia is not really abandoned; this is just an enforced detour on the path to quiescence. A part of the work required to make the specific action possible is the arresting of the onward flow of the endogenous (instinctual) stimulation towards that part of the motor system whose activation would bring about the action, since the action would be abortive if carried out in the absence of the necessary object. This is what Freud later talks about as the function of the ego in its dealings with the id, and in the Project he presents the ego as an organisation of neurones that have become differentiated in a certain manner.

> This organization is called the 'ego'. It can easily be depicted if we consider that the regularly repeated reception of endogenous $Q\eta$ in certain neurones (of the nucleus) and the facilitating effect proceeding thence will produce a group of neurones which is constantly cathected [i.e. filled with quantity] and thus corresponds to the *vehicle of the store* required by the secondary function (Freud 1895, p. 323).

This notion that individual neurones can store up excitation instead of immediately discharging it has been given great emphasis by Pribram and Gill (1976) in their work devoted to the Project, and the question of its significance will be discussed shortly, but the point I want to make here is that this store of energy, 'bound' energy, is not actually that of the instinctual drives themselves, although its accumulation is somehow the result of the endogenous drive stimuli. It is clearly the energy employed by the ego-neurones to arrest the flow of quantity in other neurones, either to prevent the premature occurrence of a specific action or to prevent an incipient 'hostile mnemic image' (the memory of a traumatic happening) from developing to the point where it would be transmitted to one of the 'key-neurones'. The 'key-neurones' lead back from the central nervous system into the body, and their activation results in an increase in instinctual stimulation and a sharp increase in unpleasure. The mechanism by which the ego-organisation does this, that is, by which it prevents certain cells from transmitting the impulse, is what Freud calls 'side-cathexis'. That is, if neurone a has synaptic connections (as they are now called) with two other neurones b and c, to either of which it could transmit its impulse, then, Freud asserts, if the cathexis (amount of excitation) in cell c is increased concurrently with the excitation in a, that will facilitate transmission at the synapse or 'contact-barrier' between a and c, thus attracting to c the energy that might otherwise have been transmitted to b. Thus, alterations of the cathexis of such strategically placed neurones can affect the direction of the flow of energy through the nervous system, preventing the occurrence of those processes which (according to memory) are followed by unpleasure. Pribram and Gill evidently regard this phenomenon of side-cathexis as being consistent with modern neurophysiological knowledge, but, be that as it may, the question is whether Freud (or anyone else so far) has managed to give a mechanistic account of the processes through which this supposed redistribution comes about *as if in order to* affect the course of excitation. In introducing the concept Freud makes this optimistic pronouncement:

It is easy now to imagine how, with the help of a mechanism which draws the ego's *attention* to the imminent fresh cathexis of the hostile mnemic image, the ego can succeed in inhibiting the passage [of quantity] from a mnemic image to a release of unpleasure by a copious side-cathexis which can be strengthened according to need (Freud 1895, p. 324).

With the best will in the world, one would have to say that this presupposes a prodigious *knowledge* in the ego of the precise layout of the nervous system, and of what was about to happen in it, and an equally unexplained ability to despatch its stored cathexis to the requisite site. Indeed, we find Freud later on in the work confessing:

How *primary defence*, non-cathexis owing to a threat of unpleasure, is to be represented mechanically – this, I confess, I am unable to say (Freud 1895, p. 370).

Pribram and Gill feel that this pessimistic passage 'must be taken with a grain of salt', but I cannot see that they show how the deficiency is to be repaired. It is the problem referred to above which plagues perceptual defence, selective attention, repression and the like, of explaining how the ego contrives not to know something when the contriving requires that it does know it, and to say what the mechanism of exclusion (as distinct from *choosing* to exclude) may be. The self-directing energies on which Freud relies here have no place in a mechanistic model.

Freud's attempt to construct a neurophysiological model for mental functioning was daring, imaginative, and requisite for a deterministic psychology. What is requisite is not in general a precise anatomical knowledge of the brain structures involved, with the specific exception that the instinctual drives cannot be identified without knowledge of their brain structures; the point is, rather, that a working model is necessarily a deterministic model and would show that the apparent purposefulness of behaviour can be explained deterministically. As Freud wrote to Fliess, about the Project, 'Everything seemed to connect up, the whole worked well together, and one had the impression that the thing was now really a machine and would soon go by itself.' To say that such a model must be possible is not to say that psychology is to be dissolved into neurophysiology. On the other hand, the *failure* of Freud's Project is not to be taken as a sign that behaviour is intrinsically and irreducibly purposive, so that the functioning of the *brain* would also have to be thought of as teleological, or not mechanistic, as suggested by Charles Taylor (1970) and Wilson (1979) – as if it were a matter of self-generating and self-distributing electrical energies, orienting themselves towards some behavioural outcome. Not even the most sophisticated cybernetic system is to be understood in that way, as we have seen, and the concept of such processes is not really intelligible

The first problem in trying to make Freud's concept of instinctual drive compatible with modern neurophysiology is to conceptualise 'instinctual tension' in neurological terms. At first, as we saw, he thought in terms of stimuli originating in the cells of the body, but then the notion gradually developed that this excitation must go somewhere, and if it could not be discharged immediately through a specific action, then it must accumulate. Is there anything in the way the nervous system functions that can accommodate that notion of a build-up of tension? Freud's own offering on this issue is at the level of the single neurone.

In an earlier paper on Freud's neuropsychology Pribram pointed out that:

Freud takes cognizance of the fact known since du Bois-Reymond's *Untersuchungen* of 1845 and Pfluger's (1859) comprehensive work on the subject, that quantity of 'electrotonic' excitation may increase or decrease in neural tissue without necessarily initiating transmitted impulses. For Freud, a neuron may 'fill' – i.e. become *cathected* – with excitation even though no transmitted activity results (Pribram 1969, p. 399).

This is elaborated by Pribram and Gill:

> In summary, quantity, Q, we believe refers to physical and chemical quantity of energy ... that $Q\dot{\eta}$ is its neuroelectric manifestation which can accrue as a *potential* within a neuron, become action currents of nerve impulses, which when they overcome the *resistances* at contacts between neurons, discharge the neuron. Contemporary neurophysiology could find little to fault in this outline of nervous system function. Thus the *Project* contains exactly what the critics of the current melange of psychoanalytic dogma are seeking . . . : a biological (physical) definition of the energy concept which can be 'meaningfully linked to modern neurophysiology' (Pribram & Gill 1976, p. 34).

I cite this not because it offers an adequate basis for Freud's thoughts about the accumulation of instinctual tension, but only in order to answer the implications some critics have drawn from the 'all or none' law of the propagation of action potentials in individual nerve cells. As Grossman summarises it, this law states that 'once a neuron has been stimulated to the point where a travelling disturbance is created, the size of this response and the speed of its conduction are independent of the intensity of the stimulation' (Grossman 1973, p. 21). A wave of depolarisation runs along the membrane of the entire cell and when this has been completed, and the very brief refractory and after-potential phases have passed, the cell returns to its normal resting state of polarisation. Consequently, it has been argued, Freud's notion of the accumulation of instinctual tension does not fit the facts of nervous functioning. But it now appears that a neurone *can* accumulate tension or electrotonic potential, lowering its threshold of stimulation, until a further discharge occurs (though not affecting the size of this discharge). As we have seen, Freud looked to this phenomenon as lending some credence to his proposal that the *ego*-cells must maintain a store of excitation to be used in establishing side-cathexes to control instinctual stimulation, but perhaps it could also be related to the notion that instinctual stimulation builds up into a persisting quantity of tension. Certainly, Pribram and Gill lay great stress on its explanatory value.

However, the conception of a certain number of individual cells accumulating energy through alteration in the permeability of their membranes is hardly flexible enough for Freud's requirements when, for example, he talks of instinctual energy being diverted from one avenue of gratification into an alternate one. Consider this passage, drawn from a much later work, but representative of many earlier ones:

> It even seems that the energy of these instinctual impulses is in a state different from that in the other regions of the mind, far more mobile and capable of discharge; otherwise the displacements and condensations would not occur which are characteristic of the id (Freud 1933, pp. 74–5).

The approach at the single neurone level is not appropriate. Some way of understanding the equipotentiality of function of much larger masses or organisations of cells is required. In any case, an important point in considering the notion of an accumulation of tension is that in all the larger structures of the brain there is continual electrochemical activity of one kind or another. Since they are always active, the conception of a greater or smaller *store* of nervous tension does not seem applicable.

However, all that is required to accommodate 'tension reduction' to the facts of nervous functioning (so far as they are known) is to translate 'more' and 'less' tension into 'different kinds', i.e. different patterns and frequencies of evoked potential in the structures of the brain. The state of 'tension' would be represented by one pattern and that of 'quiescence' by another. As a first approximation, let us call these hypothesised distinguishable patterns the drive–excitation and drive–satiation patterns respectively (remembering always that there are several drives, each having a different characteristic brain state). Further, let us suppose (with a proviso about the meaning of 'centre' which I shall shortly spell out) that there is a particular type of brain structure that functions as a *drive centre* for each drive. Then we can think that a period of deprivation of the appropriate supplies, combined probably with appropriate external stimulation, will result in an input to the drive centre causing the drive–excitation pattern to develop, displacing that of the previously prevailing drive–satiation. This, in turn, will stimulate a particular high-level motor nerve channel and give rise to characteristic types of behaviour, the specific actions, which if successful bring about (in a way yet to be specified) the cessation of the drive–excitation pattern and the re-establishment of that of drive–satiation, with the consequent termination of that particular motor output.

In this way the deterministic aspect of Freud's principle of 'tension-reduction' can be retained. Instead of an accumulation of energy, one would think, as he did originally, of a continuing input of some specific type of nervous impulse, together in the case of some drives with specific biochemical factors, to the brainstem structure of which the instinctual drive mechanism basically consists. Rather than the consummatory action using up an accumulated store of tension, it would (through some feedback loop) terminate the input to the drive mechanism. In order that the consummatory action should not run off abortively in the absence of the necessary object, the output of the brainstem structure into the motor nerve system would have to be modified by those ongoing processes in the cerebral cortex that mediate the organism's cognitions about the environmental situation; that is, its perceptions of what is present and its beliefs about the effects of possible actions. In these ways the model incorporates the motivational and cognitive aspects of the 'desire plus belief' account of so-called teleological behaviour. The details of the mechanism by which the perceptual processes modify the motor processes are as yet unknown, but at least it is well attested that there is a constant interchange of stimulation between the brainstem and the perceptual structures. I said above that the innate, specific consummatory actions are the reality underlying the 'basic goals' of conventional purposivist theories; they are, of course, not *sought*, one is driven to perform them. Just to emphasise that point, the import of this version of instinctual drive theory is that *everything one does throughout one's life, however obviously acquired, sophisticated or culture-bound it is, is some modified form or instrumental elaboration of one of the innate consummatory actions.* To put it more radically still, nothing is ever done but a consummatory action in some guise. This basic nature of learned behaviours is often heavily disguised by many layers of increasingly refined rationalisations, as I shall try to show in my final chapter, but the more one subjects such rationalisations to dispassionate logical scrutiny, the more the shape of the basic consummatory action underlying the surface behaviour reveals itself.

The 'proviso' mentioned a moment ago in connection with the term 'drive centre' is necessitated by recent research on the central mechanisms controlling eating, which calls for some modification of the long-held theory of dual mechanisms in the hypothalamus, put forward by Stellar in the 1950s (e.g. Stellar 1954). The basic phenomena are that lesions of the lateral hypothalamus cause indefinitely prolonged anorexia, whereas lesions in the ventromedial region of the hypothalamus cause hyperphagia; by and large these observations are not in dispute. This gave rise to the conceptualisation that there are two separate centres, one responsible for the initiation and one for the termination of eating. However, more precisely controlled studies of the sites of lesions, and studies employing chemical agents, neurotransmitters, and so on, administered through permanently implanted cannulas in the nervous system, have shown that the controlling mechanisms are not restricted to groups of cells in the hypothalamus, but include, for example, dopamine pathways that join the hypothalamus to other bodies, and also involve extremely complex biochemical processes affecting the functioning of nerve pathways. Consequently, some researchers have argued that the concept of 'centres' is too restricted and should be discarded (cf. Blundell & Latham 1979).

However, it is not disputed that there are systems, however complex and anatomically diffuse they may be, sensitive to the internal environment, and controlling the onset and offset of eating behaviour. That is all that is intended here by the use of the term 'centre', and in fact all that is intended by the concept of instinctual drive, or the expression 'biological engine' which I have occasionally used. After all, a car engine is complex enough; it includes not only the pistons going up and down in the cylinders but the mechanism (carburettor) that brings the chemical supplies, electrical pathways that join it to the battery and to the ignition lock on the dashboard, and so on. Any tampering with any of these can profoundly affect the on–off characteristics of the engine. But that does not show that there is anything wrong with the concept of the car engine. To call something an engine does not imply that it has some superior sort of causality, or that it is a *source* of driving energy. An engine is simply an entity that converts one kind of energy into another and applies it to a particular use. The output of most of the things we call engines is mechanical energy, and since it is more easily observable than the potential energy in whatever the input is, the illusion is created that the engine creates power within itself. But that cannot be, and is not implied by the account I have given of instinctual drives as engines. They are mechanisms that are caused to work by sensory and biochemical input, and, through their innate structure, give rise to specific bodily behaviours which as a matter of evolutionary fact are likely to terminate the input, which is all that 'consummatory' means. The output of the drive is maintained only as long as the input continues, allowing that there may be a separate satiation mechanism which switches off the excitation mechanism before any relevant biochemical condition has actually been reversed. The drives neither store nor create energy. The knowledge of how many such engines there are and what activities each produces would obviously be extremely valuable to the psychologist, just as it is valuable to the automotive engineer to know that the engine that drives the car forward also drives it in reverse, or whether the motor that opens and closes the windows is the same one that retracts the aerial, or provides the power-assistance for the power-assisted steering.

For simplicity's sake I shall assume that for each drive there is an excitation centre and a satiation centre. The excitation centre becomes 'on' as a consequence of deprivation or noxious stimulation or some sensory process; this 'on' condition is maintained by the continued input of the stimulation; consequently, it initiates and keeps on driving some more or less developed form of an innately given behaviour which, in an evolution-shaped organism, can be expected eventually to give rise to a sequence of events that will turn the satiation centre to 'on', and this will somehow disconnect the excitation centre from the motor channel. As a result, the behaviour stops.

But even if one accepts that such drive structures exist, the problems in determining how many of them there are, and what kinds of behaviour each one drives, are still formidable.

Psychological needs and physiological needs

As a beginning one may distinguish between those putative drives which may be related to physiological needs and those which may be related to psychological needs. (Of course, there may well be drives that do not function to meet anything that could seriously be called a need; and there are needs, such as that for some of the B vitamins, that do not seem to be served by any specific drive, but this division between types of need is a first step to identifying the methodological problems. The only reason for introducing the concept of need at all is that if we found that the members of a given species showed every sign of being driven to find and consume some perfectly non-nutritious, inert substance that passed through their bodies without altering their biochemical or other condition in any way, we would be inclined to feel it was implausible, we had missed something, some by-product distantly related to a survival mechanism; but it need not be so.)

Physiological needs are ordinarily thought of as needs for physical supplies or conditions that in a direct material way make adequate physiological functioning possible. The most obvious case is the literal taking in of physical substances into the body (food, air, water) or the expelling of others from it. In so far as sex is a physiological need, then it might be thought of as a need for the physiological event of detumescence, let us say. But *psychological* needs – the proposed needs for love, esteem, aesthetic enjoyment, and so on – are to be distinguished from these by the fact that there is no tangible material substance to be taken in or expelled. They are needs for psychological events, not physiological ones; essentially, for particular types of cognition, such as 'someone cares for me', and perhaps for the consequent emotional state.

The possibility of identifying drives related to the physiological needs seems more straightforward than for those related to psychological ones, for the specific reason that there are gross biochemical factors related to the former and not to the latter. A drive structure is a physiological structure, and the events that activate the excitation centre and the satiation centre must be physiological ones, whatever their more remote causes may be. For those drives whose consummatory actions bring about the ingestion of needed physical substances or the excretion of toxic ones, and the like, the excitatory event will typically involve the build-up of some biochemical condition resulting from physiological processes that have been going on since the last occasion of the consummatory action (for example, the blood changes resulting from the using up of nutrients). A great deal of information has accumulated by now about the steady states whose maintenance is necessary for adequate physiological functioning, and about the processes that tend to disrupt them and those which tend to restore them. Many of these biochemical states are capable of direct physical measurement, and when it can be shown that a deviation in one of them regularly sets in train a behavioural sequence that tends to result in that deviation being reversed, and as more is learned of the specific physiological links that lead from the excitatory state to the satiation state, then the more confidence can be felt that an independent primary drive has been demonstrated.

But in the case of the supposed psychological needs, if the exciting event is the deprivation of a cognitive state and the satiating event is the supplying of it, then the physiological substrates of these, necessary for activating the excitation and satiation nerve centres, will (one may assume) be specific patterns of nerve impulses occurring in the cerebral cortex, and the technical difficulties of identifying such patterns and relating them to the types of cognitive event in question would be immense.

In an earlier chapter I disputed the quite gratuitous assumption that the brain state that underlies the cognition of an external state of affairs is in some sense a miniature copy of that external state. Its relationship of representing is not intrinsic to its structure; and consequently, to discover the specific relationships between brain states or events and their cognitive referents would be a matter of the most piecemeal fact collecting. Considering, for example, the enormous multiplicity of individual objects that any person is acquainted with, the possibility of discovering a code that, when cracked, would short-circuit the task of deciphering the brain traces relevant to them, seems remote. Suppose that we had the services of a technologically perfect telemetric brain scanner that displayed on vast screens an ongoing record of all the action potentials occurring in a subject's central nervous system. Our subject says to us, 'I just one moment ago got the conviction that someone cares for me.' Which segment of the enormously intricate pattern of nerve impulses occurring in the brain at that time shall we guess to be related to that thought? How many repetitions will it take to establish the connection? Furthermore, we must not forget that the subject can tell us only about his or her conscious thoughts. If we must wait on some psychological interpretive technique to disclose the unconscious thoughts as well, the task becomes one of truly forbidding magnitude. (The virtually insurmountable technical difficulties of establishing such brain state to mental event correlations are brought out by Wilkes 1980.)

But let us provisionally allow that it would be possible over a period of time to collect a respectable number of such relationships between mental events and brain events, so that we would be in a position to test one of the hypotheses about psychological drives – for example, that there is an independent affection-getting drive, satiated by the belief that someone cares for one. By now it would be child's play to discover the connection between the 'somebody cares for me' event in the cerebral cortex and the consequent impulses that it sent along the nerve tracts to the postulated affection-satiation centre in the brainstem. If its arrival there caused the overt affection-getting behaviour to cease, we should feel more confident about the ontological status of the proposed affection drive; that is, if we could be sure we had not merely identified a conscious affectionate thought that concealed an unconscious hostile one, and if we could be sure that this 'satiation centre' were not just an adjunct of the basic sexual drive, or of the food-getting or temperature-control drives which a cynical person might think were the basis for an infant's developing a 'need for affection'.

But if we are to have anything like an objectively based list of 'psychological' drives, the foregoing is not just an unnecessary science fiction romance. It may seem that a type of research that has been ongoing for some years, using implanted electrodes to stimulate sites in the brainstem and so elicit particular behaviours will prove adequate to demonstrate the existence of drives of this kind, but in fact although this kind of research appears to have its basis in hard physiological data, it actually suffers exactly the same disability as the 'externalist' attempt to identify basic goals by observations of overt behaviour. Consider the following contrast between assumptions about basic and derived psychological drives, and how the issue might be tested.

Earlier, I briefly mentioned Fromm's assertion that 'man is biologically endowed with the capacity for biophilia, but psychologically he has the potential for necrophilia as an alternative solution' (Fromm 1974, p. 366). I take the first part of that to imply that there is an instinctual drive structure that when activated gives rise to affectionate, helping behaviour. Of course, Fromm is aware that there is a difference between giving and seeking affection; however, the two processes are complexly interrelated in life, and he often speaks of both of them as manifestations of biophilia, so for simplicity I shall just deal with the affection-getting aspect of biophilia. Necrophilia, on the other hand, is evidently not the function of a separate instinctual drive structure, in Fromm's view, but is rather a by-product, an 'alternative solution' as he says, of the long-term frustration of biophilia. There is a paradoxical reversal in the type of behaviour but the somatic source is that which normally gives rise to biophilic behaviour. It is as if the frustrated person gives expression to his rage and despair in the hope that the victim will recognise his need for love and take pity on him. This benign view of basic human nature is typical of the humanist approach, as typified also in Maslow's assertion (quoted earlier) that murderous and exploitive impulses are not part of the true 'inner core' of personality. It may be contrasted with the conception of motivation to be found in Nietzsche, or in Adler's early work, which postulates a will-to-power as the basic monistic motivating force, all other seemingly independent demands being merely instrumental to it, roundabout ways of gratifying the will-to-power. Let us reinterpret will-to-power as an independent drive of aggression. From the Adler-type view the direction of explanation is the reverse of that postulated by Fromm. One would try to win another person's affection only in order to gain power over that person, not because one wanted affection at all.

How could such a dispute be resolved? As I have argued before, there are no purely behavioural criteria to distinguish between 'instrumental values' and 'terminal values'. The issue as to the independent existence of the 'aggression drive' as against the 'affection drive' or vice versa could only be decided by identifying the physiological drive structure whose excitation produced each type of behaviour. Are there two drives as physiologically defined or only one? And if the latter, which?

Because of demonstrations using implanted microelectrodes, many physiological psychologists now accept that in some species of vertebrate there is a certain part of the brainstem that when stimulated in this way gives rise to a marked increase in aggressive behaviour, and that there is another part whose stimulation markedly inhibits aggressive behaviour. These tend to be thought of as an excitation centre and a satiation centre for aggressive *drive*. Certainly Delgado (1967), one of the leading researchers in this field, insists that a drive-like state can be initiated in monkeys, showing directedness and perseveration, as distinct from the elicitation of merely stereotyped and undirected motor patterns, or 'sham rage'. To define them as aggression centres is to claim that they establish aggression as an independent primary drive, thus refuting at least half of the Fromm-type position, in that he says we have no biological endowment for necrophilia (assuming that similar results could be produced in human beings). If we accepted it as a physiologically established fact that aggressive drive exists, then we could at least in principle test the other half of the Adler-type theory, that 'affectionate' behaviour is a by-product of aggression. If the aggression centre could be continuously monitored rather than just artificially stimulated, and if we found that whenever affection-getting behaviour occurred, the *aggression*-excitation centre was operating, and that the aggression-satiation centre was activated when affection was received, that would strongly confirm the Adler view, that affectionate behaviour (in its affection-eliciting aspect) is in some sense *spurious*, and is just a technique of aggressive dominance. (Of course, if that were universally so, not just in the occasional deceptive person, it would be hard to understand how the concept of 'affectionate behaviour' ever arose. There could hardly be spurious affectionate behaviour if there were none of the other kind, but I suspend that consideration for the sake of the discussion of method.)

But the discrediting of the affection drive depends on the prior identification of the aggression drive, and that is not nearly as unequivocal as the stimulation studies suggest. There are no grounds other than the observation of the overt behaviour for calling these excitation and satiation centres *aggression* centres rather than centres for affection or almost anything else, and the behavioural observations can be interpreted in a number of ways. A site in the brainstem is electrically stimulated and the animal shows aggressive behaviour. But who is to say that the stimulated site is not actually an *affection* drive excitatory centre, and the animal has been artificially thrown into such an extreme pitch of affection-deprivation that its behaviour has taken the perverse path described by Fromm – has turned into necrophilia?

Consider a striking demonstration by Delgado of the inhibition of overtly aggressive behaviour. He took some bulls of the strain bred in Mexico, the so-called 'brave bulls'. He describes them as having been selectively bred for 'ferocity', and says that 'the sight of a person, which is neutral for a tame bull, will trigger a deadly attack in a brave one' (Delgado 1969, p. 168). Consequently, he did not need artificially to stimulate aggressive behaviour, but he did prepare them with implanted microelectrodes in what he labelled the 'aggression inhibition centre'. These electrodes were activated by remote control through a small radio receiver fastened to the bull's skull (Delgado's own special contribution to technique). Delgado demonstrated his confidence in their efficacy by provoking the bull to charge him and then activating the inhibition centre when the bull was only a few feet away, upon which it would stop its charge and turn aside as though it had lost interest.

But despite his ability to manipulate the animal's behaviour, Delgado's identification of the stimulated site as an aggression-inhibition centre is less than absolutely compelling. It is possible to put forward an alternative interpretation which, though it may seem fanciful and less plausible than Delgado's, cannot be ruled out by the behavioural observations. Suppose that the strain of 'brave bulls' had unwittingly been selected, through the generations, for what was only a spurious ferocity and was actually an intense need for affection, so intense indeed that it could never be gratified in the ordinary circumstances of life, especially if each generation of parents had become so embittered by their ungratified need for affection that they had none to give their offspring. In such creatures the affection-drive could readily take Fromm's perverse path, so that it would be continually expressed in destructive behaviour. In that case the inhibition centre which stops the bull charging could be read as a satiation centre for the affection-drive, so that its activation through electrical stimulation causes the bull no longer to employ the perverse aggressive mode of expression. If the reader finds this reinterpretation (prompted by the opposition between the Fromm-type and the Adler-type theories of motivation) too frivolous, it would be quite easy to work up a more respectable one on the lines of Tinbergen's model, which represents aggression, in some species at least, as an instrumental component of the reproductive drive, defending territory against intruders, rather than as a separate drive in its own right. Plainly, the observation of just one mode of behaviour, taken in isolation from larger patterns of the animal's interactions with its own and other species, is insufficient to determine the nature of the drive involved (and may be insufficient in any case), no matter how closely correlated it is with the activation of particular bits of the nervous system.

One other conceivable way of getting independent information to help in characterising the stimulated structure would be to ask human subjects prepared in a similar manner how they *felt* when the artificial stimulation was applied. However, in the scattered reports of such investigations the outcome is equivocal. Delgado refers to a report by King (1961) of a female patient with an electrode implanted in the amygdala, who when a charge of 5 mA was delivered through this electrode, was made to act in an angry and agitated manner, verbalising her wish to control these aggressive feelings, and actually deflecting them into ripping up a sheaf of paper offered her by the interviewer. However, when the stimulation was reduced from 5 to 4 mA, which of course is still a positive stimulation of the same location (though it may spread less widely), the patient was reported as immediately changing her expression to a wide smile and a laugh, and as talking to the interviewer in a positively friendly and conciliatory fashion, endeavouring to explain away the previous aggressiveness (King 1961, p. 485). She had felt the surge of aggressiveness to be alien to her, even while she was experiencing it, but the later friendliness under stimulation in turn contrasted with her everyday pre-stimulation manner, which was withdrawn and flat in tone. How would one decide to name a structure that produced such markedly different types of behaviour, depending on the intensity of stimulation?

If one had always to rely (as is at present the case) solely on equivocal overt behaviour and verbalisations in trying to determine the character of the controlling nerve centres, or of the drive, then it would be difficult to resist the feeling that the question of what psychological drive was operating is a quite empty one, a mere verbal one. If the same biological engine can drive both 'aggressive' and 'affectionate' behaviour, what difference would it make if we call it the affection or the aggression engine? The words begin to lose their meaning. It seems senseless to argue either way, that the one strand of behaviour expresses what is 'real' in human nature and that the other is a 'spurious' or distorted derivative of it. But the trouble is that *the drive in question is not actually being specified through the identification of its somatic source*. That it has been so specified is a misleading impression deriving from the fact that the electrodes (in the bulls, for example) are implanted in a mappable part of the brainstem and that stimulation of it regularly gives rise to a certain kind of observable behaviour. But that is insufficient. The fully developed concept of somatic source includes not only the anatomical location of 'off' and 'on' centres for the behaviour, but also the specific physiological character of the excitation process and of the satiation process. As I have tried to show, it is at present impossible to identify these physiological events for the 'psychological' drives whose excitation and satiation events are cognitive happenings.

But in the case of the physiological drives, i.e. drives whose functioning is related to the maintenance of specific physiological states (though that is just their *effect*, not their *goal*), both the activating and satiating processes are much more readily identifiable because they consist predominantly of biochemical changes susceptible of direct physical measurement, as I said before. If the excitation event is a departure from some norm due to the combustion of nutrients, or the production of toxins, or an increase in the concentration of sex hormones, say, then the satiation event will ordinarily be the reversal of that condition and return to a neutral resting state, though there may also be intermediary events in the satiating process that interrupt the circuit and suspend the behaviour before the biochemical reversal, which may take some considerable time, has run its course. For example, in the case of the food-hungers, it is found that eating terminates (in mammals) many minutes before the food can have been digested to the stage at which the excitatory biochemical condition can have been reversed. The mechanism of this termination is not fully known, but it is believed that the ingestion of food causes the secretion of some chemical substance in the gastrointestinal tract, the effects of which are transmitted directly to the satiation centre without having to wait on the processes of digestion and absorption. Further complications have been revealed by the classic sham-feeding experiments in which dogs are prepared with oeso-phageal fistulas, so that food which they chew and swallow falls out of a chest opening, and the stomach can be directly loaded with nutritious or non-nutritious substances by the experimenter (e.g. Miller & Kessen 1952). If the stomach is loaded with non-nutritious substances while the dog is 'eating', the eating will terminate after about the duration expected for the deprivation period, but the satiating effect is soon suppressed and the animal resumes eating much earlier than in normal circumstances. On the other hand, merely loading the stomach with nutrients without giving the dog a chance to go through its eating and swallowing takes a markedly long time to obviate eating when the dog is given an opportunity to eat. This suggests that the motor process of eating is part of the normal consum-matory pattern, not just getting the stomach loaded, though of course some kind of acquired habituation or expectancy factor cannot be excluded.

There are even larger gaps still remaining in the knowledge of the hormonal factors in the excitation and satiation of sexuality. As far as excitation is concerned, it appears from experimental studies using non-human mammals that in the normal male testosterone plays a significant role (though not a sole one), as does oestrogen in the female. For human beings, testosterone apparently plays a similar role for men, but in women the ovaries and their products seem not to be essential for any major aspect of sexual behaviour (Davidson 1972), and very little is yet clear about its biochemical basis. With regard to the satiating factors, most researchers seem by default to have retained the Freudian notion that the behaviour terminates because it has exhausted the nervous tension in question, because there has been virtually no research into positive terminating factors; however, since we have abandoned the possibility of a store of tension, something else must be the case. One must ask, how in fact is the level of testosterone or oestrogen (where they are relevant to the excitation) decreased *as a result of* the sexual behaviour, or alternatively, how is their action on the hypothalamus (for so it seems) opposed? One possible assumption is that the sexual behaviour releases some further hormone which activates a satiation centre, thus inhibiting the excitation centre. That possibility is sketched in by Davidson:

> Situations are now coming to light in which behavioral stimuli precipitate changes in endocrine function as well as other physiological or behavioral events . . .

First, behavioral stimuli originating in individual A may affect hormone secretion in the same individual. Second, stimuli emanating from individual A may affect endocrine function in individual B. In either case the changed level of hormones can affect further behavioral events in either individual A or B . . .

The fact that ovulation in a number of species . . . occurs as a result of sexual stimuli – usually copulation itself – is well known. Stimuli derived from the act of mating activate a neuroendocrine reflex resulting in the release of pituitary LH [the luteinising hormone] leading to ovulation . . .

Interestingly enough, it has been reported that LH is released following coitus in male rats . . . (Davidson 1972, pp. 76–7).

Such secretions consequent on sexual behaviour are the kind of thing that might function in satiation. I am not for a moment presuming to suggest that the luteinising hormone is the one that closes the loop and terminates the behavioural cycle, whether in rats or in any other species. But something must do so – it is not enough to say that the organism stops because it has *achieved its goal* – and if it is something of a biochemical nature, then its identification, and the discovery of the mechanism of its action on the satiation centre in the hypothalamus, would seem to be in principle well within the scope of present-day biochemical and neurological techniques.

If such knowledge were available, along with techniques for monitoring the physiological processes involved, its explanatory value for resolving the true nature of particular behaviours would be great. For example, it would make it possible to test the psychoanalytic claim that eating can become eroticised, i.e. that in such a case the person's eating does not express food-hunger but rather frustrated sexuality. Such a person would presumably be in the position of Davidson's individual *A* (above) in that his or her own behaviour-induced stimuli affected his or her own hormone secretions in such a way as to produce sexual satiation (to some degree). If the eating began in a condition of hunger satiation as physiologically defined, and in connection with high levels of testosterone or progesterone or whatever the relevant biochemical factor in sexual excitation is eventually determined to be, and if it terminated not because of the hunger-satiation centre being turned to 'on' (since it would have been 'on', i.e. in the condition of satiation, from the beginning of the sequence, given that it is a case of overeating) but because of the *sex*-satiation centre being turned to 'on' (as revealed by the monitoring device), then that would provide the scientific test, and the actual empirical content, of the assertion that what the person was 'really seeking' through excessive eating was sexual gratification. The notion of what one is really seeking is (here and everywhere) to be recast into that of what one is really *doing*; that is, what consummatory behaviour one is engaged in.

This physiological program for the analysis of 'wants' and 'needs' is not to be thought of as a physiological *reductionism*, as if it heralded a psychology in which mentalistic terms were to disappear altogether, and the events intermediate between stimulation and behaviour were to be described in solely physiological terms. It is only in the case of discovering and listing the instinctual drives that psychology needs to turn to physiology to solve its distinctive problems, and that is because, as I have been arguing throughout this chapter, the drives can be identified only by discovering their sources and cannot be 'inferred' by studying their aims, i.e. just by observing behaviour, since the latter procedure leads to the unrestricted postulation of pseudo-explanatory constructs.

The structural bases of drives can be found only in physiological entities, not in mental ones, because as I have argued in earlier chapters, there are none of the latter to be found. 'Purposes', 'intentions', and 'desires' have traditionally been postulated as the mental structures that give rise to behaviour, but they cannot be purified of their essentially relational nature, or credited with any believable intrinsic mental properties. Mentality consists not of structures but of relations (perceiving, believing, remembering, recognising implications) into which certain brain structures enter. In 'Instincts and their vicissitudes' Freud said, speaking of the instincts, that 'in mental life we know them only by their aims' (Freud 1915, p. 123); that is, by self-observation we may become aware that we are continually thinking about a certain situation and how it might be brought about, may become aware that we are actually engaged in bringing it about, and so on, but the structural *sources* cannot appear in mental life because they are brain processes, and as I have pointed out we cannot be directly acquainted with our own brain processes, having no sense organs adequate for that function.

If mental processes are relations into which brain processes enter, as central state materialism proposes, then on the instinctual drive theory it is specifically the drive structures which, through their connections with the perceptual system, enter into those cognitive relations. Freud's theory, if his mentalistic terminology were purified, would reveal itself as a psychologically more detailed version of the mind–brain identity theory. Each instinctual drive accumulates information and misinformation about the location and means of acquisition of the objects necessary for its specific actions to be performed. It is only from a pluralistic view of this sort that one can begin to make sense of the facts of internal conflict and of repression, of the situation in which one part of the psychological apparatus knows something that another part does not know. Also, it makes possible an understanding of the fact that cognitive processes are always motivated, never perfectly disinterested and rational, even when they are clinging to the reality principle because of its generalised practical utility. These matters will be discussed further in my final chapter.

But, obviously, to say that the drive structures are physiological and not mental entities is not to say that mental processes are irrelevant to the determination of behaviour, as I tried to show, for example, in connection with the development of the basic eating program, and as will be shown in connection with higher fields of endeavour. Once physiology has provided a list of the primary drives and an indication of the basic forms of the consummatory actions necessary for their satiation, then psychology will have a framework within which, with some limitations and precautions, the language of desires and strivings will be meaningful and informative. A good deal of clinical and social psychology, as well as everyday talk about people's doings, has always treated that language as informative, but as we have seen its explanatory value rests on an implicit theory of primary drives which is conceptually ill founded and adopted by consensus rather than based on empirical tests. Without the physiological basis sketched in this chapter, explanations by basic desires (cf. Anscombe), if subjected to the smallest critical scrutiny, simply collapse and can be seen to have no real explanatory value at all. But when we have that list of drives and consummatory actions, then we will have a framework within which to approach the question 'Why did he do that?', and we will not actually need an all-seeing telemetric brain monitor trained on our subject, to reveal which of his excitation and satiation centres are operating, in order to answer it. We will still be able to employ such real-life procedures as asking the person, and perhaps witnesses who knew him or her well, how he or she conceived the nature of the action and what might come from it; be able, that is, to revert to the language of wants and intentions while being as unsentimental and realistic about it as we can, provided only that our explanatory chain reveals the behaviour as related to one of the established consummatory actions of one of the accredited instinctual drives. It would be that consummatory action, then, which we would say that the person was trying to do, in doing the action for which we were seeking an explanation. I repeat that, in a sense, everything that an organism can be said to be doing throughout its entire life will be one of these consummatory acts, if we understand such an act in the experienced organism as including the instrumental techniques that have become incorporated into it. In that case the list of drives and consummations would provide a comprehensive framework for the entire science of behaviour.

7
Higher activities and their basic meanings

Basic actions

It remains only to offer an impression of how a cognitive-determinist, instinctual drive-based psychology can accommodate a range of distinctively human behaviours that are often put forward as being *by definition* incapable of subsumption under 'materialistic' motives or explanation by mechanistic principles. These are predominantly aesthetic and ethical pursuits and cognate activities such as scientific enquiry, the betterment of society, the pursuit of liberty, and so on. To say that a person's interest in something is purely aesthetic is expressly to say that he is not using it to gratify any interest other than the aesthetic; similarly, ethical acts most positively cannot be done for any extrinsic gain – virtue is of necessity its own reward. It will not be possible for me to fill in the links between behaviours categorised in these ways and the consummatory acts of physiologically defined drives in sufficient detail to confute any possible scepticism, but enough can be said to show that some more substantial objection is required than the rhetorical question 'How can a deterministic psychology account for these activities?'

One way in which a deterministic psychology will *not* attempt to incorporate aesthetic and ethical behaviour is by postulating an 'aesthetic drive' and an 'ethical drive'. Such constructs face all the disabilities of drives specified solely by their aims to which I have referred before. To try to convert their satiating events into the neurological processes underlying the beliefs 'I have done something aesthetically good' and 'I have done something ethically good' is only a verbal pretence of converting them into drives specified by somatic source, in view of the present technical impossibility of identifying such neurological processes. On such a basis one could postulate a drive to do every kind of action that an organism could think of itself as doing, but such a theory of 'motivation' would be vacuous beyond reclaim. It is only in the case of <u>drives with measurable biochemical events as their exciting and satiating conditions</u> that one can feel any confidence in their reality as physiological mechanisms driving behaviour. Even of those there are as yet none of which it can be said that all the physiological links from excitation through behaviour to satiation have been filled in. However, enough is known to allow the compilation of a provisional short list of drives with a reasonably well attested physiological basis including some knowledge of the innately determined consummatory behaviours necessary for their satiation, none of these being especially surprising. The list would consist of sexuality, its basic consummatory actions being those which physically stimulate the primary erotogenic zones; hunger (or several specific hungers), with its consummatory action being to eat specifiable kinds of substance; thirst, satiated by drinking; the respiratory drive; pain avoidance, where pain is specified literally by reference to the activation of pain nerves, and the satiating behaviour is anything that terminates that activation; and a temperature control drive, specified in much the same way as pain avoidance, by reference to the activation of specific nerve endings.

Is it possible that an explanation of *all* human behaviour can be made just in terms of that basic equipment and repertoire, and no more? Do we not do anything but eat, drink, breathe, flinch away from pain, heat, and cold, and (to put the matter briefly) copulate in one of its real or imaginary forms? – never do kindly things, never create works of art, pursue disinterested enquiry, philosophise, worship, sacrifice pleasure for duty, act from moral conviction, and so on and so on? In one sense it would be absurd to say that we do not, because if we did not it would be meaningless to talk of relating such behaviours to the operation of instinctual drives. Yet in another sense one can argue (as suggested above) that in doing any of those things what we are really doing is one or more of the basic consummatory actions listed above, in a derived form.

That any given action is capable of a number of descriptions all of which may be true has been pointed out by a number of philosophers, one of the better known examples being Anscombe's man who is (a) working a pump handle, (b) replenishing the water supply of a house, and (c) poisoning the inhabitants, because he knows the water is poisoned, as well as producing any number of other side-effects. The question 'What is he *really* doing?' has no determinate answer; he is really doing all those things, and to prefer one answer over another reflects (amongst other limiting conditions – what he can know about what he is doing, what he is capable of doing directly) one's belief about what his main goal is. For this purpose that will be what he is 'really' doing and everything else, by and large, will be instrumental to it or accidental by-products of it. The explanatory framework I am proposing consists not of basic goals but of basic actions. The concept of 'basic action' has also received a good deal of attention in recent years, beginning with Danto's (1963) version that an action *B* is basic if there is no other action performed by the agent that is the cause of *B*. This and other proposals have been critically reviewed by Hornsby (1980). Her own version, to put it too briefly perhaps, is that an action is basic if it is unlearned, if there is an innate capacity to do it. Her main interest is to trace actions back to the bodily movements of which in her view they consist, and those to their origin in 'trying' (as she sees it) to do them. If there are some bodily actions (acquired skills) that I can only perform by finding how to put together their components, then those components must be actions that I can just natively do. That seems to me correct, as I have agreed earlier, but since my interests are in the motivational origins of actions, which Hornsby, as she is obviously entitled to do, leaves to some other enquiry, my notion of a basic action includes not only that in its most primitive form it is unlearned but also that it is consummatory in the sense I have given that term above. Every innately provided action (an action being something larger than a reflex) as it occurs in the inexperienced organism is a consummatory action; this is a merely contingent assertion. Innately provided instrumental actions such as walking occur only as part of basic consummatory actions, not for 'the sheer pleasure of it', whatever those words may mean. To say that the learning of 'new' actions is only an elaboration of the innate consummatory actions is what I mean by saying that the latter are basic to the former. But it is obviously insufficient to assert in a merely *a priori* way that actions of the order of aesthetic and ethical actions are just elaborated forms of the basic consummatory actions of the physiological drives listed above; what is required is some indication of how the connections come about, of how the one action actually functions as an elaborated form of the other.

What I am contending is not that persons who say that their works of art or virtue are self-contained and have no extrinsic motivation are consciously deceiving their audience; I am saying that because of their repressions they are unaware of the basic nature of their own activity. This should not be taken as vilifying all that is fine in human nature. From a deterministic view of human nature it can be neither noble nor base, and to represent it as other than it is will not increase the store of human understanding or fellow-feeling in the world. A great deal of valuable material would be lost to psychology if the view (Gauld & Shotter 1977, Harré 1979) that behaviour is to be understood in terms of the actor's own account of it, without speculating about *hidden* meanings of which he or she knows nothing, were to prevail. (Once the somatic sources of behaviour are fully established, talk about hidden meanings will not be speculative; they will be objectively discoverable.) Always to accept a person's account of his or her own behaviour would mean, for example, that acting according to social norms would be accepted as a final explanatory category; that morality or 'doing what is right' be accepted as if it were objectively determinable in spite of its demonstrable logical incoherence; and in general that every nice-minded rationalisation or ideological commitment be allowed to pass at its own valuation. But to justify the assertion that behaviours of this elevated kind are not simply what they claim to be, and conceal earthier motivations, it will be necessary to show in each case some objective ground for disputing the validity of the rationalisation; then to show how the activities so rationalised may plausibly be related to drive satiation.

Social rule-following and 'reasonable' behaviour

A movement prominent in recent years in British social psychology (Gauld & Shotter 1977, Harré 1979, Harré & Secord 1972), and which has something in common with American 'social learning' theory, lays great weight on the proposition that man is 'a purposive, rule-following and self-monitoring agent' (Harré & Secord 1972). A great deal of social behaviour is accounted for as 'rule-following', as if that were a sufficient explanatory category. Some of the authors in this movement have useful things to say about the concept of rule (Collett 1977) and about how widespread the influence of rules is, but they virtually all accept uncritically that rule-following entails being purposive. That is just another case of the common error (discussed in Ch. 4) of supposing that cognition-guided behaviour is necessarily purposive behaviour, and it prevents these authors from paying adequate attention to the overt and covert sanctions attached to social rules, or to what is involved in the predigested notion that rules become 'internalised'. Harré and Secord, for example, say:

> ... the analysis of social episodes and the explanation of their genesis involves reference to principles of order for the sequences of happenings different from those which are used to order items causally which derive from the immediate reference to biological mechanisms for their explanation (Harré & Secord 1972, p. 162).

That is to suppose that there is a principle of order in human behaviour incompatible with the causal one, i.e. the principle of self-direction. This holds in the psychological realm as distinct from the physiological one, but the venerable problem of explaining how the non-caused order interacts with the caused one without making nonsense of its causality is just dismissed by these authors by saying repeatedly that human nature is a 'psycho-physical mix' – it may be 'any sort of a mix of the psychic and the physical' (Harré & Secord 1972, p. 283). In general, then, although we have to cope with our biological nature, and it may sometimes upset our rational functioning, most of our behaviour is a matter of reasoned choice, as they see it.

The notion of 'reasonableness' is an ingredient in the concept of the rule-following agent for most of these psychologists, yet there are not many attempts to explain what it entails, perhaps because it is difficult to do so without committing oneself to the dualistic notion that we have a faculty of Reason which (at our best) we exercise in the choice of our behaviour. John Shotter does attempt this, but the distinctions he proposes between reasonable and non-reasonable behaviour are not clear.

Reasonable people . . . are expected not just to act in some sense appropriately to their circumstances, but to act in a socially intelligible manner, and to be *responsible* for what they are doing by being able to indicate when required what they intend or mean by their actions (Shotter 1973, pp. 154–5).

But (except when the action is a symbolic utterance) one can only give the 'meaning' of an action simply by saying what sort of action one believes it *to be*, or by naming the larger action of which it is a component. If others can see what I am doing, that is, if they believe they can see that I expect to produce a certain outcome, then nothing more is required for my behaviour to be 'socially intelligible', even though they may not approve of it. One suspects that by 'socially intelligible' here Shotter means 'socially responsible', or taking proper heed of the welfare of others and of society in general. That interpretation is borne out when he says a little later that in order to act responsibly people 'must be able to assess the value or significance of their own performances in relation to needs, goals, and interests other than their own immediate and idiosyncratic ones' (Shotter 1973, p. 155). But this is to introduce a moral consideration; if we are to be considered 'responsible', we must practise self-restraint for the common good, which is quite different from saying just that our actions must be socially *intelligible*. In the ethos of the business world, for example, it is, with few exceptions, *only* self-interest that is considered intelligible. It is quite impossible to get everyone to agree on what is socially good, and even if one settled for a majority opinion, there is no reason apart from a merely stipulative one to think that what the majority of people want is inherently desirable, and should be respected by every individual.

The fact that reciprocation and cooperation do occur does not mean that some new order of explanation for social behaviour has emerged, higher than the causal operation of instinctual drives. Social rules and contingencies are just a particular class of the contingencies of nature, which individuals discover and which then modify their consummatory behaviours. It has often been pointed out (cf. Collett 1977) that social rules basically derive their prescriptive force from the application or threat of sanctions (i.e. of the frustration of primary drives). Collett warns that we should never 'regard analyses in terms of rules as being in themselves sufficient explanations of social behaviour' (Collett 1977, p. 27). Harré and Secord, Shotter, and others do often appear to regard them as sufficient explanations, and one feels that underlying this assumption is the authors' own conviction that the maintenance of the social fabric is an ethical imperative, so that social rules making towards that end are ethically correct, i.e. embody true moral propositions about what one ought to do. According to this conception, everyone who develops into a 'rational, responsible person' will see that such rules are ethically correct and so find them binding on his or her own behaviour. This is a typical form of the concept of rational behaviour, of behaviour guided by Reason. The notion is that by the exercise of intellect the rational person calculates the probable consequences of various types of behaviour, and by the exercise of Reason derives from those facts a proper understanding of how people *ought to live*. But, however respectable such a conception of Reason may be, it is still the case that facts never of themselves imply policies, still true as Hume pointed out that we cannot derive an 'ought' from an 'is', and that although behaviour is certainly guided by knowledge of facts, the question of what that behaviour will be, and of which way the facts direct our behaviour, is determined by the primary or instinctual drives.

That is not to say that there is no such thing as behaviour dictated by the person's moral convictions; such convictions are amongst the most important determinants of social behaviour. But it is to say that they are not to be taken as *true descriptions* of the kinds of action to which they refer, and thus as being self-evidently binding on and explanatory of conduct. As Sellars put it (1952), there are *feelings* of moral obligation, but these are analysable by empirical psychology, and their existence does not mean that there is a class of actual moral obligations that must be included in any complete description of the world. Moral convictions are not only social acquisitions but social inventions, and their development calls for explanation in motivational, not intellectual, terms (cf. Henry 1980). Moralism is a special technique of social control, a special application of the concept of 'rule'.

The dynamics of moral behaviour

When a person gives an account of an action that he or she has undertaken by saying that it was done simply because it was *right*, was *what one ought to do*, then that is, of course, to deny most explicitly that it was merely an expression of material interests, merely an instance of drive gratification. But if we can show that this rationale is invalidly argued, then we may hold that it is a screen (though probably not consciously employed) for something else, and that some further explanation of the motivation is required. For brevity's sake I take 'the good', 'the right', 'the virtuous', 'the obligatory', 'what one ought to do', and all cognate expressions as being essentially synonymous, and will group them under the heading 'that which is demanded in itself'. Such expressions apply to kinds of action, rather than to objects. They are used as if they indicated a property of the actions, as the terms 'vigorous', 'clumsy', or 'communicative' indicate properties of actions. But, as has so often been pointed out, despite their grammatical semblance of descriptiveness, their actual function is not description but prescription; they are used to enjoin us to perform certain actions and refrain from certain others. They *cannot* legitimately function as descriptions because they exemplify the fallacy of constitutive relations to which I have had occasion to point in earlier chapters – the fallacy of saying that a thing's relations can be found intrinsic to the thing itself. The relation of being demanded *by someone* is a familiar enough one; we have all had the experience of having a certain action demanded of us by someone else, but when an action is said to be demanded or obligatory in its nature, then that is to represent the relation of being demanded as being internalised into the action itself, and as forming part of its intrinsic nature (Maze 1973). The moralist, in fact, expressly denies that the action he enjoins on us is demanded by himself or by any secular agency. Wishes are irrelevant; the action is supposed to be of the obligatory *kind*, and every worthwhile person should see that it is obligatory, and, seeing this, feel impelled to perform it, otherwise his worthwhileness is suspect. But if there is no such intrinsic relatedness, then there are no natural moral properties, no 'ought-to-be-done-ness', and most emphatically no 'non-natural' moral properties, since such a conception is a perfectly meaningless verbalism. The ethical demand that every person with a 'moral sense' should be able to recognise such properties is one that is impossible to fulfill. What are the sense organs of the moral sense? We know what the organs of the visual sense are, and we know what properties they can discover, colours and shapes, and so on, but we can find neither organs nor discriminanda for the moral sense. Thus, the belief in the existence of objective moral properties is to be considered as a type of *delusion*, though a corporate one, and, as with other delusions, the psychologist must look for the economic functions it serves for the person who entertains it.

They are not far to seek. The belief in the inexorable reality of 'right' and 'wrong' is acquired in the years of childhood, from those persons on whom the child is so dependent, and whose affectionate regard and good opinion are so urgently desired, the parents. In saying that the prospect of losing their affection is felt as a grave threat by the child, I am not reverting to that concept of a 'need for affection' requiring no further underpinning which I discussed before. There may conceivably be such a drive, but as yet there is no possibility of identifying an independent physiological basis for it. Nevertheless, the kind of interpersonal attitude that we call an affectionate and protective one does exist, even though its instinctual derivation may be less selfless than it seems, and it can be identified by the child. The child comes to feel that the gratification of various genuine primary drives is contingent on this affectionate attitude in its parents. Most children are likely to have experienced the frustration of their pain-avoidance drive, for instance, in the form of angry slaps, accompanied by overt signs of a failure of parental affection. In general, if a small child comes to feel (what is true by and large) that it cannot maintain its existence unaided in the face of a hostile environment, one may think that all its instinctual drives become joined in the belief that the gratification of each one is dependent on the parents' affection. Consequently, if the parents, as so many do, make the continuance of their affection conditional on the child's being 'good', and on its being able to tell the right from the wrong, then that is a strong pressure on the child to believe that it *can* see the 'rightness' and 'wrongness' on which its parents lay so much stress. Thus the delusion is established (Maze 1973).

What gives moral beliefs their binding force, what motivates people actually to behave in accordance with them, is the underlying fear that they will be punished if they do not. Those fears become unconscious, largely because the guilt-making circumstances in which they were acquired become subject to repression, whereas the moral beliefs are consciously held as objectively true, rather than as restrictions imposed on one by the threat of sanctions. The economic value of this is that it enables the person to believe that he is adopting certain inhibitions of his instinctual impulses as a matter of virtue, of principled renunciation, whereas if he retained in consciousness the realisation that he had given in to the arbitrary demands of others, that would be humiliating and painful.

The socialisation of children can readily be interpreted as the setting of instinctual drives against one another. Its aim is to bring about the suppression of specific instinctual impulses, particularly, in our society, of the expression of sexuality in its pregenital forms which are all represented as being 'dirty' (this having a long-lasting effect on the person's adult sexuality, as well), and of aggression, especially of aggression directed against 'proper authorities' (the parents themselves, in the first instance) or against some specially protected group such as younger siblings (Henry 1980, 1982). This is done by offering rewards and punishments. A reward can only be the gratification of an instinctual drive, and a punishment can only be the frustration of one. So, then, what is being put to the child is that if it gives expression to some particular one of its instinctual impulses, another will be frustrated. To take an implausible, though possible, case, a child could conceivably be told that if it went on with some pregenital sexual behaviour then it would not be given any more food. Hunger is being set against sexuality. If the threat is the more common one of the infliction of pain, then pain-avoidance is being set against sexuality. Withdrawal of affection is the derived or intermediary sanction. In general, all those instinctual drives whose gratification is dependent on the parents' good will and which is employed as reward by them are mobilised in opposition to the forbidden instinctual impulses. Thus, one subset of the instinctual drives becomes organised in competition with the remainder, and treats the blocking off of the remainder as an essential part of securing its own gratification. These acquisitions are of the same instrumental order as those gradual elaborations of the consummatory behaviour patterns that are brought about by everyday trial and error (Ch. 4 above).

This view of the developed structure of the mental apparatus in terms of the opposition of groups of instincts is very much the same as that to be found in Freud's writings up to about 1923, in which he uses the notion of the self-preservative instincts, or the ego-instincts (Freud 1910), as constituting the counter-balance to the id instincts, the libidinal impulses. The 'self-preservative' instincts would presumably include a selection from the sort of list I have proposed – they could be hunger and pain-avoidance, for example. The actual principle of division, between the instinctual drives that are to constitute the ego and those which are to be repressed and constitute the id, would be that the former were those whose expression was not subject to *moral disapproval*, that is, those which were socially regarded as legitimate constituents of a respectable person, whereas the latter were morally condemned as impulses that no worthwhile person would have. The content of a person's moral convictions, then, the list of actions and abstentions that he or she regarded as virtuous, would provide a mirror-image of the contents of the id – of the unconscious wishes (action-tendencies) that the ego is keeping at bay.

It is misleading, or at least incomplete, to say, as Freud does, that 'the ego seeks to bring the influence of the external world to bear upon the id and its tendencies, and endeavours to substitute the reality principle for the pleasure principle which reigns unrestrictedly in the id' (Freud 1923, p. 15). The reality principle, properly conceived, is not Rationality, but just seeing what is the case, as against hallucinating what one wishes to be the case. The ego functions in accordance with the reality principle, and opposes the tendencies of the id, only in so far as that is effective *in securing its own gratification*. Its policies are not dictated by Reason but by its own consummatory programs. The moral convictions that a person embraces are embraced by, or forced upon, the ego, as beliefs about what it must do in order to protect itself from frustration. These beliefs, together with the unconscious fears of punishment, constitute Freud's 'superego'.

Moral behaviour, then, is to be seen as a special sort of functioning of those drives which compose the ego. That is not to say that the person who professes morality as the ground of his or her behaviour is being self-consciously cynical and self-seeking; that may sometimes be the case but is far from typical. Further, it is not always the case that moral behaviour actually enhances the person's welfare even in an indirect way. The ego's unconscious beliefs about what is necessary to ensure gratification are unrealistic ones, acquired in childhood and preserved behind the barrier of repression. Morality functions to persuade individuals to forego real-world gratifications in favour of the assurance of 'virtue'. Some of these renunciations may be necessary for the maintenance of the social fabric but many are not. There is no lack of surplus repression. In any case, it is not self-evident that an imposed moralism is necessary to contain hostility and establish acceptable levels of social cooperation. Although one cannot find sufficient evidence of a biological basis for 'affection' or the 'social feelings' to allow them to be included *as yet* in our list of instinctual drives, I do not despair that they may eventually be established as in some sense reliable components of human nature; and it would be such fellow-feeling, if its development were not hindered in the ambivalent relation with the parents, that would provide the counter-balance to aggressive behaviour.

Art, enquiry, and the pursuit of liberty

When people give an account of their behaviour as being the socially responsible thing to do, or as trying to do what is right, what we are hearing is the voice of the repressing agency, of the ego as affected by the superego, and it is a sign of the consolidation or re-establishment of the repression. But when they insist that what they are doing is art for its own sake, or purely disinterested enquiry, or the pursuit of liberty *per se*, it is often though not invariably the case that what we are hearing is an expression of the *repressed* impulses in their minds asserting their reality, and that the activity in question is in some degree at least a lifting of the repression, a resolution of the internal conflict. The behaviour is still the work of the primary drives, though now it is a more conscious expression of the formerly repressed ones than of the repressing ones. Of course, it may sometimes be the case that these justifications of behaviour – aestheticism, disinterested enquiry, the struggle for liberty – are still merely screens for repressive forces, in so far as they may represent the behaviour as being morally superior, moralism always being a disguise for some repression. Thus, conceivably, 'aestheticism' may sometimes be a reaction-formation against anal-eroticism, rather than a sublimation of it; 'disinterested enquiry' a cloak for sadistically toned voyeurism, perhaps; 'liberty' a demand for the suppression of one's enemies, and so on. But that is not inevitably the case. To show how these activities may be the vehicle of liberation from moralism, or of the lifting of the repressions, I will consider first the case of artistic endeavour.

What I am proposing, although there is hardly scope here to develop this argument fully, is that the subject-matter of all art forms is human feelings, or the vicissitudes of human life. With regard to literature that is a fairly non-controversial view; we have the classic line that the stuff of drama is conflict and its resolution, and plainly much the same can be said of novels of a serious literary character (Maze 1981) and of epic poetry. Lyrical, abstract, and imagist poetry can often be read as dealing with problems internal to the human psyche. The proposal that music and abstract paint-ing are representations of psychological processes will meet with more resistance; however, the view that music is not only an expression of but a communication about human feelings was developed in detail by Langer (1942), and even such a professional, objective analyst as Rosen does not hesitate to describe the effect of structural variations in psychological terms. To take an example at random:

No concerto before K. 466 exploits so well the latent pathetic nature of the form – the contrast and struggle of one individual voice against many (Rosen 1971, p. 233).

Abstract painting, especially of the minimalist or geometrical kind, is supposed to have been stripped of every aspect of representationism, and the demand is to evaluate it solely in terms of what it is in itself, as a physical object. Its content is said to be nothing but relationships of a supposedly logical or mathematical kind between its shapes, boundaries, colours, and so on. However, when one considers the terms in which artists and critics try to give an account of those structural relationships in order to determine their claim to aesthetic merit, one finds that they continually employ concepts such as integrity, consistency, coherence, balance and imbalance, stress, tension, resolution, and so on. But those terms, when applied to relations between visual masses, are only metaphorical. The concepts of consistency and coherence can be literally applied only to *assertions* and the logical relations of compatibility and incompatibility between them, and whereas 'stress' and 'balance' have a clear-cut meaning with regard to physical systems, the 'masses' in a painting do not constitute a physical system of that kind. Rather they provide a visual representation of those relations, and it is at least as plausible to suggest that they represent the stresses and resolutions of conflicting *interests*, as that they are intended to show us what the literally physical relations of physical masses are like. Stokes (1947, 1961) has developed the psychoanalytic theory of symbolism with regard to the masculine or feminine import of abstract visual shapes, and related them to Gestalt properties suggesting effort or repose, and in those terms we begin to see that even an abstract painting, whatever the painter's conscious rationalisation of it, may represent the relationships between human wishes and anxieties, may represent sexual attitudes, may in general represent a state of mind or condition of life that the artist wishes to achieve (Wollheim 1965). The conception developed by Stokes is that the artist begins his or her work in a condition – one in which most of us spend our lives – of internal division, that is, of being repressed, and that the artistic endeavours are a struggle to achieve and depict personal unity; that the unity and coherence attributed to the finished work, if it is successful, is a representation of the state of internal concord that may be achieved by the human psyche no longer in conflict with itself, no longer misrepresenting itself – a condition in which moralistic self-alienation has been dissolved.

In the case of popular, sentimental, and merely consolatory *bad* art, the kind that Greenberg calls 'kitsch', what we find is actually a re-establishment of the repression. It, too, represents the gratification of repressed wishes, but does so in a perverse, aim-inhibited way rather than realistically; the repressed wishes remain unacknowledged, or ego-alien. Both artist and spectator are fobbed off with hallucinatory gratifications, the function of which is to reconcile them to being deprived of actual gratification in the real world. Genuine works of art, by contrast, insist on the legitimacy of the once-denied feelings, and body forth the situation in which the actualisation of the alienated parts of the personality is possible. At their best, they stand as criticisms of prevailing conventional morality, or in general of moralism itself. The instinctual forces that motivate the aesthetic endeavour are in the main those that have been subject to repression, but since the production of an art object also includes conscious ego-processes, then the ego-instincts must also have relaxed their defences against the repressed impulses, and joined with them in the production of the art object which symbolically expresses the state of personal integration (Dalton 1979, Maze 1981).

Turning to the concept of 'disinterested enquiry', one must ask paradoxically what interests it does serve, and what can be meant by 'disinterested'. Plainly, it is interested in objectivity and disinterested in so far as it refuses to conceal or misrepresent its findings because of interests extrinsic to that in objectivity – for instance, because of commercial or ideological pressures. As, for example, Orwell pointed out in *1984*, one of the main techniques of authoritarian control is to launch a direct assault against the subject individual's exercising his cognitive or critical faculties. The most common vehicle of assault on the young person's cognitive faculties, on the exercise of the reality principle which is necessary for the performance of the consummatory actions, is precisely the imposition of the inscrutable concept of 'what ought to be done', of moral absolutes. Thus, a dedication to enquiry, to an understanding of the way the world works and especially of the way society works, can be understood as a refusal any longer to accept the reality of unchallengeable authority, of unmentionable topics, of absolutes that must be accepted on faith. It is true that in particular cases we may find that specific interests of a more or less compulsive kind are implicated. Freud (1908) suggests, for example, that a person may have experienced the first great intellectual frustration in childhood, in enquiring into sexual matters and the facts of reproduction and coming up against the prudish 'conspiracy of silence'; for such a person it may be that the interest in enquiry is especially an expression of the demands of the sexual instinct; but there can also be a general endeavour to overcome self-alienation through achieving a wide-ranging realism.

Plainly enough, it is along similar lines that I would account for the pursuit of liberty, the defence of freedom. From a deterministic view the conception of unqualified freedom, freedom *from causality*, is simply an illusion. Everything one does is caused, not 'free'. The only empirical content of the notion of freedom is freedom *from* various things, freedom from various specific kinds of external and internal constraint. The freeing of thought from those impenetrable categorical imperatives that conceal irrational anxieties and animosities seems to me a necessary preliminary to external freedom, i.e. to the growth of a society in which every person's realistic self-monitoring will provide the main deterrent to unscrupulous competition with others in the performance of consummatory acts.

In this chapter I have been trying to dispel the sense of outrage that may greet the suggestion that not only is all our behaviour the work of instinctual drives but, indeed, is nothing but modified versions of innately provided consummatory responses. The first reaction to this theory is to feel that it gives an image of man as an unusually complicated type of battery-operated robot. What becomes of the rich variety and endless inventiveness of human behaviour, in such a theory? Perhaps enough has been said to show that genuinely informative and explanatory insights into just that rich variety of behaviour are promised by this psychology, once a physiologically determined account of the instinctual drive mechanisms has been provided as its foundation. If it still seems a gross and animalistic account of human nature, I can only point out that by no means all the manifestations of inborn animal or human behaviour patterns are brutish, self-concerned, or merely fleshly. Everything that is gracious and generous in social life, as well as everything that is violent, comes from our genetic dispositions, because there is no other source.

In previous chapters I have tried to show how empty other types of personality theory are, how at bottom they are essentially self-defeating and uninformative. Existentialism comes to nothing because its central concept is that of a self that creates itself out of nothing and still consists of nothing; purposivism in general because it defines its motive forces by their goals rather than their sources and so may postulate as many as it fancies, yet can never have enough; behaviourism because it cannot tell us why its empty organism is doing one thing rather than another, since it denies any content to its concept of 'reinforcing event'. What is required is to see that instinctual drives as conceived by Freud, divested of their unneccessary purposivistic terminology and given a local habitation in the central nervous system, are not only intelligible as working mechanisms, and entirely compatible with the concepts of neuroscience, but are indispensable as an explanatory basis for a science of behaviour and mental life. In the expression he adopted, we are *lived by* our instincts. They are the very stuff of human nature.

Bibliography

Allport, G. W. 1937. *Personality: a psychological interpretation.* London: Constable.

Anscombe, G. E. M. 1957. *Intention.* Oxford: Blackwell.

Armstrong, D. M. 1968. *A materialist theory of the mind.* London: Routledge & Kegan Paul.

Armstrong, D. M. 1973. *Belief, truth and knowledge.* Cambridge: Cambridge University Press.

Armstrong, D. M. 1978. On passing the buck. *Behav. Brain Sci.* **1**, 346.

Audi, R. 1979. Wants and intentions in the explanation of behaviour. *J. Theory Social Behav.* **9**, 227–50.

Binswanger, L. 1944. The case of Ellen West (trans. W. M. Wendell & J. Lyons). In *Existence*, R. May *et al.* (eds), 1958. New York: Basic Books.

Binswanger, L. 1946. The existential analysis school of thought (trans. E. Angell). In *Existence*, R. May *et al.* (eds), 1958. New York: Basic Books.

Binswanger, L. 1957. Introduction to *Schizophrenie*. In *Being in the world*, L. Binswanger (trans. J. Needleman), 1963. New York: Basic Books.

Blundell, J. and C. J. Latham 1979. Pharmacology of food and water intake. In *Chemical influences on behaviour*, K. Brown and S. J. Cooper (eds). London: Academic Press.

Boden, M. 1972. *Purposive explanation in psychology.* Cambridge, Mass.: Harvard University Press.

Boden, M. 1977. *Artificial intelligence and natural man.* Hassocks, Sussex: Harvester.

Boden, M. 1979. The computational metaphor in psychology. In *Philosophical problems in psychology*, N. Bolton (ed.). London: Methuen.

Bolles, R. C., R. Holtz, T. Dunn and W. Hill 1980. Comparisons of stimulus learning and response learning in a punishment situation. *Learn. Motiv.* **11**, 78–96.

Bolton, N. 1979. Phenomenology and psychology: being objective about the mind. In *Philosophical problems in psychology*, N. Bolton (ed.). London: Methuen.

Borger, R. 1970. Comment on Charles Taylor's 'The explanation of purposive behaviour'. In *Explanation in the behavioural sciences*, R. Borger and F. Cioffi (eds). Cambridge: Cambridge University Press.

Braithwaite, R. B. 1953. *Scientific explanation.* Cambridge: Cambridge University Press.

Brentano, F. 1874. *Psychology from an empirical standpoint*, L. L. McAlister (ed.) (trans. A. C. Rancurello *et al.*), 1973. London: Routledge & Kegan Paul.

Chisholm, R. M. 1964. The descriptive element in the concept of action. *J. Phil.* **61**, 613–25.

Chisholm, R. M. 1976. The agent as cause. In *Action theory*, M. Brand and D. Walton (eds). Dordrecht: Reidel.

Chomsky, N. 1959. Review of *Verbal behavior*, by B. F. Skinner. *Language* **35**, 26–58.

Collett, P. 1977. The rules of conduct. In *Social rules and social behaviour*, P. Collett (ed.). Oxford: Blackwell.

Dalton, E. 1979. *Unconscious structure in 'The idiot'*. Princeton, NJ: Princeton University Press.

Danto, A. 1963. What we can do. *J. Phil.* **60**, 434–45.

Davidson, D. 1963. Actions, reasons and causes. *J. Phil.* **60**, 685–700.

Davidson, D. 1973. Freedom to act. In *Essays on freedom of action*, T. Honderich (ed.). London: Routledge & Kegan Paul.

Davidson, J. M. 1972. Hormones and reproductive behavior. In *Hormones and behavior*, S. Levine (ed.). New York: Academic Press.

Delgado, J. M. R. 1967. Aggression and defence under cerebral radio control. In *Aggression and defence*, C. D. Clemente and D. B. Lindsley (eds). Vol. V: *Brain function*. UCLA Forum in Medical Science. Berkeley: University of California Press.

Delgado, J. M. R. 1969. *Physical control of the mind*. New York: Harper & Row.

Dennett, D. C. 1979. *Brainstorms: philosophical essays on mind and consciousness*. Hassocks, Sussex: Harvester.

Dickinson, A. 1979. Review of *Cognitive processes in animal behavior*, S. Hulse *et al.* (eds). *Q. J. Exp. Psychol.* 551–4.

Ellenberger, H. F. 1958. A clinical introduction to psychiatric phenomenology and existential analysis. In *Existence*, R. May *et al.* (eds). New York: Basic Books.

Farber, M. 1943. *The foundation of phenomenology*. Cambridge, Mass.: Harvard University Press.

Fodor, J. A. 1975. *The language of thought*. New York: Thomas Crowell.

Freud, S. 1895. A project for a scientific psychology. *Standard edition of the complete psychological works of Sigmund Freud*, vol. 1. London: Hogarth.

Freud, S. 1900. *The interpretation of dreams. Standard edition*, vol. 5. London: Hogarth.

Freud, S. 1905. *Three essays on the theory of sexuality. Standard edition*, vol. 7. London: Hogarth.

Freud, S. 1908. On the sexual theories of children. *Standard edition*, vol. 9. London: Hogarth.

Freud, S. 1910. The psychoanalytic view of psychogenic disturbances of vision. *Standard edition*. vol. 11. London: Hogarth.

Freud, S. 1915. Instincts and their vicissitudes. *Standard edition*, vol. 14. London: Hogarth.

Freud, S. 1920. *Beyond the pleasure principle. Standard edition*, vol. 18. London: Hogarth.

Freud, S. 1923. *The ego and the id. Standard edition*, vol. 19. London: Hogarth.

Freud, S. 1933. *New introductory lectures. Standard edition*, vol. 22. London: Hogarth.

Fromm, E. 1974. *The anatomy of human destructiveness*. London: Jonathan Cape.

Gauld, A. and J. Shotter 1977. *Human action and its psychological investigation*. London: Routledge & Kegan Paul.

Gibson, J. J. 1979. *The ecological approach to visual perception*. Boston: Houghton Mifflin.

Giorgi, A. 1975. Phenomenology and the foundations of psychology. In *Nebraska symposium on motivation*, J. K. Cole (ed.). Lincoln, Neb.: University of Nebraska Press.

Globus, G. 1976. Mind, structure and contradiction. In *Consciousness and the brain: a scientific and philosophical inquiry*, G. Globus *et al.* (eds). New York: Plenum.

Globus, G. and S. Franklin 1980. Prospects for the scientific observer of perceptual consciousness. In *The psychobiology of consciousness*, J. M. Davidson and R. J. Davidson (eds). New York: Plenum.

Grossman, S. P. 1973. *Essentials of physiological psychology*. New York: Wiley.

Harré, R. 1979. *Social being: a theory for social psychology*. Oxford: Blackwell.

Harré, R. and P. F. Secord, 1972. *The explanation of social behaviour*. Oxford: Blackwell.

Hearst, E. 1978. Stimulus relationships and feature selection. In *Cognitive processes in animal behavior*, S. H. Hulse *et al.* (eds). Hillsdale, NJ: Erlbaum.

Hearst, E. and G. B. Peterson 1973. Transfer of conditioned excitation and inhibition from one operant response to another. *J. Exp. Psychol.* **99**, 360–8.

Hebb, D. O. 1949. *The organization of behavior*. New York: Wiley.

Heidegger, M. 1957. *Being and time* (trans. J. Macquarrie & E. Robinson), 1967. Oxford: Blackwell.

Heil, J. 1981. Does cognitive psychology rest on a mistake? *Mind* **90**, 321–42.

Hempel, C. G. 1965. *Aspects of scientific explanation*. New York: Free Press.

Henry, R. M. 1980. A theoretical and empirical analysis of 'reasoning' in the socialization of young children. *Human Devel.* **23**, 105–25.

Henry, R. M. 1982. *The psychodynamic foundations of morality*. Basle: Karger.

Hochberg, J. 1970. Attention, organization, and consciousness. In *Attention*, D. Mostofsky (ed.). New York: Appleton-Century-Crofts.

Honderich, T. 1981a. Psychophysical lawlike connections and their problem. *Inquiry* **24**, 277–303.

Honderich, T. 1981b. Nomological dualism: reply to four critics. *Inquiry* **24**, 419–38.

Hornsby, J. 1980. *Actions*. London: Routledge & Kegan Paul.

Hull, C. L. 1930. Knowledge and purpose as habit mechanisms. *Psychol. Rev.* **37**, 511–25.

Hull, C. L. 1934. The concept of the habit family hierarchy and maze learning: part I. *Psychol. Rev.* **41**, 33–54.

Hull, C. L. 1943. *Principles of behavior*. New York: Appleton–Century–Crofts.

Hull, C. L. 1952. *A behavior system*. New Haven, Conn.: Yale University Press.

Hulse, S. H., H. Fowler and W. K. Honig (eds) 1978. *Cognitive processes in animal behavior*. Hillsdale, NJ: Erlbaum.

Husserl, E. 1913. *Ideas* (trans. W. R. Boyce Gibson), 1931. London: George Allen & Unwin.

Husserl, E. 1929. *Cartesian meditations* (trans. D. Cairns), 1973. The Hague: Nijhoff.

Husserl, E. 1950. *The idea of phenomenology* (trans. W. P. Alston & G. Nakhnikian), 1970. The Hague: Nijhoff.
Hyslop, A. and F. C. Jackson 1972. The analogical inference to other minds. *Am. Phil Q.* **9**, 168–76.

Kant, I. 1781. *Critique of pure reason* (trans. J. M. D. Meiklejohn), 1943. New York: Wiley.
King, H. E. 1961. Psychological effects of excitation in the limbic system. In *Electrical stimulation of the brain*, D. E. Sheer (ed.). Austin: University of Texas Press.

Laing, R. D. 1960. *The divided self.* London: Tavistock.
Langer, S. K. 1942. *Philosophy in a new key.* Cambridge, Mass.: Harvard University Press.
Liddell, H. S. 1944. Conditioned reflex method and experimental neurosis. In *Personality and the behavior disorders*, J. McV. Hunt (ed.). New York: Ronald.

MacCorquodale, K. 1970. On Chomsky's review of Skinner's *Verbal behavior*. *J. Exp. Anal. Behav.* **13**, 83–99.
MacKay, D. M. 1960. On the logical indeterminacy of a free choice. *Mind* **69**, 31–40.
MacKay, D. M. 1967. Freedom of action in a mechanistic universe. In *Good reading in psychology*, M. S. Gazzaniga and E. P. Lovejoy (eds). New York: Prentice-Hall.
MacKay, D. M. 1971. Choice in a mechanistic universe: a reply to some critics. *Br. J. Phil. Sci.* **22**, 275–85.
MacKay, D. M. 1973. The logical indeterminateness of human choices. *Br. J. Phil. Sci.* **24**, 405–8.
Mackie, J. L. 1974. *The cement of the universe.* Oxford: Clarendon.
Mackintosh, N. J. 1977. Conditioning as the perception of causal relations. In *Foundational problems in the special sciences*, R. E. Butts and J. Hintikka (eds). Dordrecht: Reidel.
Malcolm, N. 1958. Knowledge of other minds. In *The philosophy of mind*, V. C. Chappell (ed.), 1962. Englewood Cliffs, NJ: Prentice-Hall.
Maslow, A. H. 1962. Some basic propositions of a growth and self-actualization psychology. In *Personality: readings in theory and research*, E. A. Southwell and M. Merbaum (eds), 2nd edn, 1971. Belmont, Calif.: Brooks/Cole.
Maze, J. R. 1954. Do intervening variables intervene? *Psychol Rev.* **61**, 226–34.
Maze, J. R. 1973. The concept of attitude. *Inquiry* **16**, 168–205.
Maze, J. R. 1979. Dostoevsky's problems with the concept of conscience: Svidrigailov and Raskolnikov. *Int. Rev. Psychoanal.* **6**, 499–509.
Maze, J. R. 1981. Dostoevsky: epilepsy, mysticism, and homosexuality. *Am. Imago* **38**, 155–83.
McDougall, W. 1936. *Introduction to social psychology*, 23rd edn. London: Methuen.
McGinn, C. 1979. Action and its explanation. In *Philosophical problems in psychology*, N. Bolton (ed.). London: Methuen.
Merleau-Ponty, M. 1963. *The structure of behavior* (trans. A. L. Fisher). Boston: Beacon.

Miller, N. E. and M. L. Kessen 1952. Reward effects of food via stomach fistula compared with those of food via mouth. *J. Comp. Physiol Psychol.* **45**, 555–64.
Morgan, M. J. 1979a. Motivational processes. In *Mechanisms of learning and motivation*, A. Dickinson and R. A. Boakes (eds). Hillsdale, NJ: Erlbaum.
Morgan, M. J. 1979b. The concept of drive. *Trends Neurosci.* **2**, 240–2.
Morgan, M. J., D. F. Einon and R. G. M. Morris 1977. Inhibition and isolation rearing in the rat: extinction and satiation. *Physiol. Animal Behav.* **18**, 1–5.
Morriston, W. 1979. Kenny on compatibilism. *Mind* **88**, 266–9.

Nagel, E. 1961. *The structure of science*. London: Routledge & Kegan Paul.
Neisser, U. 1967. *Cognitive psychology*. New York: Appleton–Century–Crofts.
Neisser, U. 1976. *Cognition and reality*. San Francisco: W. H. Freeman.
Noble, D. 1967. Charles Taylor on teleological explanation. *Analysis* **27**, 96–103.

Penfield, W. 1975. *The mystery of the mind*. Princeton, NJ: Princeton University Press.
Pettit, P. 1978. Rational man theory. In *Action and interpretation*, C. Hookway and P. Pettit (eds). Cambridge: Cambridge University Press.
Pettit, P. 1979. Rationalization and the art of explaining action. In *Philosophical problems in psychology*, N. Bolton (ed.). London: Methuen.
Pribram, K. H. 1969. The foundations of psychoanalytic theory: Freud's neuro-psychological model. In *Adaptation: selected readings*, K. H. Pribram (ed.). London: Penguin.
Pribram, K. H. and M. Gill 1976. *Freud's 'Project' reassessed*. London: Hutchinson.
Puccetti, R. and R. W. Dykes 1978. Sensory cortex and the mind–brain problem. *Behav. Brain Sci.* **3**, 337–75.

Rosen, C. 1971. *The classical style*. London: Faber & Faber.
Rosenblueth, A., N. Wiener and J. Bigelow 1943. Behavior, purpose and teleology. *Phil. Sci.* **10**, 18–24.
Rozeboom, W. W. 1965. The concept of 'memory'. *Psychol Rec.* **15**, 329–68.
Rudy, J. W. and A. R. Wagner 1975. Stimulus selection in associative learning. In *Handbook of learning and cognitive processes*, W. K. Estes (ed.), Vol. 2. Hillsdale, NJ: Erlbaum.
Russell, E. S. 1945. *The directiveness of organic activities*. Cambridge: Cambridge University Press.
Rychlak, J. F. 1975. Psychological science as a humanist views it. In *Nebraska symposium on motivation* J. K. Cole (ed.). Lincoln, Neb.: University of Nebraska Press.

Sartre, J.-P. 1943. *Being and nothingness* (trans. H. E. Barnes), 1956. New York: Philosophical Library.
Searle, J. R. 1979a. What is an intentional state? *Mind* **88**, 74–92.
Searle, J. R. 1979b. The intentionality of intention and action. *Inquiry* **22**, 253–80.
Sellars, W. 1952. Obligation and motivation. In *Readings in ethical theory*, W. Sellars and J. Hospers (eds). New York: Appleton–Century–Crofts.
Shaw, R., M. Turvey and W. Mace 1981. Ecological psychology: the consequences of a commitment to realism. In *Cognition and symbolic processes*, W. Weimer and D. Palermo (eds), vol. 2, Hillsdale, NJ; Erlbaum.

Shiffrin, R. M. 1976. Capacity limitations information processing. In *Handbook of learning and cognitive processes*, W. K. Estes (ed.), vol. 4. Hillsdale, NJ: Erlbaum.

Shotter, J. 1973. Acquired powers: the transformation of natural into personal powers. *J. Theory Soc. Behav.* **3**, 141–56.

Skinner, B. F. 1957. *Verbal behavior*. New York: Appleton–Century–Crofts.

Smith, A. D. 1977. Dispositional properties. *Mind* **86**, 439–45.

Sommerhoff, G. 1950. *Analytical biology*. Oxford: Oxford University Press.

Sommerhoff, G. 1974. *Logic of the living brain*. London: Wiley.

Spiegelberg, H. 1960. *The phenomenological movement*. The Hague: Nijhoff.

Stellar, E. 1954. The physiology of motivation. *Psychol Rev.* **61**, 5–22.

Stokes, A. D. 1947. *Inside out: an essay in the psychology and aesthetic appeal of space*. London: Faber & Faber.

Stokes, A. D. 1961. *Three essays on the painting of our time*. London: Tavistock.

Taylor, C. 1964. *The explanation of behaviour*. London: Routledge & Kegan Paul.

Taylor, C. 1967. Teleological explanation – a reply to Denis Noble. *Analysis* **27**, 141–43.

Taylor, C. 1970. The explanation of purposive behaviour. In *Explanation in the behavioural sciences*, R. Borger and F. Cioffi (eds). Cambridge: Cambridge University Press.

Taylor, R. 1950. Comments on a mechanistic conception of purposefulness. *Phil. Sci.* **17**, 310–17.

Taylor, R. 1966. *Action and purpose*. Englewood Cliffs, NJ: Prentice-Hall.

Tolman, E. C. 1932. *Purposive behavior in animals and men*. New York: Century.

Tuomela, R. 1977. *Human action and its explanation*. Dordrecht: Reidel.

Turvey, M. T. 1977. Contrasting orientations to the theory of visual information processing. *Psychol Rev.* **84**, 67–88.

Ullman, S. 1980. Against direct perception. *Behav. Brain Sci.* **3**, 373–415.

Westcourt, K. T. and R. C. Atkinson 1976. Fact retrieval processes. In *Handbook of learning and cognitive processes*, W. K. Estes (ed.), vol. 4, Hillsdale, NJ: Erlbaum.

Wilkes, K. J. 1980. Brain states. *Br. J. Phil. Sci.* **31**, 111–29.

Wilkes, K. J. 1981. Multiple personality and personal identity. *Br. J. Phil. Sci.* **32**, 331–48.

Wilson, E. 1979. *The mental as physical*. London: Routledge & Kegan Paul.

Wilson, E. 1981. Psychophysical relations. *Inquiry* **24**, 305–22.

Wollheim, R. 1965. Preface. In *The invitation in art*, A. D. Stokes. London: Tavistock.

Wollheim, R. 1971. *Freud*. London: Fontana.

Woodfield, A. 1976. *Teleology*. Cambridge: Cambridge University Press.

Wright, L. 1972. Explanation and teleology. *Phil. Sci.* **39**, 204–18.

Wright, L. 1976. *Teleological explanations*. Berkeley: University of California Press.

Wright, L. 1978. The ins and outs of teleology. *Inquiry* **21**, 223–37.

Author index

Subject index